Foster Cares

A Novel

Steven Paul Wilson

Double-D Ranch Books

The Steven Paul Series
Hindsight
Vertigo
Wayward
Poached
Cash-and-Carry
Vegas Peach

The Eddie Winston Series
The Girl in the Attic
Foster Cares

Double-D Ranch Books—Austin, TX

This book is a work of fiction. Names, characters, places and incidents either are the product of the author's imagination or are used fictitiously. Any resemblance to actual events or locales or persons living or dead, is entirely coincidental.

Foster Cares © 2019 by Steven Paul Wilson

Printed in the United States of America

Cover Art provided by Scottie Dixon

ISBN: 13: 978-0-9981651-2-7

Acknowledgments

I'd like to thank the newest members of our small team: Editor and Graphic designer, Cari Stanhope; IT and Web Administrator, Jim F. Zwiener; and General Assistant, Heather Greeson. I'd also like to thank and acknowledge past contributors Brad Kelly, Maria Kennedy, Peter Hughes and Jini Smith. And, finally, I'd like to thank my family for their encouragement and continued support, making all things possible.

Note from Author

The Russian language contained herein is spelled phonetically and is mostly slang and not what they teach you in college. The most important thing when it comes to pronunciation in Russian is stress. Once you find the correct syllable in a word, the rest of the pronunciation should fall into place. In this book, stress is indicated in the transliteration line by capital letters.

"Cautionary note: Don't repeat the words herein lightly." (Dirty Russian, Erin Coyne & Igor Fisun, Ulysses Press, 2009)

Chapter One

"How's she holding up?" Detective Amy Foster asks as they stroll the upscale outdoor strip mall, the Arboretum in North Austin.

"The question is, how are you holding up?" Eddie Winston counters as Bobo, his dog, strains against his leash.

Amy draws them to a stop before the windows of the Gap. She looks up at Eddie, the dimple in his right cheek nearly discernable. But for a smile, Amy thinks. And God is this man handsome. A gust of the cool, spring breeze blows a long lock of brunette hair across her pretty face. She tucks it behind an ear and shrugs.

"My near-term fate will be decided today. My rep says there's 50/50 chance I'll be fired. After that, he says it's a long, drawn-out appeal process. Again, he puts my odds at 50/50." Foster shrugs once more. "Fuck it, that's what I say." She smiles wanly. Eddie's own smile brings out his dimple. It's enough to make a gal weak at the knees.

"You're alright, Amy," Eddie says. He's really come to care for Amy. "Whether they fire you or not, you'll always be Detective Amy Foster in my books." He gives her shoulder a squeeze.

"Thanks. You didn't answer my question. So, how is Ms. Lori Pritchet holding up?"

"Considering she was kidnapped by a sociopath, I think she's doing well. She's young and resilient and tough. Yeah, I think she'll be alright in the long run."

"Has she ever said how she got all her injuries? You know, the autopsy of her abductor revealed that he had quite a few injuries himself."

Eddie chuckles. "I believe she gave him a hard time. Came close a couple of times to kill him herself."

"Good for her. How about this outfit, Eddie? You think Lori would like something like this?"

Eddie looks past Amy and through the store-front window. "I think she's more of a jeans type of girl. Maybe you can pick her out some makeup that she'd like."

"Poor thing. Her eyes will be black for a good minute with that broken nose of hers."

"The doctor said it set well. At least she won't need any surgeries of any kind."

"Thank God for the little things." A small dark-headed child stops before Bobo. She clutches her teddy bear tight. "Um Eddie, it looks like we have company," Amy says.

Eddie turns to look down at the cute girl standing before Bobo. She has a determined expression on her face. She can't be more than three or four. And she appears to be unaccompanied by an adult. Eddie scans the immediate area. No one seems to be paying the child any attention. "Amy..."

"I'm with you, Eddie," Amy says kneeling beside Bobo and before the child. "Where's your mommy, pretty little girl?"

The girl remains silent, her azure blue eyes are large and doe-like.

She clutches her teddy bear even tighter.

"Okay, Eddie. Not good. I think she's lost."

Eddie kneels down beside Amy. Offers his disarming smile.

Eddie has a way with most everybody—his appearance instantly melting the hardest of hearts. "Are you lost, honey?"

The little girl remains silent. Thirty yards beyond, Igor spots the child. He turns his back for 60 seconds and the little snot disappears. "piz-DYTE!" He turns to his comrade. "Fuck!" he repeats and points. He puts the back of his hand to Erik's chest stopping him in his tracks. "Let me handle this to-VA-risch, comrade." Erik nods. Igor's the leader, the alfa-male among them.

"Yeah. No more fuckups, nyet," he says despite the fact.

"Yeah, yeah, no more fuckups," Igor mumbles. He puts on his best smile as he moves through the sparse shoppers. He pulls up just short of the kneeling Eddie and Amy. "ZERA-sstye!" Igor says and clears his throat. "Um... Howdy. I see you found my precious little girl. They're quick to walk off, da?... I mean, turn your back ten seconds." He gestures walking off with two fingers. "Gone." He offers his hand to the child. "Come along DYEvoch-ka ... Um, little girl."

Eddie rises slowly. "Little girl?" That's an odd way of addressing the child even if she is a little girl. Eddie stands to his full 6'-2". The man before him looks scruffy. He sports a several-day growth and appears to be 40 plus and a mite too old to be the child's father. Not to mention, Eddie thinks, the guy's smile seems strained. Amy stands, her cop hackles raised. She too is leery of the sudden development. The man takes another step closer. The little girl moves to position herself behind Bobo who growls at the man. Bobo never growls at anyone.

"Well, that explains why this living, little doll doesn't speak. I take it by your heavy accent that you're Russian," Amy says.

The man nods, "Da," he says and again reaches for the girl's hand.

3

Eddie raises his own. "Hold up a second pardner. What's your hurry?"

Igor drops his smile and all pretense of friendliness. He's growing tired of playing nice. It goes against his grain. Piss off, he thinks. He grabs for the girl's hand. "i-Di ti NA fig!" Eddie snatches him by the wrist. The little girl recoils, backs into Amy. Amy lays comforting hands on the girl's shoulders. The men lock eyes.

"I said hold on there, pardner. Something doesn't sit well here. You got any ID?"

Igor reddens. Who does this fucking American think he's talking to? He snatches his hand free, "na khu-YU VI-dyet. Go fuck yourself." Igor doesn't like the way things are playing out. It was stupid to make the exchange in such a public place. He should have never agreed to it. Igor shakes off the thought. What's American saying, "No sense in crying over spilled milk?" He looks down at where his wrist was once encircled, looks back into the eyes of the arrogant American. His former military training comes to the forefront of his mind. He grins at the American. He'll dispatch of him in a quick manner. He chuckles. And get the fuck out of Dodge. American movies very good, the best, he thinks.

Eddie watches the Russian before him. Registers the resolve in the man's eyes. Eddie's pulse spikes. This might get messy, he thinks.

"Last chance," the Russian says.

"Dial the police," Eddie says.

The Russian jabs with surprising speed—nearly catches Eddie's flush on the jaw.

Eddie counters with a straight right, misses, and catches a hook in the gut.

Eddie grunts—wraps his arms around the Russian and takes him off his feet and drives him into the pane-glass window. It's like grappling a bear after waking him up from a long sleep, Eddie thinks, as they bounce off the window and he slams the Russian to the concrete.

The Russian gains his feet with surprising agility. They square off.

The girl begins to cry.

Bobo barks, bares his teeth, and growls—his pit mix surfacing.

Amy struggles to retrieve her phone from her purse while maintaining a protective arm around the girl. They're starting to attract attention. She can't find the damn thing. Did she bring it with her? "911! Someone call 911! Officer needs assistance!" she yells.

Eddie and the Russian circle each other. Measure each other. If he can just hold the big fellow off until the police get here.

Eddie takes a shot to the left eye. Hold him, off, yeah right. His own left jab connects, rocks the Russian.

The Russian spits blood and grins. They circle.

Erik quickens his pace—pushes through the gathering crowd.

He pulls from his inner pocket a led, telegraphing zap. He presses the release button. It triples in length.

Erik steps in behind Eddie.

Amy's eyes grow round. "Look out, Eddie!" she calls out. Erik zaps Eddie behind the ear.

Eddie crumbles as if his spine were yanked out of him. Igor steps over Eddie—moves beyond Bobo's snaps and backhands Amy across the face slapping her off her feet.

Amy hits the ground with a thud. Her head bounces off the concrete, her vision clouds and her eyes roll up in her head. Igor chuckles. He's not remotely disturbed by the situation. Hell, he doesn't even hear sirens yet. He spits at Amy—yanks the girl off her feet. Her teddy bear falls to the ground. He takes a bow.

"SU-ka zio-ye-BU-cha-ya! Fucking bitch!" Igor carries the girl by one arm—her other flailing—her feet kicking. The girl's sobs fall on deaf ears. He steps before an oncoming Buick, rounds to the driver's side door, calmly opens it and yanks the blue-haired woman from within. He tosses the girl in and slides in after her.

Igor pulls the door shut at the same time as Erik's passenger's side door shuts. The tires squeal as they make for the nearest exit.

Eddie moans—rolls to a sitting position and gingerly touches the rising lump at the base of his skull. What the fuck did he hit me with Eddie wonders as he watches the Buick disappear? He looks over at Amy. She's stunned but making it to her feet. Her face is red on one side but otherwise, she appears unharmed. "You okay, Amy?"

"They got the girl, Eddie."

"I know." Eddie staggers to his feet. Moves to the elderly lady. She too seems unhurt, just stunned. Eddie helps her to her feet. "You okay, ma'am?"

"They took my car."

"I know, ma'am. The police will be here shortly. They'll help you get it back."

"My purse, too. My purse is in my car."

"Yes, ma'am. They'll help you with that, too. You okay?"

She nods. "Yes, I think so. It happened so fast."

Another woman takes the elderly lady from Eddie's arm. Tells him that she'll look after her until the police get here. Eddie returns to Amy's side. Amy picks up the dropped teddy bear.

"What just happened, Eddie?"

"I'm not really sure."

Amy frowns—eyes the teddy bear in her hands. "Eddie, look at this thing. This is an expensive teddy bear."

"Is that real leather. What do they call that outfit?" "'Lederhosen.' They're traditionally worn by boys."

"And by beer-drinking men at Oktoberfest."

"Well, yeah, that's true, too. And yeah, it's real leather. How's your head?"

"I'll live. Who hit me?" Eddie asks still rubbing the base of his skull.

Amy purses her lips before answering. "The second guy."

"I figured that much." Despite the situation, they both laugh. Seemingly cheating death does that to you somehow. The short laugh feels good to both.

"Well, the good news is," Amy says, "once we tell the police what we know, our involvement with the pair will be history."

"Thank God," Eddie says. They'll soon come to learn—learn the hard way—how deadly wrong these words will be.

"Thank God," Amy concurs as multiple police cars begin to arrive on the scene. They spend the next 30 minutes repeating what little they know. Amy turns over the sole piece of physical evidence, but not before she notes the "Made in Germany" tag. A tag that raises more questions than it answers.

The three step into the Gap to buy Lori something nice to wear for her pending release from the hospital. They settle on pair of 501 Levi's, a retro jean and a cream-colored blouse. Footwear is a little more challenging. Eddie only knows boots, cowboy boots, that is and the Gap doesn't sell cowboy boots. Thus, Eddie defers to Amy's judgment as to the shoes but insists on helping Amy in selecting the appropriate bra and panties.

Amy gives Eddie a disapproving look for the bra Eddie selects.

She reads the tag. "36C. Are you sure she's that large?"

Eddie nods enthusiastically. "Absolutely. You'll have to trust me on this one, Amy."

Amy smirks at Eddie. "Well, I happen to be a 36C too, you know."

"Okey-dokey," Eddie mutters turning away. "If you say so."

Amy scowls and playfully swats Eddie above the knot on the back of his head. "I am, darn it!"

Eddie turns back. "And you sound a bit frustrated, too." This time he sees the scowl.

"Only because of you, Mr. Eddie Winston," she says causing them both to laugh. Eddie turns serious.

"If you want, you can drop me off at the hospital—take my truck to your appointment ..."

"Hearing."

"Hearing—and come back to the hospital when you're finished, seeing how you went and got your own vehicle shot up."

"Shot up! It got shot up because I was trying to save you!" They stop before the cashier—drop their selections on the counter. The cashier smiles at them, checks their respective ring fingers and turns most of her attention back toward Eddie.

"We're married, honey," Amy says. "And we're in a hurry, too. Think you can focus on ringing us up?"

Eddie shrugs and mouths "bitch." Amy punches him in the shoulder.

"I heard that. Can't take him anywhere with me these days."

"You were doing really good, sir," the cashier says, "before the other guy hit you from behind. For what it's worth, it was a cheap shot.

"Thank you."

Amy stomps her foot. "Would you just ring us up please."

"Yes, ma'am, sorry." She turns her attention back to Eddie.

"You're the guy that rescued the kidnapped woman, aren't you? You look taller in person."

Amy snatches Eddie's wallet out of his hand, plucks two, $100 bills from within and tosses them on the counter.

"Correction. We rescued her." She takes Eddie by the elbow and pulls him toward the door. "Keep the change," she calls back over her shoulder. Eddie's laugh carries them all the way to the exit. Amy hides her smile. God she could get used to Eddie's presence.

Eddie opens the passenger door to his late-model, 4-wheel drive GMC and helps Amy up into the cab. He opens the rear door for Bobo and rounds the truck to enter on his side. The diesel rumbles to life. Eddie sets a course for the hospital.

Foster Cares

Chapter Two

Igor punches the dash. "Will you shut her the fuck up so that I can think!"

"us-po-KOI-sya, calm down Igor. She wants her fucking teddy bear."

"Why didn't pick the fuckin' thing up?"

Erik sighs. "I didn't see her drop it. We need to ditch this car."

"Call our contact. Tell him price just went up. The price is $15,000."

Erik wipes his face with his hand. "Igor…"

"Call him!"

"o-POM-nis, Come to your senses."

"VSYO tut pod kon-TROL-yem."

"Everything is not under control, Igor!"

Igor reaches across the crying child and slaps Erik in the back of the head with an open hand. "past za-KHLOP-ni."

Now you're letting him tell you to shut your pie-hole, Erik thinks. One day Igor will go too far and I pull my piece and I pop a cap in his ass. But not today. Dutifully, Erik pulls out his phone and makes the call. He'll appease Igor a little longer.

Igor listens to Erik's side of the call and he doesn't like the whine he detects in Erik's voice. If he wasn't his brother-in-law, he'd have killed him long ago despite the strict, Russian Mafia code of conduct. Igor grows more impatient by the second.

The garage door to the north Austin warehouse rattles open and Igor drives in. The door closes after them. Igor reaches over and snatches the phone out of Erik's hand. Igor's hand shakes.

"Now listen you fuck. The price went up. It's $15,000 and that's non-fuckin' negotiable. Put it together. And I better hear back from you within 30 fuckin' minutes." Igor hits end and tosses the phone into Erik's lap.

"What about the car?"

Igor runs his hand across the dash, admires the curved contours. "La Crosse, shit, this thing is going into container and out Port of Houston. Think what she bring. Fuck shut kid up! Bring in Istanbul. Hell, even China. Chinese love Buicks."

Erik takes the child in one arm and pushes open his door. Igor is nuts, that's what he is. If they weren't brothers-in-law, he'd consider killing him. Fuck the code. He kicks the door shut, mindful not to mar or dent it. Igor remains in the car and rifles through the old woman's purse. Inside the checkbook, he finds several crisp hundred-dollar bills. He takes that as a good sign. Life is good in America. Americans, so stupid. Not only do they invite you in but they cut you a check for a couple of years. "Stupid fucks," he says to himself. Then he can't help but chuckle and shake his head. The only acclimating he'll be doing is acclimating to how the police operate. Igor pushes his door open and exits the Buick.

~~~

Eddie hates the antiseptic smell of the hospital and the endless mopping and buffing it takes to keep the place looking clean. It's ironic, Eddie thinks, that so many patients die from staph infections at hospitals despite the best efforts at cleanliness. Eddie comes to a stop before the nurse's station for Lori's wing. He clears his throat. Margot peers over her shoulder at him.

"Hey, Eddie. Be right with you." Margot bends slightly more at the waist, her scrubs pulling taut across her rear. Eddie smiles. Margot straightens, turns to face Eddie. "Hey, Bobo." She steps before the counter and grins—her teeth straight and white.

"How's my girl this afternoon?" Eddie asks.

"Lucky girl. Looks like you've been shopping. The Gap—nice Eddie. She's doing good. She's asleep at the moment."

"Any visitors?"

"You just missed her mother." Margot nods at the Gap bag. "She went to go buy her something to wear."

"New hairdo? I like the new color, too."

Margot offers her hand for inspection. "Manicure and pedicure, too. You'll have to take my word about the pedicure."

"What's the occasion?"

Margot blushes slightly. "No occasion. Whatcha' buy her? Can I see?"

Eddie sets the bag on the counter. Margot pulls out the bra first. "Nice. A little small for me, but I'd wear it." She pulls out the panties next.

"Little small for you, too?" Eddie asks with a smile.

"Nooo. Good one, Eddie. Nice blouse, too. And the jeans and shoes work as well. Do you cook and clean, too?"

Eddie winks. "I better leave something to the imagination."

He picks up the Gap bag and starts toward Lori's room. Oh, there's plenty left to the imagination, Margot thinks, as she leans over with elbows on the counter—her face cradled in her hands. She adds a sigh.

Eddie opens the door to Lori's private room and sticks his head in to confirm she's sleeping before stepping in. Eddie doesn't want to disturb her. God knows she needs her sleep and he doesn't mind sitting with her while she sleeps.

Bobo precedes Eddie into the room. Eddie gently pulls the door shut, careful not to make any noise. He scoots the visitor's chair nearer the bed and sits. Eddie takes Lori's bandaged hand. The poor girl. Bobo eyes the end of the bed. Eddie gives him a mock stern look. Bobo yawns wide and casually looks in another direction—sits. Eddie shakes his head. What a character he has for a dog. When Eddie's visiting, usually a nurse borrows Bobo and takes him up to the children's ward to visit and comfort the kids. Funny thing is, it's always a different nurse. Must be a coincidence—not.

Like clockwork, there's a light rap on the door which cracks open and a never-before-seen nurse sticks her head in. Like all that have preceded her, she's a looker too. She mouths "may I?" Eddie snaps his fingers and points. Bobo hops to attention. He knows the routine and disappears from the room dragging his leash.

Eddie turns his attention back to Lori—perfectly content to sit with her as he has for the past three days. As he watches over her, Eddie doesn't know what will become of their relationship considering how short they'd been together before her abduction—one night to be exact. Not to mention, he's 20 years her senior. Eddie smiles—not that he's complaining. What man in his position would? Well, whatever happens, he'll be eternally thankful to Lori for saving him from his downward spiral and giving him hope and reason to live once more. Yes, he'll be forever thankful for that.

Eddie's mind drifts to Holly, the love of his life three years prior who ironically appears to have been abducted by the same man. The DNA results aren't in yet, but there's little doubt that one of the decomposing corpses recovered from an inoperable freezer at the crime scene was that of Holly. Whatever doubt there might have been was quashed when a tearful Lori handed him a necklace belonging to Holly that she had found in the abductor's home, the same necklace that he had given to Holly for her birthday.

Lori's eyes flutter open. She gasps before realizing where she is. She squeezes Eddie's hand and winces. "Hi, handsome," she says. "Been here long?"

"Maybe 15 minutes. How are you feeling?"

"Oh, you know, kinda' dreaming some weird shit."

"Understandable. You don't want to talk about it do you?"

"Nah, Eddie, I think I'll just sleep a bit longer if that's okay

with you."

"Sure, I'll be here when you wake up."

"What do you have in the bag?"

"Amy and I went shopping. Picked you up a few things."

"Thanks. I'm going to sleep now, okay."

Eddie leans in kisses Lori lightly on the forehead, "I'll be here," he says.

"But you did sleep with him, correct?" asks the internal affairs officer for the fifth time.

Amy blows out her breath. How much clearer can she make it for the imbecile? "Again, I slept at Mr. Winston's house, but that was only after my investigation confirmed to me one, that Mr. Winston was not involved in Ms. Pritchet's disappearance and two, only after it was apparent to me that my so-called partner was trying to frame Eddie... Mr. Winston."

"Eddie? Y'all are on a first-name basis?"

"That's is his name," Amy snaps.

"Still..."

"What difference does it make what she calls the man?" interjects Amy's Rep, Mark.

"Sounds intimate..."

"But we were not intimate. It got late and I got tired. That's simply the truth."

"And still highly inappropriate. According to the officers that accompanied Detective Johnson that morning you were seen approaching Mr. Winston with two cups of coffee. That Mr. Winston was still in bed and that you were wearing nothing but a T-shirt."

"Was that a question?" asks Mark. He waves his hand. "Never mind. As Amy has stated, Mr. Winston was in the living room sleeping on his sofa sleeper because he insisted that she sleep in a real bed."

"And," Amy adds, "you can't overlook the fact that Mr. Winston was in fact innocent and helped to rescue Ms. Pritchet. Johnson went out of his way to frame Eddie. Yeah, frame Eddie. That's his name."

"Be that as it may..."

"Be that as it may," Amy mimics. "I don't even know what the hell that means." Mark pats Amy on the hand indicating that's enough. Mark speaks up.

"She does make some valid points. To the city, she and Mr. Winston are heroes. Not only did they rescue the young lady, but they took a serial abductor and killer off the streets. That has to factor into this situation."

"Humph," says the IA man that seems to be asking the bulk of the questions. "Be as it may," he begins again, "Mr. Winston was a suspect. Policy dictates you don't sleep with the suspect."

Amy feels like blowing her top. Things are not going well. She looks over at her Rep who continues to pat the top her hand. Well, do something, say something, she wills. He finally does, goes all in.

"If need be, we will take our case to the public. My brave client is a hero and if you treat her any less than that I believe the proverbial shit will hit the fan."

"Is that a threat?"

Mark shrugs. Though he did step over the line, the recorder can't record his shrug. And to say he's "pissed" at the moment would do a disservice to the word. The truth be known, he's fucking pissed. He counts to ten. "I think we've stated our case." He turns to face Amy. "Any final thoughts?" Mike asks. He stops patting her hand but squeezes it.

17

"I think Johnson should have been brought before the board, complacent before I was. My so-called 'partner' went out of his way to frame an innocent man. Thank God I did what I thought was right. Not to mention he tried to kill us."

"Detective Johnson has yet to be released from the hospital..."

"He's milking it," Amy says.

"You blew his knee out..."

"He got lucky..."

"...and he'll be facing criminal charges, as well. He'll be dealt with just as fairly as you," the IA man says. Amy would love to slap the smug look off his face. She suspects he has the "short-man" complex. The IA man stands. To Amy, his pistol and badge appear ridiculously large on his belt. She shakes her head as Mark and her stand—this phase of the meeting clearly over.

"If you'll just wait out in the hall while we deliberate," the IA man says with a know-it-all smile. "It shouldn't take more than a few minutes."

Mark takes Amy by the elbow and steers her toward the door before she can say anything. He pulls the door gently shut behind them. Amy stomps her foot. Gives the door the finger.

"What an asshole. How'd we do?" she jokes.

"There's always your appeal."

"That's what I thought." Amy begins to pace. She's tempted to chew a nail but won't give in to the urge. She's trying to grow them out a bit—take a little more pride in her appearance. Not that she hadn't before, mind you, but ever since Eddie came into her life...

The door opens interrupting Amy's chain of thought. Their wait sure was a short one, she thinks. She has the urge to giggle as she steps back into the room. She doesn't bother taking a seat.

"After duly considering all the circumstances in this case," the IA man says, "I'm disappointed to advise you, Mrs. Amy Foster, your position with the Sheriff's Department has been terminated. Of course, you'll continue to receive your pay while your appeal is pending. So," he stands up to his full height of five foot nothing in her eyes, "that terminates today's hearing." He adds his smile once more, "Good luck to you."

Amy leans across the desk—invades the IA's space. She pushes stop on the minicorder. "News bulletin asshole. Go fuck yourself!" Mark chuckles. The other two hearing officers struggle to stifle their own chuckles. The IA standing before Amy turns beet red.

Amy pushes away from the table, spins on her heels and stomps from the room. "Ugh!" she says as Mike catches up with her. "That man!"

Mike chuckles again. "Did you see how red the little shit got?"

"Little men with big guns, big badges and little dicks. There should be a law against them."

Mark punches the button for the elevator. "That there should be." The door opens, they step in. "We'll get them on appeal, Amy."

"Thanks."

~~~

Bobo's toenails click on the tiled floor as he's let back into the room. The nurse drops Bobo's leash and whispers thanks before silently seeing herself out. Sensing a second pair of eyes on her, Lori slowly stirs. She smiles up at Eddie.

"Still here?"

Eddie raises her hand and kisses her fingers. "Yep."

"My mom hasn't made it back yet?"

"Haven't seen her."

"Oh. Hey, Eddie, there's something we need to talk about."

It's Eddie's turn to say, "Oh?"

The door opens interrupting them. "Speaking of the devil, here she is. Mom, this is Eddie. Eddie meet mom."

"Gloria," the bleach blonde says. The scent of cigarettes precedes her. She offers a hand that's prematurely wrinkled and that matches her smoker's rasp. Eddie estimates her age to be about his own, but she looks ten years older. Eddie's stunned, to say the least. He shakes her hand. Gloria holds onto his hand longer than necessary. He manages to mask his shock at the contrast between mother and daughter.

"Nice to meet you, Gloria," he says.

"Wow, she said you was a handsome rascal."

"Mother."

"Well, you did say that."

"In confidence."

Gloria waves her bejeweled fingers. "Well, the man knows he's drop-dead gorgeous. If you ever get tired of him, Lori..."

"Mother!"

"I'm just saying."

"Mother, would you please give us a few more minutes alone. Go down to the cafeteria and get a coke or something to spike your whiskey."

Gloria laughs. "Such a kidder. Okay, I'll be back in a few."

She finger waves to Eddie. "Ta-ta." Eddie waits until the door closes. "I would have never guessed her to be your mother."

"Tell me about it. She can be challenging at times. Used to try and steal my high-school boyfriends."

Dreading the words, Eddie asks anyway, "Is there something you wanted to talk about?"

Lori grasps Eddie's hand in both of her bandaged hands. She sighs heavily. "Eddie, I've asked to be discharged and that's been approved. All my physical injuries are superficial. I look like shit, but I'll heal. Mentally, I think I'll be okay, too. Anyway, you might have noticed that mother and I are not much alike. Our relationship has been a strained one for many years. And that is something I'd like to fix... mend. My abduction taught me that life is precarious. A number of times during my ordeal I thought this is it, it's over. What ran through my mind during these moments is how many people I would miss and how many people would miss me. And that includes you, Eddie. And when I saw my best friend Jennifer on the news it broke my heart. I cried my eyes out.

"What I'm trying to say, Eddie, is I need to patch things up with my mother and this is the perfect time to do so. I can take time off from work and school for a while and nobody will fault me. Plus, I do believe I need some time to heal mentally. Just a bit.

"When I went home with you that night, Eddie, I was so lonely. I could see the loneliness in you as well and I think we both needed someone desperately in our lives. And you know, Eddie, you're a great guy..."

"But?" Eddie interjects remembering the Seinfeld episode with the George Costanza "It's me not you" breakup.

"...but I need to fix this relationship with my mother before I can give my all to another relationship. Hey, don't look so glum. I'll be back. You're not mad at me are you, Eddie?"

"At you, how could I ever be mad at you. You pulled me out of a downhill spiral and I'll always be grateful for that."

"And you'll always be my hero. You know I dreamed about you. First it was Tom Cruise as Jack Reacher..."

"Lee Childs."

"Yeah, I know. Anyway, the image morphed and there you were, my, Jack Reacher. And you spoke to me. You said, 'hold on, Lori, I'm coming for you.' And you did. You came."

Eddie's taken back by Lori's words. A number of times when he was searching for Lori, he used just those words, or close to them. "Hang in there, Lori. I'm coming for you," Eddie whispers.

"Yes, that's them! Those were the words. You're telling me that's what you were saying?"

"Aloud and to myself."

"That's surreal. I heard you, Eddie." Lori grows serious. "Hey, can I tell you something else?"

"You changed your mind," Eddie half jokes.

"Noooo. You haven't noticed that Detective Foster is crazy about you?"

"I have gotten that impression."

"She lights up in your presence. When she comes into the room, she always manages to rest her hand on your shoulder, casually, but nevertheless. I'm sure you've noticed she's a nice-looking woman...

"Where are you going with this, Lori?"

"And, no ring. What's up with that?"

"The ring?"

"Yeah."

"Divorced."

"Then I say go for it, Eddie."

"My priority is you."

Lori squeezes Eddie's hand once more. A tear threatens. "That's sweet," she says. Ever since her abduction and even more so after her rescue, her emotions have been on a roller coaster. Talk about confusing, she thinks. Here she's encouraging Eddie to be with another woman and yet at the same time she longs to be in his arms again. Lori struggles to find the right words. They don't come. On one hand, she needs to patch up the relationship with her mother and time to heal and on the other hand, she can't bear the thought of losing Eddie. Lori has to release Eddie's hand to wipe the tear from her cheek. "Sorry, Eddie," she finally manages.

Lori sucks in a deep breath and exhales. It makes her almost sick to her stomach to say the words. "I think I need time to heal."

Eddie frowns and smiles at the same time. He wants to take her in his arms and hold her until she changes her mind. Eddie brushes the hair from her forehead instead. "You have to do what you think is right for you, Lori."

Unabashed, this time Lori's tears do come. Eddie's eyes blur as well. A light rap on the door precedes Amy's entrance. Lori hastily wipes the remaining tears from her cheeks.

"I hope I'm not disturbing anything," Amy says pulling up beside Eddie. She rests her left hand on Eddie's shoulder. Lori grins. "How's the patient... What?"

Lori sniffles. She wipes her nose with the back of her hand. "Nothing. I'm being discharged here in a bit. I'm going to go to Dallas and stay with my mom awhile."

"Oh," Amy says looking between the two.

"How did the hearing go?" Eddie asks.

Amy gives it a thumbs down. "Canned. Can you believe it?"

"Are they nuts?" Lori says. She can't believe it.

"There's the appeal process and the good news is I get paid during the time the appeal is pending." Amy puts on a brave face. "It's like being on paid vacation."

"Sorry to hear it," Eddie says. "What now?"

Amy shrugs—sighs. "Fuck 'em. They'll give me my job back or they won't."

"Well, at least the vacation part's okay. Amy, would you mind locating my mom and tell her I'm about ready to go. She went down to the cafeteria. You can't miss her. Mid 4Os, bleach blonde with way too much makeup. You'll probably have to pry her from some doctor's leg. She's on the prowl for her fifth husband." Lori chuckles. "She tends to outlive them. Maybe on second thought, Eddie, you should go. Give us girls a few minutes alone."

Eddie leans in and kisses Lori on the lips, sad to think it might be their last. "Gotcha. Be right back."

Chapter Three

"I see how you are around Eddie," Lori says.

"Oh," Amy says for the second time. "Sorry, I hope I didn't do anything to upset you."

"Relax. It's all good," Lori says not knowing if it's actually true or not.

"I'm not sure I'm following you. You know Eddie's crazy about you and 100 percent loyal. He's a great guy."

"I've always believed that myself, but that's not where I'm going, Amy. I've made a really difficult decision. I'm going to patch up things with my mother. Meaning, I'll be going to Dallas for a spell. I need time to heal, too. Eddie was deeply scarred resulting from the loss of his previous girlfriend and he needs someone in his life now. Not at some future date when I decide to return. That's not fair to Eddie. So, though it hurts me to say it, you two have my blessings."

Amy sits in the chair vacated by Eddie and takes Lori's hand. She at a loss for words as her eyes begin to tear. All she can do to is offer a goofy smile feeling like a heel for practically throwing herself at Eddie. Strike that, for throwing herself at Eddie. Amy doesn't know what all Eddie may have said to Lori, but she decides some things are better left unsaid. She settles with thanks.

They both cry, each for their own reasons.

Bobo barks as the door opens and Eddie and Lori's mother return. What a silly dog, Lori thinks. She'll miss him, too and the thought is enough for the tears to flow once more. Gloria waves the discharge papers.

"Cheer up, honey, you're free to leave this dreadful place."

Lori chokes back a sob and tosses the sheet off her. She's wearing only the hospital gown that ties in the back and leaves everyone's ass exposed and socks with little rubber beads on the bottom. She rolls around and plants her feet on the floor – still a little wobbly. Lori pats her knees and Bobo instantly responds.

He does his best to get in her lap. Lori laughs and hugs him dearly. She kisses him on the snout. "I'm going to miss you, boy."

"For heaven's sake. It's not like you're going away forever," Gloria says. She's itching to go—needs a cigarette badly.

"Yes, mother." Lori's already having second thoughts. It's going to be a long drive to Dallas. She stands and hugs Eddie for a long minute. She trembles in his arms. God is it hard leaving this man behind, she thinks. She kisses him long and hard before giving him one last hug. Lastly, she hugs Amy. "Thanks," she says and whispers, "You better not hurt him."

"I won't, girlfriend," Amy whispers back.

Eddie takes up Bobo's leash and opens the door. He looks back one last time as he follows Amy out. Though their time together was short, Eddie knows he'll never forget Lori. Never.

~~~

Igor throws a shoe at Erik. "Turn fuckin' TV up, Erik." He points at the TV. "That's the khu-ye-SOS, the cocksucker from this morning!"

Erik leans in as if that will give him a better view. He only saw the man for mere seconds, but it sure looks like the guy. "You may be right. That looks like him."

"Would you shut fuck up. I'm trying to listen."

"Today the DA's Office has announced that all charges against Mr. Eddie Winston have been dismissed with respect to the disappearance of North Austin resident Lori Pritchet, whom Mr. Winston assisted in rescuing this past Thursday evening. A Source at Brakenridge Hospital tells Channel 7 News that Ms. Pritchet is recovering nicely and is expected to be released sometime today. Our hearts go out to Ms. Pritchet and everyone here at the station prays for her speedy recovery.

"In other news..."

"Yeah, that's him alright," Igor says, "I'd recognize anywhere. A worthy opponent. He make Igor very angry." Igor turns on the old woman's I-phone.

"They can track that phone, Igor."

"Siri, address and phone number for Eddie Winston, Austin, Texas." The phone instantly dongs and displays the info. Igor smiles and turns off the phone. He scowls over at Erik. Erik thinks he's stupid. Of course, he knows they can track the phone, but with it turned off once more, they'll only know the tower it pinged.

"What you want information for?"

"Shut fuck up, would you!" Igor snaps. How did he end up with idiot for a brother-in-law? His sister, could wring her chicken neck.

Erik remains silent. He knows when Igor's in a foul mood and it's not good to tempt fate when he's in such a mood. *I'll kill him someday,* he silently vows for the hundredth time. Erik closes his eyes to watch the first of dozens of scenarios in which he handily dispatches Igor. He smiles to himself. *Da, someday.*

~~~

"Hey, Eddie, I think I'll buy a nondescript car."

Eddie eyes Amy for a second and continues to drive. *She's up to something,* he can see it in her devious look. *But what?* Eddie can't fathom.

"Go up to 183 North and stop at the first dealership."

"It's after 5:00, Amy. It's getting late. Shouldn't you go check on your house plants or something?"

"No need, they all died months ago. Besides, why would I want to rush home to an empty house? And, besides, it's not too late for a dealership. They can always bail me in a car and we can do the paperwork tomorrow."

"The true American consumer, are you Ms. Amy Foster?" Eddie jokes. "Tell me, Amy, how much do you plan to put down?"

"The whole insurance check, of course. I want low payments." Eddie takes the 183 exit. "Wrong answer. You go in with zero down, let them crunch the numbers and then after you settle on a number, you hit them with the down payment."

"Why on earth for?"

"Otherwise, you'll likely pay thousands more for the car. They'll back into the deal and take as much of that $7,000 in profit as they can."

"And how would you know that?"

"Been a finance manager and have sold cars, too. I know. Believe me."

"A used car salesman?"

"And a damn good one at that."

Amy shudders. "And to think I almost slept with you."

Eddie's dimple appears. "Now that you know, I should be relatively safe around you."

"Hardly, there's a dealership. Take this exit. It's on the feeder."

"Hardly?"

"It's like sleeping with the gardener. It's both taboo and exciting."

"Ever slept with your gardener?

Amy frowns. "My gardener is my neighbor's ten-year-old boy and he's the only gardener I can afford."

"What about your mailman?"

"She's a dyke. Nice enough, but a dyke nevertheless. Hey, stop right here. Let me out."

"You're going to buy a Ford?"

"Ford Focus. They drive them in NASCAR."

"And what do you know about NASCAR?"

"That I'd sleep with Jeff Jordon."

"Tramp." They both laugh. Eddie pulls to a stop behind a row of Focuses.

"Right here. Just drop me off. You want me to pick up something for dinner?"

"We have dinner plans?"

Amy steps down. Leans back into the truck. "Of course. I've been given the green light." The slam of the door cuts off Amy's laughter. Eddie shakes his head. What kind of talk did the girls have? He almost feels cheapened. The key word being "almost." Eddie laughs. He can't help but smile. Women—he might not ever fully understand them, but God you can't help but love them.

Bobo replaces Amy in the passenger's seat. Eddie rolls down Bobo's window and hollers out at Amy. "Yeah, pick us up something on your way home, honey."

Amy smirks but her pleasure's discernable. "Yes, honey," she hollers back dutifully. There's a new spring in her step. She feels like hugging herself not recalling when she's been so happy. So what, she's been fired. That's nothing if she ends up with Eddie. Amy shudders at the thought. Is it possible? Could this be the beginning of a relationship? God, she hopes so. She knows Eddie's attracted to her but was too much a good guy to act upon it. At least she hopes she's reading him right. Surely, she is. Amy smiles recalling climbing into bed with Eddie wearing nothing but one of his T-shirts and a smile. Had Eddie not been a good guy he would have taken advantage of the situation. But for his overriding concern for Lori and giving their budding a relationship a fair chance and his conviction that he was going to find and rescue Lori, he would have acted upon it.

He as much as said so and surely, he wasn't just saying so as not to hurt her feelings, was he? Of course not, Amy. Don't be foolish. You're still a desirable woman in your own right. I mean, you jog several times a week and things have yet to turn south, mostly.

Hell, you even take pride in your looks—especially here lately. A new cut with dirty-blond highlights. Amy shakes her head. Yes, she likes her new just-fucked look. She chuckles. God, it's been a long time—too long. And she's been with virtually no one but her ex-husband since high school. Wow, talk about a long time. She chuckles, "I hope it hasn't grown shut!"

"Can I help you ma'am."

Amy jumps. Shit, the salesman scared her. I hope I wasn't speaking out loud, she thinks.

"You we're saying, ma'am?"

Amy reddens, turns to look at the car beside her. "I'm looking for a low-mileage Ford Focus at a decent price."

The salesman smiles—aren't we all. "I think we can help you with that. How's your credit look?"

"800 plus."

"Good enough for me." He eyes his watch, offers his hand. "Chuck."

They shake, "Amy Foster."

"And how much down were you looking to put?"

Amy smiles. "Zero." She's not sure, but she thinks she might have taken some of the wind out of his sails.

"Oh. It's getting late. The finance department is closed for the day."

"So, we pick out a car. You take a copy of my driver's license. And then you bail me in the car. We'll do the paperwork tomorrow."

"Ouch," he says good-naturedly.

"Ouch," Amy replies.

Forty-five minutes later, Amy's on the road in a one-year-old blue Ford Focus with less than 20,000 miles. She'll have to kiss Eddie and then some for his input. Yes, and then some. Slut, she thinks.

~~~

"Couldn't get the car back, boss," one of Igor's men says. "Why fuck not?"

"Cops got it surrounded."

Igor hammer's the coffee table with his fist. "pit-DYETZ!" Shit, he thinks and that really pisses him off. That fucking slimeball attorney. Now he owes for car, too. His cell phone rings. Speak of moron. He answers in his gruff voice.

"Dorbandt, you stupid fuck. Had to meet in a public place! Now you owe me for car, too."

"But they insisted," Dorbandt whines.

"You owe another ten large," Igor says doing his best not to laugh. He heard the "ten large" saying on some American gangster movie and he was hoping he'd get to use it someday. In reality, he could care less about the fucking car. Hell, it was stolen out of Dallas and so were its tags. Something Dorbandt need not know. "Did you fucking hear me!" Igor screams at his cell phone.

"I... I hear you. I don't have ten more thousand. I'm broke!"

And stupid. "Give me what you have today and you can owe me." He hears Dorbandt's groan on the other end and again fights his urge to chuckle. "Listen," he says sounding more reasonable, "let's get deal done and we work on what you owe." The kid's constant crying is beginning to get to him—fraying his nerves.

"The H.E.B. on Burnet Road. Know where it's at?" Dorbandt asks.

"Yeah." Another fuckin' public place.

"Meet me there in 30 minutes."

"No more delays or fuckups. Understand Dorbandt?"

"Yeah, I'll be there," Dorbandt says. Igor taps end—looks up at his man who's still hovering over him.

"What?"

"Boss, what about the car?"

"Go steel another one, you moron." Fuckin' idiot. All around him, fuckin' idiots.

~~~

"Don't fall out boy," Eddie tells Bobo. Bobo sticks his head back in the truck long enough to ascertain there're no treats involved before resuming his precarious position of sticking halfway out the window. Eddie shakes his head. He loves his goofy dog. His thoughts turn to Lori. He never expected the bombshell she dropped on him this afternoon, but he doesn't blame her. She does need time to heal. And there's their 20-year age difference to consider.

Eddie takes the Burnet Road exit—heads south. And not to mention, he's not without baggage. A borderline alcoholic who self-loathes at the loss of his true love, Holly Austin. Now there's no doubt what became of Holly. Eddie can't help but to still think her abduction and soon-confirmed murder was his fault. How could he not? It was his insensitive remarks that had her crying and storming out of the house that day three years ago. But for that, she would have never been abducted and murdered. And now everyone will say, "at least there's closure." Eddie doesn't buy into it. There is no such thing as "closure" as far as Eddie's concerned. Perhaps time will heal. And Lori, bless her, came into his life when things for him were most dire. Their lone night together gave him hope. I hope that he'd be able to love someone and himself again someday.

Eddie pulls Bobo's tail. Bobo contemplates Eddie for a long second. "Someone to love other than you, boy, that is," Eddie says. He sure loves his dog, he thinks, not for the first time today. Bobo's unconditional love is Eddie's true savior. But for him, Eddie would have cashed it in years ago. Bobo's a handsome dog, eye patch and all.

The traffic on Burnet is heavy as always at this time of day, but Eddie pays it no mind. He passes H.E.B. on his right as he nears his home, the same cream-colored Santa Fe home where he's been living for the past dozen years. Eddie's thoughts turn to Amy. He smiles. She sure is in a good mood and he suspects he knows what that's about—the "green light" Lori gave her. Eddie's still stunned over the development. He sure didn't see that coming.

Maybe Amy will stop and buy some beer and try to get him drunk again. He chuckles. That didn't quite work out for her last time, though she did lose her clothes. Not that it wasn't a close call, Eddie thinks. Amy's a nice gal in her own right—brains, looks and yes body, too. Having been awoken with one of her breasts cupped in his hand, a rather firm breast at that. "Yes, a close call," he says to himself. Another lonely soul desperately searching for love.

Eddie wonders what in the world Amy is really up to as he takes a right on Woodrow. Two blocks up on his right rests his home on its corner lot with a large, fenced-in backyard. It's a decent house and Eddie likes it with its hardwood flooring throughout and Spanish tiled kitchen.

Eddie pulls into his short drive and kills the engine. Bobo loses interest in his window and turns to look at Eddie. Eddie grabs him by the loose skin on his neck and gives him a good shake. "We're home, boy." Bobo yawns wide and licks his snout. He's a funny dog.

Eddie climbs down and Bobo jumps down behind him. They enter the house through the garage. Eddie's kitchen phone blinks. He has messages and quite a few of them it turns out. He deletes them all in turn—mostly reporters wanting to do a story on him. Eddie's not interested. Though he is interested in one call from his lawyer, Buzz Myers, who informs him that the charges have been dropped against him with the exception of the assault charge he picked up while in jail. And, that Eddie no longer owes him the million that Buzz posted for him. As for the assault charge, Buzz is of the opinion that that will be dropped soon, as well.

Well, that's something positive, Eddie thinks, as he opens the fridge for a Bud Light, his first of the day. Eddie eyes the clock on the microwave, he's set a new record for the latest in the day for his first beer of the day. Hell, that's something, too. A little light at the end of the tunnel. And perhaps, too, something to build on.

Eddie sits at the kitchen table and opens the external CD Rom Drive plugged into his new laptop and drops the DVD in. He'll watch the short, 15-minute video one last time before putting it away in storage. Eddie pushes the drive shut. The DVD begins to play.

Chapter Four

Amy's cell phone rings on the seat beside her. She recognizes the number as being an extension of the County's. She pulls into the next commercial entrance to take the call.

"Foster here."

"Amy, it's Howard. Heard the news. Sorry to hear it." "Thanks, Ron," she says calling him Ron like all those that are close to him because he looks so much like Ron Howard, or more aptly like Opie. Amy's glad he called, too, because Howard was her inside man in the Sheriff's Department during her suspension and she wants to thank him again for all the assistance he provided with respect to her and Eddie's search for Lori.

"I'm glad you called, Ron. I wanted to thank you again for your assistance on the Pritchet case. But more importantly, for trusting my instincts about Eddie."

Howard chuckles. "Eddie, it's like that, is it? So, the allegations are true?"

"No, not yet. But if I have anything to do with it... I mean, you've seen the guy. He's absolutely gorgeous."

"That's superficial, Amy," Ron says in mock disapproval. "Looks are not everything. You do realize I'm still single and available?"

"I think of you more like a brother."

"Thanks, now I feel better about the whole situation."

Amy laughs. She pictures Ron at his desk making a stupid face. "You're my second choice. Does that make you feel any better?"

"No. Hey, Amy, the reason I'm calling, have you heard the other news?"

"Other news?"

"Your partner, Johnson...," he draws it out.

"Mike? What about Mike? Come on, quit teasing me."

"Begging, that's better. Anyway, Johnson posted bond."

Amy drops her phone, scrambles to pick it up and puts it back to her ear. "You're shitting me!"

"I shit you not."

"But... How's that possible. Can he even walk? And what did the DA go with?"

"Apparently with crutches."

"After a knee replacement? Christ, I blew his fucking knee out."

"I guess so. Obstinate old bastard. Anyway, two counts: attempted murder and a third-degree obstruction of justice."

Amy's jaw drops, literally. "You've got to be kidding. Two lousy counts. I thought he was still in the hospital."

"Have you heard that Matty and Tae song where they sing 'he's madder than a hornet in an old Coke can?' Well, that's what I hear. Watch yourself, Amy."

"Thanks... Unbelievable. It's hard to wrap my mind around this one. Wow."

"I know. Well, I thought I better give you the heads-up."

"Well, shit, okay. You're the best, Ron."

"That's what the ladies say."

Amy smiles. "Right. I'll try not to picture that. Later, Ron."

Amy hits end and tosses the phone back onto the passenger's seat. The new development's unnerving. How could the court allow Johnson to post bond? The guy has clearly gone off the deep end. Not only did he try to kill Eddie, but he tried to kill you as well, Amy thinks. She puts her car back into drive and cuts across the lot toward the other entrance/exit. That should be two counts of attempted murder at a minimum, the way Amy sees it. If you count Johnson T-boning her Expedition, that would be four counts because Johnson tried to kill them both twice. Oh well, they'll just have to be careful.

Amy inhales deeply. She likes the smell of her new ride—well, her slightly used car. Somebody detailed it nicely. She'll have to buy some Weather Tech mats and an old blanket for the back seat for Bobo.

Listen to yourself, Amy, already making plans. Isn't that a little presumptuous of you? "Hell yes," Amy says out loud. She turns her rearview to check herself in the mirror. "And this time you shall be seduced, Mr. Eddie Winston," she says winking at her reflection.

She turns the mirror back. "Yes, you have met your match... Well, hopefully."

Amy giggles and decides she better stop and pick up a 12 pack of beer and touch up her makeup. It's called "hedging your bet." In other words, it can't hurt. But you better not drink so many beers this time, Amy, she thinks.

Amy puts on her blinker and turns into the 7-11 store.

~~~

Igor spots Dorbandt's 80's era Mercedes diesel toward the back of the lot. He points. "Over there, Erik." Igor has nothing but contempt for the lawyer. Judging by his car, he must not be much of a lawyer, either. He'd love to slap Dorbandt around a bit to remind him who's boss. Igor smiles at the pleasant thought as they pull in beside Dorbandt's car. "Erik, go get money first. Come back. Then you bring girl and give to PAD-la, to bastard." Igor, never one to pass up an opportunity to teach Erik new words adds, "Capisce?"

Erik nods as Igor alights from their 80's era Cadillac Fleetwood.

Igor fails to register the irony in that their car is a relic, too. He slips into the passenger seat of Dorbandt's car. Dorbandt passes him an H.E.B. paper bag containing the money.

"H.E.B. bag, how fuckin' clever. Did you go shopping, too, while you were at it?"

"No," Dorbandt answers softly. He's scared shitless of the guy—Igor with his beady, close-set eyes that seem capable of exposing your deepest, darkest secrets. Dorbandt swallows—feels his temples grow hot. How did he ever get into this situation, he wonders yet once again? Because you're a shitty lawyer and an even worse gambler, he need not remind himself.

"Do I need to count this, Dorbandt?"

"Uhm... I got most of the money. I'll make up the rest. I swear."

Igor laughs. "And you actually passed bar?" He shakes his head in disgust. Americans. In Russia, it's who you know—not some stupid test that counts. He eyes Dorbandt, cocks his head, closes one eye partially. He's practiced the look in the mirror and can smell the fear the look instills in Dorbandt. Igor sighs heavily for effect.

"Okay, this time, I'll let you make up. Speaking of, I have this blue-eyed Syrian boy on the way. Very cute." He turns his latest Galaxy to show Dorbandt the kid's picture. "Maybe you keep this one for yourself, nyet? You look like you might like little boys. Huh? You can tell Igor."

"No," Dorbandt says. He can hear the tremor in his voice and it disgusts him. He pulls out a handkerchief—mops his brow.

"Eh? Seven, eight?" Igor laughs with gusto. "I hear he's well behaved. A favorite among his Syrian smugglers. They like buggering boys. Russians no like, but Americans, eh? Da?"

"No... I... I don't think so. Is... Is he going to be healthy?"

"Maybe you take some picture first. Maybe a little video." Igor taps on his phone, summons up his app, Pediscope, and begins to record. Dorbandt puts up his hands, attempts to block the lens with one hand, his face with the other.

"Stop... Please!"

Igor laughs again. "Relax. I'm just fuckin' with you." He leans over, pats Dorbandt on the knee and whispers in his ear. "Hey, it's been fun, gotta run." Igor chuckles as he exits the car. God the man is fun to fuck with, he thinks. Such idiot. And maybe, too, Dorbandt like little boys. Igor shrugs before getting back into his car. Igor could care less. What's it to him, as long as they pay, nyet?

"Everything okay, Igor?"

Igor grunts—nods in the direction of Dorbandt's car. "Give him girl."

Igor's grubby fingers open the paper bag and dump the contents in his lap as Erik transfers the girl to Dorbandt. All new bills, some still wrapped in the bank's wrappers. Igor grins—winces. Fucking toothache. He reaches for his bottle of vodka at his feet, uncaps it and takes a long pull. Better.

~~~

The image is shaky, to say the least, but every now and then Eddie managed to catch Holly's smiling face as she turned back to see if he was still behind her. Eddie smiles as he watches and recalls how difficult it is to snowboard and follow the skiing Holly while filming and laughing at the same time. Holly, so pretty, so sweet. And talk about the perfect snow bunny.

Eddie downs his beer and wipes a tear with the back of his hand. The video is nearly over. The grand finale—Holly crashing as she turns back one last time to see if he's still behind her. Eddie's smile broadens recalling purposefully crashing too. The camera is all but forgotten as they tussled and rolled and laughed in the fresh snow.

Eddie opens the drive and removes the DVD and places it in its protective casing. It's time for it to go into storage, not forever, but at least for now. It's time he gives life a chance once more. Lori did that for him. Gave him the will to give life a second chance. She showed him it's possible to love again. And for that, he'll be ever grateful.

Perhaps, Lori was just the door, Eddie considers and Amy's the answer. Maybe Amy can fill that hole in his heart that's been there for so long.

A horn blows outside in the drive. Bobo scrambles to get his feet under him on the slick tile. He barks once and looks to Eddie for confirmation he's done the right thing—a single bark. Eddie shakes his head in amusement.

"Let's go see who it is, boy." Bobo's ahead of the game. He paws at the garage door—urges Eddie to speed things up. Bobo barks once more as he bangs off the door jam and disappears from view. What a goofy and lovable dog. Eddie follows him out. He whistles at the sight of a beaming Amy standing beside her new ride.

"What a beauty," he says. Amy runs her fingers through her hair puffs it up a bit.

"It's the new cut-and-color that does it for you, huh, Eddie?"

"I'm talking about the car." They both laugh.

"So, what do you think?"

"Ford Focus. I've never ridden in one, but I like her lines. She's a good-looking car."

"He's a good-looking car. Just look at the masculine lines."

"And what size engine does it have?"

Amy twirls a lock of hair as she studies her car. She hasn't a clue. Eddie steps over and covers the window sticker with his hand. "Well?"

"Well, I know this, it's the largest of the Eco-boost engines that Ford makes."

"At least you're trying to save the planet," Eddie says.

Amy smirks. "Yeah, right. Hey, check out the interior," Amy says opening the driver's door. "Though it's a year old, she... Umm, he has the upgraded In Touch system which is run on Black-berry software."

"Is that a good thing?"

Amy shrugs. "Hell, I don't know. That's just what the salesman said. But I like it—the touch screen, blue tooth and as you see, it's got two USB ports. That ought to be worth something."

Eddie drapes his arm over Amy's shoulder. "Actually, I like your new car, Amy. You did well."

Amy wraps her arm around Eddie's waist and leans in. Damn the man feels good, she thinks. "Thanks."

"And you bought beer, too. Plan on getting me drunk again?"

"Yep."

Eddie can hear the smile in her voice. "And how did that work out for you last time?"

Amy pinches Eddie's side causing him to flinch. "It got one of us naked and that's half the battle." She looks up to admire Eddie's jawline. Now that's a masculine line, she thinks. "Eddie, I don't suppose you picked up anything for dinner? I... kinda forgot."

"Nope. I had one last thing that I needed to do."

Amy waits for him to continue, but he doesn't and she doesn't want to pry. "Good, let's take a ride—pick up some burgers and fries at Top Notch. I was so excited about the car I forgot about the food."

"And that kind of food won't go straight to your thighs?"

Amy pinches him again." Noooo, I'll have you know." She kisses his jaw. "Come on, let's go. You too, Bobo."

Amy's enthusiasm is contagious, Eddie thinks as he rounds the car to the passenger side. He opens the door and pushes the seat forward for Bobo to hop in and lets it drop back into place and slides in. The interior is nice, the seat comfortable.

"You did good, Amy," he says for a second time and he means it. He's never owned a Ford, albeit, for a 90's Lincoln Town Car that he bought used many years back and it turned out to be a very dependable car. Amy cranks the car and it's so quiet compared to his diesel that he wouldn't know it was running but for the tach.

Amy backs out of the driveway and turns toward Burnet. She's clearly pleased with her purchase and he's happy for her. Eddie wonders what else she has up her sleeve, excuse the cliché, but there's something else definitely on her mind.

Top Notch, the hamburger joint, is only a couple miles north and on the right. They ride the short distance in silence, both preoccupied with thoughts of the other, both in need of someone in their lives. Eddie passes a $20 across to Amy to pay for their order. The aroma of hot fries fills the car. Bobo's paws and snout appear between them. He licks his snout.

"Don't worry," Amy tells him, "we got you burgers and fries, too."

She's not sure it's the best meal for him, but he's a difficult dog to deny. Amy pulls back into the waning traffic.

"So, what do you really think of my car?"

"Nice, but you didn't order anything for dessert?"

"Oh, I have dessert planned for you, never fear," Amy says not believing she actually uttered the words. She's never been shy, but also has never been so brazen. Eddie's just easy to be around, she decides. Nevertheless, she reddens some, once again nervous about the evening's prospects.

Eddie studies Amy as she continues driving. He likes what she's done with her hair. He feels a tinge of remorse at the thought. It was Holly's new cut that lead to Eddie's insensitive words and Holly's fleeing the house in tears. And that's still a hard pill for Eddie to swallow.

"Home," Amy announces as she pulls into the drive and kills the engine. She can picture a life with Eddie and that prospect, as well, makes her nervous. Nervous for no other reason than she hasn't wanted anything so bad in as long as she can remember. Go slowly Amy, she silently tells herself. Don't be too pushy and scare the poor man away. But don't let him get away either. Amy hides her smile as she pushes her door open. Eddie gathers up the food and twelve-pack as Amy lets Bobo out on her side. He's got a live one on his hands, but he's fine with that, he realizes. He too smiles as he alights from the car. Yes, he's perfectly fine with that.

~~~

The clanking of the industrial garage door opening draws Erik's attention. He checks his watch. Right on time. A repurposed Ryder truck pulls through and rolls to a stop. A hiss of air precedes the quieting of the diesel engine.

"The shipment has arrived, Igor."

Igor runs the blade of his Uncle Henry once more down the length of wet stone before closing the blade against his leg and sliding it into the leather casing at his side. It's a shame he didn't have his knife with him earlier today, he thinks, because if he had, he'd a cut the American a new asshole. He chuckles, "never leave home without it." Igor walks the short distance to the back of the truck and impatiently waits for the locks to be undone and the cargo door to be rolled up. He snaps his fingers and several of his underlings hop up into the back of the truck and manhandle the pallets, one by one, to the end of the truck to be unloaded by the forklift operator.

The pallets consist of hundreds of pounds of bundled used clothing and their only purpose is to conceal the small hidden compartment toward the front that conceals the true cargo—human cargo. Igor screams at his men to hurry up. He's eager to see what today's shipment has brought him. Maybe he'll keep one out of this bunch for himself, he thinks. Teach her what Russian men like. But she's got to have nice teeth, too. Bad teeth—bad breath. He spits at the thought.

The last of the pallets are removed and they begin removing the fake back which is no simple feat having been so carefully constructed to appear authentic.

The foul smell precedes the half-dozen woman as they're led off the truck. Though they were provided with a chemical toilet some refused to use it. Something about modesty. Stupid fucks—would rather shit themselves than use the toilet. He spits once more as the first of the women is brought to stand before him. Igor can only see her eyes because her hair and face are covered by whatever the fuck they call it.

Igor reaches for the black cloth and the woman visibly shrinks before him. "SHLYU-khu!" whore, he screams at her and grabs a handful of the material and yanks good and hard. It takes some effort. She's not giving it up easily. A few more tugs and it's his. Igor throws it to his feet and grinds his boot into the material.

Igor backhands her for his trouble. The sooner they learn to mind, the better. The others will likely be more pliant after seeing how the first one's disobedience is dealt with, Igor thinks. And in this regard, he's seldom wrong.

Igor studies the cowering woman before him. Not bad. She'll clean right up. And she'll be a real money maker for him. Igor feels the elation that always comes with a new shipment. Ever since Putin opened an air base in Syria and began bombing everyone into oblivion, business has been good. Not to mention Europe's tightening of its borders after a wave of New Year's Eve sexual assaults by young, migrant men assimilating to their host countries as they see fit. Igor shakes his head in disbelief. And Germany welcoming them with open arms only to be shit on. Free housing, fat checks, smartphones. Stupid. He'd send everyone capable of fighting back to fight.

Igor likes the first one the best. He suspects she has no kids, meaning if she hasn't been raped by a relative or a smuggler, she'll still be a virgin. He stirs at the thought. He orders his men to have her cleaned up first and brought back to him.

One good thing about Syrians is most speak some English and he has an Arab interpreter to lay down the rules for the rest—the cost of safe passage to America. Of course, they'll never get out from under Igor unless he sells them outright or they become so undesirable they can no longer command the price of even a blow job, at which time they'll simply cease to exist.

Igor returns to his recliner before his big screen. He loves American TV and movies. So much to be learned.

Chapter Five

Eddie pops the top on another Bud Light and passes it to Amy before taking a seat beside her. They've knocked a sizeable dent in the 12-pack but Amy seems to be holding her own this time and remains fully clothed. "Impressive," Eddie says.

"What?"

"You're still fully clothed."

"I'm playing hard to get this time."

Eddie grins. "Well, good luck with that."

Amy punches Eddie in the arm. "Hey, I've been thinking..."

"'Bout what?"

Amy takes a deep breath, exhales slowly. "I'm thinking we make a pretty good pair..."

"Is this a proposal?"

Amy gives Eddie her quit interrupting look. "We followed the clues and found Lori. Anyway, now that I'm fired and you're unemployed, why don't we start a detective agency together?"

"That's it? That's what you've been working yourself up to tell me?"

"We make a good team. You have to admit that."

"Is there any money in it?"

"I imagine. Look, if nothing else, it will be fun."

"Doing what?"

"I don't know. Following cheating spouses around -surreptitiously videotaping them."

"How about this? I can follow the woman into the bar and see if I can pick her up, take her home, and test her to see how faithful she is."

Amy pouts. She doesn't care much for that idea. She brightens. "Well maybe not that, but I am serious."

Eddie thinks it over for a long minute. He's never considered being a PI. In fact, he hasn't contemplated ever working again unless necessary and at this point, he's financially set from his years working at Dell Computer and some lucky investments. Thus, work at the present is unnecessary for him. Still, Eddie considers that maybe doing something purposeful might give his life some meaning.

"Well?" Amy prods.

Eddie turns to study Amy closer. She does seem serious in a slightly buzzed kind of way. And at the same time, quite desirable. "Don't you have to have some kind of license?" he says.

"Of course. No biggie. I've got a concealed weapons permit, so getting a license shouldn't prove to be much of a problem. I imagine you shouldn't have a problem either. Please! It will be fun." Amy's eyes grow large. She tucks her hands between her knees. "Come on, Eddie, please!"

"Winston and Foster's Detective Agency," Eddie says. "That does have a nice ring to it."

"Foster and Winston's," Amy counters.

"And I suppose you'll want the dominate position in the bedroom, as well?"

Amy hides her smile behind a slow sip of beer. Hell, any position will be a welcome change at this time, she thinks, her face growing hot at the thought. She fidgets in her seat before placing her beer on the coffee table, Eddie's gaze making her uncomfortable, uncomfortable in an exhilarating kind of way.

"You going to make me sleep by myself tonight, Eddie?" she asks, surprised to hear herself voice the question. Amy's green eyes are piercing, penetrating and sparkle as they reflect the light from the end table. Eddie pulls Amy onto his lap, hugs her tight and kisses the top of her head.

"Not a chance," he whispers into her ear. Amy melts in Eddie's arms. She turns her head and looks up at Eddie longingly, their lips mere inches apart. Amy wills Eddie to kiss her and he does and it's enough to curl her toes. The kiss is everything and more than she imagined. She grows hot again, this time in a different place.

Their tongue's meet and explore. Eddie works his hand under her blouse to cup a breast. He feels the nipple grow hard beneath the sheer fabric. His heartbeat grows strong in his chest. He grows hard, their kiss more impassioned and needy. Amy comes up for air.

"Wow!" she says breathlessly.

"Damn, girl!" Eddie says.

Amy works herself free of Eddie's arms, stands to tower over him. "Hold that thought, Eddie. A quick shower and I'm all yours."

Eddie stands and just as quick hoists Amy up and over his shoulder. "Fuck the shower," he says as he carries the giggling

Amy toward the bedroom. Bobo jumps up to follow. "Stay," Eddie says. Reluctantly, Bobo sits. Eddie kicks the bedroom door closed behind them.

~~~

Pavel, a brute of a thug, one of Igor's meanest, leads the freshly bathed struggling woman by the nape of her neck and a twisted arm behind her back. She eyes her discarded burqa in despair and realizes that life for her will never be the same as before the war.

Igor's man brings her to stop before Igor. She's clothed with nothing but a bathrobe pinched from a Hilton Hotel somewhere. Igor grins, his beady eyes moist, his breath foul with the stench of stale cigarettes. Igor reaches for the knot securing the robe. The woman grabs his wrist with her free hand—stares at him in fear and defiance.

Igor wrests his hand free. He likes a challenge. He likes a feisty woman.

"Hold the bitch!" he snaps. Pavel secures the woman's other arm. Better, Igor thinks. He reaches for the knot. The woman kicks out at him, spits.

Igor wipes the spit from his cheek. He backhands her, snapping her head to the side. Follows up with a punch to her gut. She'd have folded double but for Pavel. Igor grabs a hand full of hair, forces her to look at him, dares her with his eyes to spit on him again. Maintaining his stare, again he moves for the knot. This time there's no struggle. She's resigned herself to her fate.

Igor laughs with gusto. "Better," he says with a grunt as he works the knot. The bitch sure tied it tight. Igor withdraws his blade, flicks it open with a practiced flip of the wrist.

The woman's eyes grow large, but her resistance has fled her. Igor licks the trickle of blood from her lip as his knife easily slices through the sash. His eyes trace the parting robe down. He swallows. Her breasts are firm and upright, her stomach flat and the vee between her legs a bush—a hairy bush.

Igor releases the parted robe in disgust. "This one needs a Li-za!" He plops back down in his recliner. The room laughs.

"Carpet muncher," the brute says, "good one, boss."

Igor waves his hand. "Get her out of here. And do something about mop. Erik go with him. Make sure she's not touched. Igor may keep this one for himself." He lights a cigarette and returns his focus to his big screen. He laughs at one of Gilligan's antics.

~~~

Eddie flops the giggling Amy down in the center of his king- sized bed and tugs at her boots as he toes out of his own and kicks his to the side. Eddie wastes no time stepping out of his jeans and shucking his shirt. Amy unbuttons and unzips her own jeans. Today is the first time in a long time that she's worn jeans and boots and she did so for Eddie's benefit, wanting to please him.

A couple of good tugs and off comes Amy's jeans. She's no longer giggling but breathing hard in anticipation and anxiety. She silently hopes she doesn't disappoint Eddie even though she knows it's a silly thought.

The room's dim; lit only by the light cast from the open bathroom door. Still, there's enough light for Eddie to appreciate the sight before him—Amy's firm legs and thighs, a mound prominent beneath plain-white panties. Eddie's breathing matches the rise and fall of Amy's chest. Hastily, she unbuttons her blouse and works her arms free of the garment. Her bra follows. Eddie steps out of his boxers. Amy gasps at the sight of his hardness. Fuck the foreplay, she wants him inside her now, right this very second.

Amy pushes her panties down below her knees. Eddie tugs them the rest of the way down and free. He tosses them to the side as Amy draws her knees up and apart. It's a welcoming sight and Eddie moves in between them and positions himself above her.

Amy grabs him, guides him near, urges Eddie to enter her. "Winston and Foster," Eddie whispers. Amy slaps Eddie on the chest, nods vigorously. She releases him as he enters—her nails dig into his shoulders and a moan escapes her lips.

"Eddie!"

A moan escapes Eddie's own lips as he buries himself in her. God, she feels good, Eddie thinks and abnormally wet. Eddie loses himself in the rhythm of making love to Amy and the sound of her whimpers. Beads of sweat form at his temples.

Amy pulls him down on her, wraps her legs around him and draws his lips to hers. Neither of them can hardly breathe. Their kiss needy, impassioned.

Amy guides his hands and fingers to her breasts and nipples. The caressing of her breasts and the kneading of her nipples take her to the edge—an edge she can't recall ever reaching. Oh, it's good to her—God is it good.

"Come in me," Amy moans into his mouth. It's all Eddie needs to hear. He buries himself inside Amy one last time. She gently bites his lower lip as he releases deep inside her.

Amy feels Eddie's release—his throb—and she too releases in an orgasm that wracks her body -makes her whole being shudder. Tears cloud her vision. Tears of happiness—tears of joy.

Breathless, Eddie collapses on top of her. He's spent, at least for now, sated. "Damn, that was good, woman," he finally so manages between breaths.

Amy lightly bites Eddie's shoulder stemming the flow of words that threaten to overwhelm her—suddenly afraid to read more into their sexual encounter than there possibly might be. She answers Eddie with an intense hug and a barely perceptible nod.

There's a scratch at the door. The door pushes open and Bobo slips through. He hops to the corner of the bed, does several spins and settles with his mug on his paws. Eddie and Amy laugh.

~~~

Former Detective Mike Johnson winces with every step. He hates his walker, but at least he's mobile. And the Oxies and whiskey help. Help a hell of a lot.

Johnson studies his reflection in the bathroom mirror. When did his hair turn so gray, grow so thin? he wonders. Months shy of 30 years of dedicated service in law enforcement and he gets canned. Not only canned but facing some serious felony charges as well. How did it all go so wrong? Hell, he can sum it up in one word, well, one name, Eddie Winston.

The fact that Eddie Winston was innocent all along never crosses Johnson's mind. "Well, I've got something for you, pretty boy," he tells his reflection. He takes a long pull of his Jim Beam, sets it on the counter and begins to wrap his knee with a fresh ace bandage. A fucking knee replacement at his age and for that he can thank his former partner, the slut Amy Foster. I've got something for you, too, he thinks.

Johnson wraps the bandage extra tight. He's purchased himself a knee brace similar to what J.J. Watt wears on his arm. To even be up and about after a knee replacement is a miracle, in and of itself. Not to mention getting out on bond. He had to call in a lot of chips to make that happen.

Satisfied with the bandage, Johnson struggles to step into his slacks, but he manages. If there's a will there's a way. Johnson straps on his knee brace. He tentatively puts some weight on his leg. Not bad. The pain's been reduced to a dull ache and he can live with that.

Johnson collapses the walker and leans it against the wall and out of the way. He wishes he'd have bought himself a cane, but what do they say? "Shit in one hand and wish in the other and see what you get." Or something fucking like that. Slowly, Johnson makes his way through his spacious home with its lofted ceilings, its large open floor plan, its multi-colored brick facade and its gabled roof. It's a lonely house, big and lonely. Johnson doesn't have so much as a dog to keep him company and he's okay with that. Well, he was when he worked 20 fucking hours a day.

Johnson makes it to the kitchen. Just him and his bottle. He looks over at the clock on his oven: 10:00 p.m. on the dot. And he's not even remotely tired. Hell, he's beginning to feel pretty damn good. Yeah, even good enough to take a little ride. He downs the last of the bottle. No matter, he has some more Beam in his truck.

Johnson gets up. He'll cut through his garage, take inventory of what's in his garage before heading out. He snickers, "one never knows what will come in handy if the opportunity arises."

~~~

"Hey, Erik. Look there's that fuck again. Making him out to be some kind of hero," Igor says. "YOB te-BYA!," fuck you, he tells the man on his TV. Erik moves to stand beside the recliner, but not too close. The screen changes to a still shot of Detective Amy Foster. Erik points.

"That's the bitch, too, nyet?"

"Shut fuck up. I can't hear what they're saying." Igor listens intently. Why he should care, who knows. He just does. So, she was a cop. "Hmm," he grunts. Igor gestures holding up a big set of breasts. "u nye-YO KLASS-na-ya grud. Fucking nice, nyet?"

Erik nods "kra-SI-vi-ye gla-ZI-sche," he says. Igor scowls up at Erik. He feels like slapping him.

"You and the 'beautiful eyes.' You sound like fucking poet. Poets, PI-dor, faggots-da." Igor laughs at Erik's discomfort. He likes getting his brother-in-law's goat. He jumps up. "Let's take ride, Erik. piz-DA, pussy. That's what make world go around."

~~~

Amy stirs, yawns wide. She's still snugged tightly in Eddie's arms and she can't recall the last time she was so happy. She slept well and slept in late.   Bobo, still on his corner, offers his own yawn. We're a little family, she thinks. And now Eddie and she are partners, as well. Amy recalls Eddie's words while poised to enter her, "Winston and Foster." She smiles to herself. Not fair. She'd have agreed to anything at that point to have him enter her. Of course, he was only teasing her. She grows wet just thinking about Eddie inside her.

Amy reaches behind her and takes Eddie's piece in her hand. He grows instantly hard at her touch. She strokes him until she feels his breath turn hot and ragged against her neck. She giggles, she's got his full attention.

Amy releases Eddie long enough to snatch the sheet free of them and toss it over Bobo, who scrambles to free himself and hop to the floor.

Amy rolls in Eddie's arms and pushes him onto his back. She straddles Eddie and reaches behind her once more to take Eddie in her hand. Good morning, she tells Eddie rubbing the tip of his cock against her clit and then barely parting her lips with it.

Amy takes just the head of Eddie inside her. She can feel the pulse in his cock and see the lust in his eyes. She smiles down at him.

"Foster and Winston," she says.

"Foster and Winston," Eddie croaks. They both laugh.

Amy drops taking Eddie all the way inside her. She almost comes at the sudden pleasure. She grinds her pelvis into him one good time as Eddie's mouth finds her left breast then her right. She closes her eyes and loses her breath at the added sensation.

Eddie bucks his hips. Amy takes her cue—begins to ride and meet Eddie's thrusts. God she could get used to making love to Eddie.

Amy's breasts turn hot and damp in Eddie's hands. Damn, Amy feels so damn good. Too damn good this early in the morning and the way she's riding him. Man, this woman's hot.

Amy blows the bangs from her face. She's almost there. It's going to be a short ride, but a powerful orgasm is in the works. She sucks in her lower lip—concentrates on all the stimulus.

The morning sunlight from the east-facing window highlights Amy's sheen of perspiration. Eddie's at awe at the sight of Amy's athletic body. He knew she had a nice body and has had glimpses of it, but this is the first opportunity for him to really appreciate the effort Amy must put into keeping herself in such good shape. Eddie's own efforts to think of anything other than the sex he's having to prolong the inevitable is not working for him. Amy's moans don't help the effort much either. Damn this woman's hot, Eddie thinks.

Amy clutches Eddie's hands and wills him to squeeze her breasts harder. "Now, Eddie!" she moans as she sucks her bottom lip in once more and her head lulls to one side.

Amy bottoms out on Eddie and contracts against him. Her whole body quivers with her release. It's enough to drive Eddie over the edge. His hands go to her ass, pulls her in tighter. Eddie comes—and comes hard. It's Amy's turn to collapse on Eddie and she does. They both gasp for breath. Both drenched with sweat despite the coolness of the room.

Amy's first to catch her breath, "Damn, Eddie. That was good. A gal could sure get used to that in the morning."

"Do you cook breakfast too?" Eddie says catching his own breath.

Amy lifts up and pinches him on both sides—laughs. "Actually, I do and I will. Not to mention now that you're growing soft inside me. You're not much use to me here any longer, so we might as well eat."

Eddie bucks Amy off of him, wrestles her to her back, straddles her and pins her arms above her head. He kisses her good and hard and lifts back up to study her. His grin matches hers.

"Then breakfast it will be, woman," he says. Eddie lets her up, smacks her ass one good time for the hell of it.

"Ouch!" Amy screams. She studies the print on her ass. "That better not bruise, mister," she says, giggles and disappears into the bathroom.

Eddie leans back into his pillow. He feels like the luckiest man in the world at the moment. And it's a damn good feeling.

Chapter Six

Johnson struggles to lift his head from the kitchen table. His head throbs, his mouth so cottony he couldn't work up a good spit if he had to. For some reason, he's clutching the keys to his truck and he smells like gasoline. A second empty bottle of Beam lays on its side on the table before him. What the fuck did you do last night, Johnson? he asks himself. He strains to remember but not so much as a glimpse of last night can he recall. "Shit!" Johnson mumbles and runs a hand through his thinning hair. His hand comes away greasy. Johnson realizes he hasn't washed his hair since before he was shot. Fucking Foster, I owe you bitch for shooting me. And pretty boy Eddie, you've got it coming, too.

Johnson pushes away from the table, attempts to stand. Pain slices through his knee and he drops back into his chair. Fuck, his knee hurts! Again, what did you do last night? he wonders. He looks down at his knee. Blood has seeped through his trousers. Uh-oh, he'll need to take a look at it, but of course, he's left his walker in the bathroom. That he can remember clearly. He remembers, too, taking an Oxy. Beyond that, he comes up blank.

Johnson lets his head settle back on the table. He'll just sit here a little longer, he decides.

~~~

Igor kicks the end of Erik's cot. He chuckles. "Rise and shine!"

He can't recall where he heard the phrase, but he likes it. He likes it mostly because it pisses Erik off. Not that Erik says anything, but

61

Igor can see Erik's anger in his sleepy eyes and the set of his jaw. His crew stayed out late last night drinking vodka and playing poker, but that's not Igor's fault. While they played poker, Igor busied himself thinking about all the money his American operation is making. Land of opportunity. His comrades back in Russia weren't fucking kidding when they told him that.

Erik rolls to plant his feet on the concrete floor. He reaches for his pack of cigarettes, shakes one out and tears the filter off. He wishes he had one of his Russian cigarettes made with Turkish tobacco. He'll have to settle with his filterless Marlboro. He lights it and fills his lungs and expels a plume of thick smoke before acknowledging Igor's presence. He spits a piece of loose tobacco.

"What time is it, Igor?"

"Time to get happy ass up."

Erik steps into his black, low-topped, low-heeled boots with zippers on the side as the smoke from his dangling cigarette causes him to close one eye. Boots on, Erik stands.

"So, Igor, what's so important that you need me up this morning."

"The pregnant one, whore, water broke. Come see. I think she shit out bastard child any minute now," Igor says with obvious pleasure.

Igor taps a finger to the side of his head. "Igor smart business man," he adds. Erik falls in behind him. The last thing Erik wants to see is a whore give birth. He's not sure his stomach can handle it. Erik snatches a bottle of vodka off a table as he passes and shrugs.

But what can he do? Someday he'll kill Igor and be boss. That's what.

If Erik gets sick at the sight, all the better, Igor thinks. And he is a smart businessman. He supplies none of his whores with condoms and no contraceptives of any kind and it's not because he's Catholic. If the whore should get pregnant all the better. When baby come, he sell—big money. And if they get disease, he's got penicillin. And if they get AIDS, so be it, he's not fucking whores.

Smart rules: don't fuck own whores and don't do own dope. He opens the door to the warehouse's office and let's Erik precede him. In the middle of the office, on the floor, on a bare mattress, lay the pregnant migrant with her knees up and thighs parted. Before her, a Mexican midwife encourages her to breathe and push in both Spanish and in English, though the woman likely understands neither.

The room stinks, but that doesn't deter Igor any, a good ten or 15 grands making its way into the world. It all depends what the baby looks like, Igor thinks. And sometimes whether boy or girl.

The Mexican midwife looks over at Igor and Erik. She's scared of them, but mostly of Igor. To her, he looks like Vladimir Putin. She hopes her face doesn't reveal her disgust.

"The baby coming, si," she says. And it is, out pops the head. The midwife gasps, her hands begin to tremble. This is not good, she thinks.

"What? What is it?" demands Igor. The midwife does the sign of the cross.

"Retardado," she says softly though that's not exactly what's wrong and what she's seeing she's only read about. Apparently, the woman before her has been exposed to the Zika virus and the baby being born has an unusually small head. "Microcephaly," she thinks it's called.

"Umm," she says pulling the baby free of the mother. Igor snaps.

"What?" He positions himself to see better. His blood pressure spikes as he spots the baby's head. "chto za BLYAD-stvo, what the hell's going on here?" he demands, though the cause of the deformity is already registering. Fucking mosquitoes. Probably stung by an infected mosquito during her layover in Cuba. But for a fucking can of bug spray, Igor thinks, 15 grand down the drain. He feels like hitting someone or something. "Erik, get rid of damn thing," he says turning toward the door.

The woman screams as Erik orders the midwife to wrap the baby in a towel and put it in a trash bag.

~~~

Eddie mops the last of the egg yolk with the remainder of his buttered toast and pops it into his mouth. It was a simple breakfast of eggs, bacon and toast, but a satisfying meal, the good company making it that much more so. He swallows and wipes his mouth with a paper napkin and drops it onto his plate.

"Thanks," Eddie says as Amy gathers the plates.

"You're welcome... You know, Eddie, about the PI business, I'd understand if you didn't really want to do it," she says as she sets the plates into the sink. She turns on the hot tap to keep from having to face Eddie, not wanting Eddie to see how much, in fact, she does want it to happen. Eddie pushes away from the table, turns his chair to watch Amy. He's not sure how profitable the business will be, but that's not much of a consideration at this stage in his life because, despite the recent volatility in the market, his simple portfolio has fared relatively well. What the hell, Eddie thinks, it's obviously important to Amy—the apprehension that he'll say no evident in her abrupt movements as she awaits his answer. Eddie smiles.

"About the name..." he begins.

Amy turns and nervously dries her hands on a towel.

"Eddie, the name's not really all that important."

Though he knows he shouldn't, Eddie laughs at Amy's discomfort. "I'm just messing with you," he says. "Let's do it."

Amy's shoulders relax. She throws the towel at Eddie, pulls the string on her apron and smiles seductively.

"Well, I guess we better consummate our partnership," she says moving to straddle Eddie.

"What was that last night and this morning then?"

Amy traces with a finger the strong outline of Eddie's jaw—her finger coming to rest on his dimple. "Practice," she murmurs. And practice makes perfect Eddie thinks, growing hard beneath Amy's weight.

"You drive a hard bargain, Ms. Amy Foster."

Amy giggles and gives Eddie a quick smack on the lips. She reaches for her car keys on the table—turns curious. "Hey, Eddie, what's this forth button on my key fob?"

Eddie eyes the fob. "Looks like you can crank your car remotely."

"Huh," Amy says. "Seems like the salesman said something about an after-market alarm."

"There you go, then."

"How far away can you be?"

Eddie shrugs. "A thousand feet, maybe."

"And it works through walls and all?"

"That's the beauty of it."

"The car's so quiet, we might not even hear it crank from in here," Amy says. She debates on whether to try it out and curiosity gets the better of her. She depresses the button.

The explosion is deafening—shakes the entire house. Amy spills to the floor as Eddie scrambles to get to his feet. Bobo yelps and takes cover under the table. Eddie smells smoke. He grabs Amy's outreached hand and snatches her to her feet. Eddie blows out his cheeks hoping to stop the ringing in his ears. The smoke's coming from the living room. Eddie ducks through the door. The living room curtains are on fire.

"Fire extinguisher! Under the kitchen sink!" The thing's been under the kitchen sink since he bought the house and likely doesn't work.

Eddie's socked feet crunch on broken glass as he reaches the first of the curtains, the flame already licking at the ceiling. Eddie yanks it free and tosses it out the window. He does the same with the next three. "Hurry!" Eddie yells as he crosses back across the broken glass.

"I'm looking!" Amy screams back, pulling years' worth of accumulation from under the sink and tossing it to the side. She finds it. "Thank God." It's pitifully small, she thinks tossing it to Eddie. She pushes to her feet as Eddie disappears out the garage door. She's shocked to see the bloody footprints Eddie leaves in his wake. Amy hurries after him.

Eddie pulls the pin on the embarrassingly small extinguisher. Amy's car is engulfed and it's starting to blister the paint on his truck. Like it really matters seeing how all his windows have been blown out.

The heat's intense. "There's a hose under the bush," Eddie yells over the roar of the flames. He nears at a squat, aims and pulls the trigger. The thing actually works. A cloud resembling talcum powder shoots from the small funneled end. He directs it at the hottest spot of the fire, the interior. The spray lasts all but 30 seconds but it retards the flames some.

Amy turns the spigot on high. The branches on the bushes scratching her arms and legs coming and going. Eddie reaches for the hose's end and takes it from her. She watches in vain as Eddie douses what's left of her new car. What the fuck happened? A bomb? Johnson? Johnson made bond? She blows the hair from her face. The bastard!

"Call the fire department," Eddie yells, his face beet red from the heat. Amy hurries back inside to make the call. Tears sting her eyes. What if she hadn't tried the stupid remote? One, two, or possibly all three could be dead this morning. She makes the call from her cell phone and rejoins Eddie outside. In the distance, she hears the first of the sirens. Maybe she should put something on besides Eddie's T-shirt, she considers, but decides, fuck 'em if they can't take a joke. She'll cross her arms nevertheless, for the cameras that is.

~~~

Johnson lifts his head once more. He's beginning to shake now that the alcohol is wearing off. His hands go to his head. He can't believe his head's hurting the way it is. How much did you drink last night, Mike? And more importantly, what in the hell did you do?

Johnson pushes to his feet. If he doesn't get something to drink, he believes he's going to die. Using his chair for a crutch, he inches to his refrigerator. He's breathless by the time he reaches it, but he makes it. Johnson opens the fridge's door and is relieved to see a tall six-pack of Miller High Life. At least he didn't drink the beer, too.

"Thank God," Johnson mumbles. He pulls one from the ring and pops the top and turns it up. His lips are numb to the touch of the can. The escaped beer drips off his chin and onto his soiled dress shirt. He tosses the can into the sink. "Ahhh." He smacks his lips reaching for another beer. "Now that is good." His head clears a bit. He downs the second beer and tosses the can into the sink as well.

Johnson grins inanely. "Maybe you'll live after all, boy," he tells himself. He holds onto the door handle until a dizzy spell passes, then closes the door and opens the freezer door for the chilled Vodka. One good pull from it and he'll be set to go. The vodka burns all the way down. Hair of the dog, the surest hangover remedy by far.

Now what? Johnson returns the bottle and shuts the freezer door. He puts a little extra weight on his leg. Though it's aching, it holds up pretty well—well enough to get him to the living room for some TV and some rest. He decides to take the remainder of the six-pack with him.

Johnson makes it to his favorite recliner, clicks on the TV. "BREAKING NEWS," the screen says. Johnson turns up the volume, sets the beer in his lap and reclines. The screen changes to a view from the station's helicopter and zooms down on Eddie's house. Johnson's beer misses his lips. "Shit!" He pushes the recliner forward and turns the volume up some more.

"...initial reports coming in—there's been some kind of explosion involving at least one automobile and possibly two. As you can see, Barbara, fire units are just arriving on the scene. The area we are talking about here is a residential area in the north. Austin Woodrow vicinity just east of Burnet.

"If I'm not mistaken, Barbara, this is the residence of Mr. Eddie Winston..."

"It does appear to be so, Sam..."

"Let's see if we can get a better angle and zoom in a bit. That's better. And I believe it to be Mr. Winston manning a water hose, though it appears the vehicle that he's dousing is a total loss. It also appears the house suffered some damage, as did the truck parked in the drive. At this time, I think it's safe to say only one vehicle is involved."

"Anything else you can tell us, Sam?"

"If I'm not mistaken and I hope I'm not going out on a limb here, but the woman you can see off to the right, I believe her to be Detective... Former Detective Amy Foster."

"Thank you, Sam. And we'll check back in with you as this story continues to unfold."

Johnson runs both hands down the length of his face. "Shit!" he says for the second time in less than a minute. What have you fucking done, Johnson?"

~~~

"Igor, come quick!" Erik calls out, his voice echoing in the spacious warehouse, as a photo of Eddie momentarily fills the screen.

"What is it, Erik?" Igor asks coming to stand beside him. Erik points at the TV screen. The screen changes to a view from the news chopper. They both chuckle.

"Someone try and burn Mr. Eddie, the American," Igor says fighting to control his mirth.

"Blow up, perhaps," Erik says. "Look at car." They both chuckle again. "Looks like American no hurt, da," Erik adds.

"Nor his woman." Igor bites the tip off an expensive Cuban, spits it to the concrete. He points at the screen with his cigar. "American, very lucky man, it seem. Maybe Igor will run into Mr. Eddie again. Teach him no fuck with Igor."

"Very lucky American," Erik agrees, though he sees no good reason to fuck with the American. After all, they're meeting and skirmish was only a chance encounter. He shakes his head and walks away. Igor's one crazy PAD-la, bastard, he thinks. And someday, Igor not so lucky.

~~~

"Stand clear!" the fireman yells at Eddie as he uncoils a short length of hose.

Eddie tosses the hose to the ground and joins Amy a good 30 feet away. He drops to the grass and Amy kneels in front of him.

"Your feet..."

Eddie nods. "I know," he says pulling one sock free. The second snags on a shard of glass. He picks it loose and frees the sock. Amy studies his foot. There are several pieces of glass embedded in his foot, the largest of which buried deep into his heel. She frowns up at Eddie. "This may hurt a bit." Eddie nods. Thankfully, she's not chewed her nails in a while, a whole week and they've grown out a bit. It takes a couple of tries but she manages to remove the piece. Eddie flinches but doesn't make a sound. She removes a couple of smaller shards and moves to the other foot. This one too has several small shards, but enough to have made his foot bleed through the sock, as well.

"The good news is I don't think you'll need any stitches," Amy says.

"And the bad news is someone blew up your new car."

Amy sits down in the damp grass before Eddie. "Correction, the bad news is someone blew up the dealership's car." She smiles wanly. "Think they'll be mad?"

Eddie laughs. "If they were in my position they surely wouldn't be."

Amy follows Eddie's gaze downward. Blushes slightly. Right, no panties. Well, at least no one can see her but Eddie and why am I blushing, she wonders. She tugs at the hem of her T-shirt at the sound of approaching feet.

"Any idea what happened? Hey Detective... Uhm, I mean good morning Detective Foster."

"Hey, inspector. Funny seeing you here."

"Huh?"

"I'm joking. Anyway, if I had to theorize, I'd say my ex-partner, the ex-Detective Mike Johnson, tried to blow me up, or us up."

The inspector winces. "Wow, that's one serious allegation."

"Well, I did shoot him, after all."

"Yeah, I can see how that might have rubbed him the wrong way."

Mr. Winston, would you like EMS to look at those cuts?" "Nah, I suspect I'll live."

"You share Detective Foster's belief that it was Johnson that blew up the car?"

"That's how I read it, yeah."

The inspector nods. Looks around as if searching for something. "I don't note any security cameras around here. Is that a residence across the street? It looks more like a fire station."

"It's a residence," Eddie says. "An older couple I see occasionally coming and going." Bobo makes his appearance. "There's my brave dog. Decide to come out, boy?" Eddie scoops him up and rough-houses him a minute before letting him loose. Bobo trots off around the front of the house.

"I don't suppose y'all heard or witnessed anything suspicious yesterday or this morning?"

"Sorry, can't help you there," Eddie says. Amy nods her assent.

"Not much to go on then. I'll knock on a few doors, tow the vehicle in and have forensics give it a good going over."

Amy lamely hands the inspector the keys. "When I pushed that fourth button, the car blew up."

"Sounds deliberate. Let's see what forensics comes up with. You might consider investing in some security cameras. So, your dog didn't bark or anything?"

"Speaking of, where did the rascal go? Nah, he mostly forgets to bark."

"Well, I guess there's not much left I can ask. Sorry about your truck. It may be a little wet inside. The windows are all blown out except the front windshield. Paint's a little blistered, too."

Eddie plucks a blade of grass and twirls it between thumb and finger before tossing it to the side. He pushes to his feet and offers Amy his hand. Pulls her to her feet. "Thanks." He brushes the grass off Amy's rear. "If there's nothing else."

"Nope, we'll be in touch."

Eddie takes Amy's hand and leads her toward the garage opening.

He waves up at the news chopper before ducking inside. "Well, partner, it looks like our first case is trying to figure out who's out to kill one or both of us."

"Sit down, let me get something to treat your cuts."

"There may be some iodine in the master bath. Seems like I recall seeing some there."

Amy leans in and kisses Eddie on the mouth. "Is it too early to drink a beer? I think I could use something to drink."

One step forward, two steps back, Eddie thinks. But hell, they could have been blown up. "It's 12:00 somewhere."

"Jimmy Buffet?"

"And the Zac Brown Band, I believe."

Amy smiles. "Two beers, coming right up."

Chapter Seven

Johnson watches Eddie and Amy step into the garage. He rubs his hands down his face once more. "Shit, what did ya do, Mike?" he asks himself. There'll likely be a knock on his door shortly, he thinks. Gotta get your story straight. Hell, he doesn't even know if he went anywhere last night. And, these days with cameras everywhere, they'll spot his truck passing somewhere if he did, catch him in a lie. Of course, he has no alibi either way.

Johnson heaves himself from his recliner. Figures he better check his truck for evidence. Fucking Eddie and fucking Amy. It's all their fault. Just look at the mess they got him in. He pulls a beer from the ring and pulls the tab. The beer goes down smoothly. Hell, he's almost starting to feel better. Not about his situation, but his headache's beginning to recede. He takes a tentative step. His leg is holding up. Hurts a mite, but holding up.

Johnson limps his way toward his garage. Seeing Eddie's garage on TV is spurring some kind of memory, but try as he may, Johnson can't bring the memory to the forefront of his mind. Then there's the fact he smells of gasoline.

Johnson steps through the garage door. He must have been in the garage because the light's on and he always turns it off as a matter of habit when he's not in it. He scans the garage, specifically seeking the gas can for his mower—gone. "Shit." Johnson swallows and looks around the garage some more. Several of his storage boxes are pulled out from their storage and some of the contents are spilled on the concrete floor. He limps nearer. What in the world would he have been looking for? What in the hell did he find? And what in the hell did he do? The last question he can't shake. He clearly did something, but what? Johnson almost dreads checking his truck out but has no choice. He's already in deep shit and if he gets arrested again, there'll be no bond this next time.

Johnson depresses the up button to his garage door opener. His truck's there, not too straight in the driveway, but there nevertheless. And, thankfully it doesn't appear to be wrecked.

Johnson approaches his truck cautiously, why he can't say. Terrified perhaps he'll find something he doesn't want to. Now is no time to go to jail, Johnson. Not until you get better and are able to right two wrongs. He snickers despite himself. "Right two wrongs," he mumbles. He likes the sound of that.

Johnson looks up and down the street. No one's paying him no-never-mind. He downs the rest of his beer and tosses the can in the yard. The windows of the truck are down. He pulls the driver's door open to his ten-year-old Ford F-150. The passenger floorboard is cluttered with empty carryout bags and a few empty beer cans, but nothing out of the ordinary seems to be present. Johnson lets out his breath, wipes the sweat from his forehead on his shirtsleeve. He peers into the backseat area. It too is cluttered, but again nothing out of the ordinary strikes him. That leaves only the bed. Johnson limps the last few paces and peers into the back.

His heart skips a beat. At least he thinks it does. Among the typical trash are a roll of duct tape and a partial spool of wire and he knows that they're out of place. They have no business being in the back of his truck. But, as for a gas can, there is no gas can. So where did the gas can go? And why does he believe the tape and wire represent evidence? Because a car in Eddie's drive just happened to blow up, that's why. "Shit!" He's not much of a reader, but he remembers reading a novel a few years back, "Hindsight," he seems to recall the name of it, wherein the young thugs, juvies, made an IED, improvised an explosive device with some wire, a spark plug and gas can. But, in the novel, it didn't quite work out for them; it only created a big fireball.

Did he have any extra spark plugs in the garage? Who are you trying to fool? Of course, you did—for your lawnmower.

Johnson wishes he hadn't left his keys on the kitchen table because he has some evidence to get rid of. Namely, the wire and duct tape. Today they can match the fibers in the damn tape and can tell not only who produced it but for Christ sakes, if it was from the same run, same lot.

"Time to get moving Johnson. They could be already on their way." He'll just grab his keys and maybe a little somethin' for the pain—a fresh bottle of vodka. Yeah, a little vodka because this party ain't over until the fat lady sings. And the fat lady ain't going to sing, by God, until pretty boy Eddie and his whore Amy Foster cease to exist. Johnson chuckles as he limps back into the house – limps but with renewed purpose.

~~~

Igor takes a long pull from his bottle of vodka and kills the TV. It's time to make a few rounds, check on some of his investments.

"Erik! Where fuck are you!" he yells. He's still pissed about the whore shitting out a deform. "Mikhail! Where fuck is moron?"

Mikhail, one of Igor's top muscles shrugs. "Don't know, Boss."

"Go find moron. Let's take ride. You too."

"Sure boss, take ride. You want Pavel, too, boss?"

"Da. Get Pavel." Pavel a bit slow, but strongest and meanest and loyal. A good man, Igor thinks. Unlike Erik, he never questions an order and will kill at a drop of a hat. Igor chuckles, "Drop of a hat." Americans, so many good sayings, but stupid people. Got a fucking socialist running for president. Yeah, promise everyone free everything. Dumb fucks. Just look at Venezuela, Igor thinks, long lines, no food and 2,000 % inflation. Then look at Cuba and their two-dollar whores. No money, no profits for business men like Igor.

Igor thumps himself on the chest. "And Igor the best business man. Make big money."

"kak de-LA?" What's up? Erik says.

Igor works his arm through his shoulder holster, dons his black leather jacket. "What's up, huh? What's up? We take a fuckin' ride, that's what fuckin' up."

"nor-MAL-no," fine, Erik says sensing Igor's in usual ill mood. Igor points to the driver's door of the Caddy. "Pavel, you drive."

"Sure, boss. Whatever you say." They all pile into the Cadillac.

"Did you get rid of trash, Erik?" Igor asks taking shotgun.

"Da."

"And the whore?"

"Give her a few days before go back to work, da."

"Three days, she go back. Hear?"

Erik nods as the garage door opens and the morning sun spills in. The Cadillac pulls out into the day. Pavel need not ask. He knows Igor likes to check out the eastside action first. Collect that money first so his whores aren't tempted by too much money and get funny ideas.

Pavel takes the on-ramp to I-35 South. The traffic's thinned some, but this stretch of highway traversing Austin is some of the worst congested roadways in the state, not to mention the country.

Igor rolls down his window to enjoy the cool morning air. Fires up a Cuban. Inhales deeply. Igor loves his Cuban cigars and when in Cuba some good Cuban "Culo," ass. Well, actually, pussy. Igor just likes the way "culo" sounds.

Pavel takes the Caesar Chavez exit and heads east. Their organization's property is a dilapidated apartment building from which they've slowly pushed the low-rent tenants out and have replaced them with the lower-end whores and dope pushers.

Pavel turns into the apartments and stops before the apartment they keep for on-site muscle. Some of the loiterers disperse at the sight of the Cadillac. A cop does a slow drive-by. Igor gets out of their ride and stretches. He takes a look at his surroundings as Erik and Mikhail disappear into the apartment.   Pavel steps beside Igor.

"Looks kinda quiet, boss."

Igor tosses what's left of his cigar to the curb, reaches inside his jacket for a pack of Marlboro and shakes out a cigarette. Pavel lights the cigarette for him. Igor takes a long draw from his cigarette and exhales slowly. He waves at a group of Mexican kids, some on lowrider bicycles.

"Hey, hey, yo. Come here a minute."

Several of the braver peel off from the group and ride their bikes over.

"Hey, boys. The cops been hassling folks around here lately?" "Si, si," the older of the boys says. He points to the far end of the lot.

"Some negros drinking beer. Cops took two of them to jail. Maybe have some dope, too, si."

Igor nods, digs into his front pocket, pulls out a wad of bills and peels off a $20 for each of the three boys. "Want to make some dinero, si?" The boys nod eagerly. Igor hands each a $20. "Pick up all the beer cans and trash in the lot and...," Igor points two fingers at his eyes, "... you see trouble, you knock on this door. Comprender?" The boys nod enthusiastically. Igor shoos them away like flies. "Go clean, da."

Mikhail and Erik join Igor and Pavel outside. "Lost another one, boss," Mikhail says. "And last night's take not so good."

Igor takes a last hit from his cigarette and flicks it away. "Fuck. What else?"

"May have taken off with black John-junkie-smack."

"Heroin. This John, he buy from us?" Igor asks.

"They say he buys mostly Mexican tar, but sometimes he buys our dope. Probably traded our whore for dope."

Igor nods, opens the passenger's door and slips inside. No respect, that's the problem, Igor thinks. Maybe it's time to bust some heads. Establish this our territory, our town and if you want to sell dope, you sell ours. The others enter as Igor continues to stew. The doors all slam.

"These Mexicans and blacks think we're weak," Igor says. "Pavel, drive the neighborhood."

Erik senses where Igor's going and he doesn't like the thought. "Igor, this black tar, it's controlled by Mexican mafia..."

Igor pounds his chest. "And we fuckin' Russian mafia. What do we care about a bunch of spics? Huh, Erik, you tell me that? When you going to let your nuts drop?"

"I'm just saying…"

"Fuckin' pussy. Drive Pavel."

"Where to?"

"You no fuckin' listen. Fuckin' neighborhood."

"Gee, boss, sorry."

"Gee, boss, sorry. Fuckin' drive."

Pavel backs out of the parking spot and heads out the other entrance/exit. Man, Igor can be hard to deal with at times, but if you work for Igor, he'll take care of you, Pavel thinks. Plus, Igor kept his promise and got him out of Russian Gulag where the two had met and for that he'll never forget. Yes, Pavel thinks, if necessary, he'll follow Igor to the grave. Pavel continues east at a slow pace. Two blocks up a small group of brothers are posted up, one holding a white rag to signal to passersby there's dope to be bought on this corner. Dope, as in crack. Another brother has his back turned away from them, but there's no mistaking the dreadlocks. It's a brother they've been looking for the past week.

"I see him, boss," Pavel says.

"Yeah, that's khu-ye-SOS, cocksucker," Igor says. "Get punk in car. We need talk."

The brother with the rag taps Washington on the shoulder and Washington turns slowly, spots the black Cadillac and bolts.

"Get fuck!" Igor screams.

Pavel stomps on the gas and the Caddy roars. The group scatters.

The Caddy bears down on the fleeing brother with the dreadlocks.

The impact sends him flying over the hood. He shatters the windshield and is thrown to the side. Pavel lays on the brakes and the Caddy skids to a stop.

"Get him, hurry!" Igor shouts.

Washington's on Mikhail's side. He opens his door and scrambles back 15 feet where the moaning Washington lies. Mikhail's amazed at how light the man weighs as he drags him back to the car and tosses him into the back seat. He slides in after him and slams the door shut. Pavel pulls away. Mikhail and Erik prop Washington up between them. Igor turns in his seat, pulls his pistol, taps Washington on the head with the barrel.

"We've been looking for you, you fuckin' cocksucker."

"Oh God! My leg's busted. Man, I need a hospital."

Igor laughs. "Funny guy. He think he need hospital now. Where's my fuckin' money?"

"I got robbed. I swear."

"Check his pockets." Igor holsters his pistol while they search Washington. Mikhail comes up with nothing but a half of a stem that's been smoked so hard that the glass has cracked away leaving not so much as a push, a last hit.

"A fuckin' smoker. Didn't I tell you no smoking. Stop the car, Pavel."

"Here?"

"Yeah, here."

Pavel pulls to the curb.

"Don't..." Erik begins as Igor exits the car and opens the rear door. He takes a quick look around, reaches beyond Erik and drags Washington by the dreads across and over Erik as his right hand unsheathes his knife and flicks it open.

"No!" Washington pleads.

Igor yanks Washington free of the Caddy and cuts Washington from ear to ear. Igor lets Washington drop dead to the asphalt. He wipes his blade clean on Washington's shirt, steps across the spreading pool and gets back into the car."

"Drive."

"Are you fuckin' crazy? We're in a neighborhood for..."

Igor pulls his piece and spins in his seat. He cocks the hammer and sticks the barrel in Erik's face. "Shut fuck up, pussy."

"Shit," Mikhail says.

"ti CHO KHO-chesh piz DI po-lu-CHIT! Huh, do you want a piece of this?"

"You're crazy, man," Erik says softly. Igor laughs and turns back in seat.

"Back to shop, da."

~~~

"There," Amy says with satisfaction after applying the last Band-Aid. "I think you'll live."

Eddie smiles and takes a sip of his beer. "I think you might have enjoyed applying the iodine a little too much," he says.

"Moi," Amy says unable to contain her own smile. "So, what now, Big Boy?"

"Call a glazer to replace the windows in the living room and then go out and survey the damage to the truck. You know who you remind me of, Amy?"

She straddles Eddie hiking her T-shirt in the process. "No, who?"

"Stephanie Plum."

"Because she's hot and horny all the time."

"No, because she always manages to get her car blown up."

Amy kisses Eddie on the lips, tastes the beer on his breath. "Technically, it wasn't my car and my truck wasn't blown up, so we'll have to go with 'hot and horny,'" she says willing Eddie to look down where's she's exposed and inviting. And Eddie does look and likes what he sees.

"'Hot and horny' will work," Eddie says thinking he's clearly got a live one here. Just a week ago, he would have never imagined he'd be sitting on one of his kitchen chairs with a panty-less Detective Amy Foster straddling him and he can't say he's not happy with the development. Eddie lifts the T-shirt up and off Amy and lets it drop to the floor. "Now, you were saying?"

A scratch at the door draws their attention. "Bobo," they say in unison. They both laugh. They had forgotten all about Bobo in their excitement.

"I'll let him in," Amy offers. She hops off Eddie's lap and moves to the door and opens it. In pops Bobo with a toy or something in his mouth. It takes a second to register. Bobo drops it at Eddie's feet and gives it a good lick knocking the little kitten over.

Amy kneels before the kitten whose fur is wet where Bobo carried it. "Where did you find the kitten, Bobo?" she asks picking the kitten off the floor. "Look, Eddie. It's a Persian and its little eyes aren't even open yet." She looks to see if it's a little boy or girl. "I think it may be a little boy."

"Is it hurt?"

"It doesn't look like it."

Eddie frowns, "Bobo." Bobo paws at the kitten. Amy lifts the kitten higher

"No, Bobo. Ah, he's so cute. Can we keep him?"

"Where? Here or at your house?"

Amy makes a face. "Ha, ha." She brightens. "Here, of course, with us."

Eddie can't help but smile. It looks official. He's never met anyone quite like Amy and has never made such a rash decision before. But the hell with it, why not? Shit, you only live once and Eddie wants desperately to live again.

"First, we need to at least see if we can figure out where he got the cat."

"Okay, let me get dressed." She hands Eddie the kitten.

"What about 'hot and horny?' What happened to my Stephanie Plum?"

Amy laughs as she disappears from the room. "It can wait. It won't grow shut," she calls back. "Promise, I know."

Eddie shakes his head. Knocked out of the saddle by a kitten. He scratches the little kitten behind the ear. Moves to the sink to run some warm water. Eddie gently cleans the mucus from the corners of the kitten's eyes. The eyes turn into little slits. The kitten meows surprisingly loud for such a small thing. Great, Eddie thinks. This cat probably thinks I'm his mother now. Well, he is a cute little thing. Eddie goes to find his flip-flops, waits on Amy.

Chapter Eight

Unbeknownst to Johnson, he just misses the arriving detectives. He takes a hit off his bottle, but only a small nip, because he needs to keep his wits about himself. No matter how hard he tries, though, he can't remember what he did last night. But it can't be a coincidence that somebody blew up a car in Eddie boy's driveway, and his gas can's missing and he wakes up after a blackout smelling like gasoline and he finds a partial roll of wire and duct tape in the bed of his truck. That'd be a hell of a lot of coincidences to ignore, wouldn't it, Detective Johnson? He takes another small nip. And you weren't born yesterday, he thinks.

By luck or grand design, Johnson finds himself crossing the 360 bridge and murky Colorado below. He rolls down the passenger's window and slings the roll of tape out and then the roll of wire.

"Find that you fucking smartasses," he says to himself. He finds a place to pull off and turn around and heads back the direction that he'd come. You'll have to be more careful from now on, Johnson thinks. And the next time you'll have to be successful. Successful, meaning pretty boy and the slut dies but you don't get arrested. Then, not only will he be rid of them, but there'll be two people that can't testify against him. He chuckles. Hell, he didn't spend all these years in law enforcement for nothin'.

~~~

Igor feels wonderful as they pull back into their warehouse and the garage door rattles shut behind them. A justified killing always puts him in a good mood. He alights from the Caddy and takes in his surroundings. Sticks a fresh cigar into the corner of his mouth and awaits someone to light it for him. Yes, he's a powerful man who's getting richer by the day. He snaps his fingers as his cigar's being lit.

"Pavel, new one, one Igor like with hairy MAN-du..."

"Muff, da..."

"...put her Igor's apartment, da."

Pavel nods. Igor feels good, needs pussy, Pavel thinks. So be it. It means nothing to him. He goes to the shipping container where yesterday's batch are currently being housed and where they'll be kept for the next few weeks until all vestige of hope is gone and they'll begin their new life making money for the organization.

Pavel lifts the bar that seals the container and opens one side. The women instinctively huddle toward the rear. Pavel points at the one Igor wants and signals her to come forward. Still defiant, the woman shakes her head and says something in Arabic. Erik, standing behind Pavel, laughs. Pavel's scowl shuts him up. Erik wants no part of the big brute. He's just there for the show, if there happens to be one.

Pavel steps up into the container. Steps around all the bedding. The woman cowers in the farthest corner. There's simply nowhere for her to go and her resolve is suddenly without a spine. Pavel lifts her by the hair and drags her kicking and screaming back to the edge of the container. He cuffs her once good in the head.

"Shut fuck up!"

Pavel, maintaining his grip of the woman's hair, pushes her out of the container and hops down beside her. He yanks her back to her feet, wrenches an arm behind her and steers her toward Igor's apartment, which isn't an apartment at all, but a second elevated office overlooking the warehouse. What little fight the woman has left in her all but leaves by the time they reach the base of the stairs. Pavel walks her up the stairs and pushes her through the office door and pulls the door shut. He unplugs the phone line leading into the office and heads back down the stairs in search of Igor.

"Done," he says upon finding Igor. Igor grunts, pushes past Pavel and snatches a fresh bottle of Russian vodka from an open case. He whistles a Russian tune en route. Sometimes he misses the motherland and its long-legged whores, but not today, not when he has some blue-eyed Syrian pussy to fuck.

Igor finds the woman pacing and clutching her robe together. "gdye MOZH-nona-i-TI SHYLUY-khu?" Where can I find a whore, he jokes, uncapping the vodka and taking a pull. He offers the bottle. The woman shakes her head. He points at the robe. "Off, let Igor see." The woman shakes her head. Igor sets the bottle down, closes the short distance to stand before her.

"Off!" he yells in her face. He threatens her with a backhand. The robe slips to the floor. Igor's eyes move down her body, settle on her crotch. He smiles—the pussy now neatly trimmed. He unbuckles his belt, unzips and pushes slacks and boxers down past his knees and forces the woman to the floor and on all fours.

"Da," he says positioning himself behind her. "Da."

~~~

"Ready," Amy announces. "Oh, look, he can see now."

"Yep, but I'm afraid the little fellow now believes I'm its mama."

Amy laughs, "And your family's growing exponentially."

Eddie hands the kitten over, crosses his arms and drums his fingers on his left shoulder. "Yes, there is that," he says good-naturedly. "Assuming we can't find this kitten's real mother."

"Smoky. Let's name him Smoky."

"Are you even listening?"

"Huh?"

Eddie chews the inside of his cheek, tucks a tuft of Amy's loose hair behind her ear and studies her. She's getting prettier by the minute, Eddie thinks. "Ready?"

"Huh? Uhm, sure. Hey, Eddie, let's not try too hard, okay?" They spend the next 20 minutes walking the neighborhood but don't locate the source of the kitten, and where exactly Bobo found it—he ain't giving it up. He just happily trots here and there sniffing and marking his new territory.

Despite a rocky start, the day's poised to be a nice one. They stop beside Eddie's truck and survey the damage.

"Sorry about your truck," Amy says meekly. Eddie pulls open the driver's side door and little squares of safety glass spill to the drive. Eddie frowns at the sight of two inches of water puddled in the floorboards. Eddie leaves the door open. Amy cuddles the kitten, stops short of chewing a nail.

"Not good," she says.

"They won't total it though." He sighs. "Oh, well. It's a beautiful day. Why let one bombing ruin the whole day."

Amy twists the toe of her sandal on one of the cubes of glass. She looks to the sky. "It is nice. What are you suggesting?"

"Zilker Park. This evening's Blues of the Greens."

"Who's playing?"

"Marcia Ball. It's been years since I've been to an outdoor concert. I miss it."

"Cool. And we'll be harder to kill being in a public place and all."

"There is that too. Plus, we can take a cooler of beer and Bobo and Smoky, too. Do you have cutoffs, boots and a halter top to wear? We might as well fit in."

"Right. Halter tops skipped my generation altogether."

"Scared to wear one, are you?"

"Nooooooo. But don't have one. Will you settle for a bikini top?"

"And cutoffs, where the cheeks of your ass hang out."

"Eddie, I'm not 20, you know. Besides, nothing on my ass hangs out."

"Okay," Eddie says turning to look at his truck, "If you say so."

"Hey, what's that supposed to mean?"

Eddie laughs. Amy punches him in the shoulder. "Fucker," she says and laughs with him. "Let's do it. We'll have to swing by my house, though."

Eddie turns and hugs Amy, careful not to crush the kitten. He kisses her on the top of her head. "Deal, let's do it. Call a glazer for the house and I'll clean the truck up some."

Amy lifts up on tiptoes and kisses Eddie on the mouth. "Deal." She hurries on into the house. Eddie heads to the garage to get his portable drill. He'll just punch some holes in the floorboards to allow the water to drain and dry the rest of the interior the best he can. Eddie looks to the sky. "Thank you for keeping us safe," he says.

~~~

An unmarked detective's car is parked in Johnson's drive upon his return with two detectives standing outside and waiting on his return. He recognizes both, of course, and the recognition of the lead detective brings Johnson some relief. Johnson pulls in and makes a big showing of getting out of his truck.

"Boys, how's it going?" he asks leaning against the fender of his truck.

"Johnson," they both say.

"Can one of you boys get my walker out of the back. Can't much get around without it, you know. You see with the knee and all. It's nice of you boys to stop by and check on me."

The lead detective, Whitaker, gets the walker out of the back and expands it. "Not solely a social visit, Johnson. Though we go way back, I got a job to do as well." He winks with his back still turned to his partner.

"I can appreciate that. What's this about, Donny?"

"I'm sure the Fire Marshall will be around to see you at some point, too."

Johnson feigns confusion. "Oh? Not sure where you're going with this."

"Fair enough. Can we take this in the house for a minute? We need to ask a few questions, then we'll be on our way."

"Sure, may even have a couple of extra beers in the fridge." Johnson takes about ten minutes to inch his way into the house taking numerous rests breaks and doing his share of moaning along the way.

Finally, he makes it into his living room and into his recliner. He catches his breath.

"Now what can I do you for, boys?"

"I take it you haven't seen the news?" Whitaker asks. Johnson shakes his head.

"Can't say I have."

"Well, it seems somebody blew up a vehicle this morning in Eddie Winston's driveway. I don't suppose you know anything about that, would you?"

"Gosh, no. I hope no one was injured."

Whitaker smiles. "Right, anyway, did you go anywhere last night or early this morning?"

"You know I did go for a ride last night. I needed to get out and get some air."

"Did your ride take you by Mr. Winston's house by chance?"

Johnson was afraid the questions would lead there. Hell, he doesn't remember, but he must have. And the big question is: what do they already know?

"I can't remember exactly where all I went, but surely I wouldn't have gone by Eddie's house. Truthfully, when I got home, I took one of my pain pills and drank a little too much Jim Beam and it makes my memory a little foggy."

"So, you really don't have an alibi, correct?"

"You said it was a vehicle. Eddie drives a truck. I've never known him to have a car. Hell, if it was me, I'd blow up the truck. Whose car was it anyway?"

"Your ex-partner's. She just bought it the afternoon before."

"Well, there you go. I would have never known that. Plus, as a condition of my bond, I'm to avoid all contact with Foster. Hell, Eddie, too."

Whitaker snaps his notebook closed. "Sorry to have had to ask questions like this." He turns. "Partner, have any questions for Johnson?"

"Nah, you pretty much covered all my questions."

Whitaker nods, stands. He shakes Johnson's hand. "I hate things went down like they did. Hope you can beat the rap."

"Thanks. Y'all take care now, you hear," Johnson says watching them take their leave. He waits until he hears the door shut before he audibly exhales and wipes the beginning of the sheen from his forehead.

Johnson stands, knocks the walker out of his way and moves to the kitchen and refrigerator for the remainder of the vodka. Hell, he needs a good strong shot after the encounter. Fortunately, his old buddy was assigned the case. But, there's still the Fire Marshal to deal with and that might not go so well. He takes a long pull from the bottle. Hell, not much he can do about that. Fucking Eddie and that whore Amy Foster. If it weren't for them, he wouldn't be in the mess he's in. And he can't delude himself. He's in a hell of a mess.

Well, if he's going down, he's going take two with him. And they can take that to the fucking bank—to the fucking bank.

~~~

"Da," Igor says pulling out. He stands and pulls up his boxers and pants. He puts his boot on the cheek of the woman's ass and shoves her prone—laughs.

"Pussy good to Igor, da. Igor keep whore for himself."

The woman lifts herself from the floor and rolls to sit. Her eyes flood with contempt—hate. Igor renews his laughter. "What, you no like big Russian slong?"

The Syrian spits at Igor. Igor reddens.

"Fuckin' bitch!" he screams pouncing on her—straddling her.

His left hand goes to her throat. His right hand begins to pummel the woman with blows. She scratches at his hands and squirms and kicks under his weight.   She can't breathe. Still Igor's fist pummels which flattens her nose, cuts gashes in her cheeks, and knocks her front teeth out.

Blood pours from the woman's injuries. Her kicking abates. Her struggles abate. Still Igor's fist bears down on her. Igor beats her until he's breathless and the woman's nothing but a lifeless rag doll beneath him. Strong hands grip him under the arms and lift him off the woman.

"Fuck, what you do, Igor?" Pavel asks with a shaky voice.

Igor shakes his head, stares down at the woman—a woman that's no longer recognizable. "Whore, da mnye ab-so-LYUT-no fi-o-LYE-to-vo!" He spits. "Whore make no diff to Igor." Igor flexes his hand. The knuckles are cut and already beginning to swell. He thinks he might have broken some bones in his hand, in addition to destroying a valuable asset. He shrugs.

"Pavel, get rid of whore, da."

Pavel nods slowly. He's seen Igor lose his temper before, but nothing like this since the days they were imprisoned together.

"Sure, Igor. I take Mikhail. We get rid of."

Igor plucks the bottle of vodka off the table and leaves Pavel to clean up yet another mess. So be it. It's Igor's world.

Chapter Nine

"Acquiring a PI's license doesn't appear to be all that problematic," Amy says scrolling down the page a little farther. Eddie comes to stand beside her and view the computer's screen. He pulls the tab on a fresh beer and sets it down before her.

"They're almost finished replacing the glass in my truck. It took a little bit to run down the glass. It's seldom, it appears, that they get a call to replace all four side windows in a vehicle, absent a major hail storm or vandalism. The truck still looks like shit on the driver's side, though."

Amy takes a sip of her beer. She pats him on the leg. "And that's why I'll be riding shotgun until you get it painted."

Eddie puts his arm around her, pulls her to him and gives her a squeeze. "Such a thoughtful old gal."

"Old!"

"Ol'. Ol' gal."

"Oh, okay, I think. It sure sounded like you said 'old', though."

"Sometimes we hear what we want to hear."

"Huh? Never mind." Amy exits the site having seen enough for one day. "Hey, I'm getting hungry. We haven't eaten anything since breakfast. How about we stop on the way to my house and pick up a greasy bucket of fried chicken?"

"You suddenly embarking on an ultra-high calorie diet, are you?"

"Having survived a near-death experience again today, I've decided you only live once." She looks up at Eddie and smiles. "Know what I mean?"

Eddie leans over and types "cellulite" into the search area, taps enter. He clicks on one of the search results. "There you go. Read up while I put on my boots and shirt."

"Fucker," Amy calls after him. She clicks on a link—is repulsed by the images. Never, she vows then and there. Though the photos do give her some pause and misgivings about fried chicken, they're not enough to alter the fact she's settled on fried chicken to eat. To do otherwise would be the same as conceding the point. She closes out the window and giggles. What point?

Eddie drags the cooler out to the truck. Hoists it into the back. "Cool," Amy says. "The thing has wheels on it."

"You'll appreciate the fact it pulls as easy as it pushes."

"Ha, ha, I don't think so. I have this kitten to look after." Eddie moves around to the passenger's side door—opens it for Amy. He helps her up and in and then opens the rear door for Bobo. He shuts both doors and moves to his side and climbs in.

"It smells like burned rubber in here," Amy says.

"The residual effect of your car burning in the drive next to it Stephanie."

"Which begs the question: how is it that you know of Stephanie Plum? I can't picture you curled up on the couch with a Janet Evanovich novel."

Eddie only smiles. Some things are just better kept a secret. They stop by a KFC along the way. Amy's house is off South First, deep in the heart of South Austin. Amy points out the drive. It's a nice little brick house with a giant oak in the center of the small front yard. Amy shows Eddie around. The house is quaint, a three-bedroom with a single garage, screened-in back porch and a huge backyard in need of mowing. "Nice," Eddie sums up.

"And only 15 more years of mortgage payments and I'll own it free and clear and will only have to pay taxes on it for the rest of my life."

"I believe your taxes will go down when you hit 65," Eddie says.

"Great. Here hold the kitten and I'll change," she says leaving Eddie standing in the living room. Eddie picks up an AT&T Uverse remote and clicks on the flat screen. He settles on the couch and flips through the channels—stops on tennis. He hasn't played since high school, but he still enjoys watching it. And, Federer, one of his favorites, is currently playing.

"Is this slutty enough for you," Amy says entering the room.

She's wearing faded cutoffs, a Bud Light cap with a ponytail pulled through the back, an American flag inspired bikini top and a pair of red lizard cowboy boots. She spins for Eddie. He whistles.

"Good enough to eat," he says.

Amy smiles. "I'll hold you to that."

Eddie returns the smile. "Well, if it's anything like riding a bicycle."

Amy swaps at him. "Let's go, lover."

They stop for ice and beer and beef jerky en route to Zilker Park. The truck now has an irritating whistle caused by the heat damage to the rubber molding around the windows on his side. He rolls all the windows down—rests his elbow on the door's edge. It's a beautiful day, he thinks once more. And despite the morning's excitement, he feels good about life in general.

They pay to park and head toward the concert area falling in with hundreds of party goers heading their direction. The grounds are green and the diversity of people is unparalleled. Eddie shucks his shirt and drops in on the cooler as they continue on. Bobo strains against his leash. The kitten kneads against Amy's breast.

The area's filling in rapidly towards the stage. Eddie nods. "How close do you want to get?" Eddie asks.

"Close to the front. Uh-oh, don't look now," Amy says. "It's my ex and his new bimbo." She reaches in and takes Eddie's hand, the hand that holds Bobo's leash.

"Hey, Frank. Funny seeing you here. I didn't realize you like live music. Hey Sara."

"I do now." He sizes Eddie up and feels a tinge of jealousy, though he's the one that left Amy. Sara smiles broadly at Eddie. She feels a tinge of jealousy, too. Damn, he's handsome, she thinks.

Eddie nods at the pair; offers an amused smile.

"So, I see the rumors are true," Frank says. Amy lets go of Eddie's hand, loops her arm through his.

"Yep. We're living together now. See you around."

"Yeah, whatever," Frank says.

Eddie chuckles when they're out of earshot. "So, we're officially living together now," he says.

"Well, I had to say something," she says causing them both· to laugh. "I mean, did you see the woman? God, she's beautiful."

"Oh, I saw her alright."

Amy pinches his side. "I was being... You're not supposed to agree with me. You're supposed to offer comforting words."

"I prefer older women. How's that? Ouch."

"Not comforting. Let's spread our blanket here. Here... Hold the cat."

Eddie sets the kitten on his shoulder and digs in the ice for a couple of Bud Lights. He admires Amy's ass as she bends to spread the blanket. He has to give it to her. She does have a nice ass. Hell, she has a nice body period. And the looks and personality to match. He can picture himself happy in a relationship with her.

Amy turns. "Enjoying the view?"

"Me and everybody behind me."

She lifts the kitten off Eddie's shoulder. Takes the offered beer and sits on the blanket. Eddie takes a seat next to her, puts his arm around her. Amy leans into him. Rests her head against him. They sip their beers as the crowd settles in and Marsha Ball's band finishes setting up. This is too cool, Amy thinks. This is living.

The sun begins to dip and Marsha begins to bang out a piece on her piano. A joint's passed Eddie's way. He rarely smokes weed, but what the fuck. He takes a lung-expanding hit, chokes back a cough and passes the joint to Amy. She shrugs and takes a hit. Well, she no longer has to worry about drug tests. It's been 20 years since she's smoked any marijuana and boy does she cough. Amy passes the joint along as another joint comes to their direction.

The music's loud and captivating. Amy giggles and whispers into Eddie's year. "God, I'm fucking stoned."

Eddie laughs. He's stoned too and he can't help but laugh at Amy's slits for eyes. He digs them out another beer and passes several out to his neighbors. They drink and smoke and enjoy the rest of the show.

"That was too fucking cool," Amy says. "When can we go to another?"

"Yeah. Marsha Ball's the shit, alright. I think she only plays once, but I don't see why we can't go to all the outdoor concerts."

Amy folds up the blanket as the people around them begin packing up and dispersing. They begin the long trek back to the truck, Amy taking Bobo's leash so she can hold Eddie's free hand.

Amy squeezes Eddie's hand. "What the..." she nods, "look, Eddie, I can't be that stoned."

Eddie looks expecting to see Amy's ex again but doesn't see him. "The little girl, Eddie! The little girl!"

Thirty feet ahead of them, a little girl's head is turned to stare at them. She's holding hands and being walked between a man and a woman. Eddie squints in the dim light—attempts to see the little girl better.

"Eddie, stoned or not, tell me that's not the same little girl."

The girl turns, but Eddie's seen enough of her and he's near positive it's the same girl. He shakes his head. "What the fuck!" He picks up the pace, closes the distance between them. "Hey excuse me! Hey, hold up there a second!"

The man and woman turn for a second. "Yeah, you," Eddie says.

They turn back, continue on. "Hey, I said hold the fuck up there for a second."

~~~

As the evening wanes, Johnson, despite his best intentions, leans heavier of his second bottle of Jim Beam. After the detectives left, Johnson made himself a liquor run. He charged him a case of

Beam and picked up two bottles of vodka to fill the hole in his freezer.

Johnson twirls the pill bottle in his hand, wonders whether he's taken a pill or not in the past four hours. Probably not, he decides, shaking out another Oxy. He chases the small pill with a shot of Beam. Talk about feeling no pain. Shit, he wishes he'd discovered the little pills years ago. Shit, he wishes Eddie and the slut were already dead. Johnson wonders where he went wrong. He chuckles, probably when he didn't know what the fuck he was doing. Having not succeeded, what the fuck does he do now? Because of his fuckup, he ought to lay low for a day or two. That's what he should do.

Johnson takes another pull from his Beam. His vision blurs around the edges. He blinks and squints and tries to focus on the TV. What the fuck is he watching anyway? His bottle slips from his hand as he nods off, spilling in his lap. He grunts, rights the bottle only to nod off again. His head lulls back and a raspy snore escapes his gaping mouth. The knock on his door goes unanswered.

~~~

Igor loves the nightlife. Loves slinging money around. Playing the high roller. There's a lot to love about Austin as well. Namely, the strip joints, Igor thinks. Austin's a town full of college-aged girls, thanks to the University of Texas. Of course, not all of the dancers dance to pay for their educations. Some have fallen to the wayside thanks to alcohol and drugs and these are the ones that Igor specifically seeks out. For one, they're a good source of income—and two, they're a good source for high-end pussy.

"Where to, Boss?" Pavel asks. "The Yellow Rose?"

"Nyet. XTC."

Pavel grins, he likes XTC because it's BYOB (bring-your-own-bottle) and it's a totally nude club. Pavel especially likes the shaved girls - shaved girls with little tits, though that's a hard combination to find. Most of the girls opt for bigger tits if they can find some sucker willing to pay for them.

"How come you no get window fixed?" Igor says pointing at the windshield.

"Sorry, Boss. It's not so bad at night. I fix tomorrow, nyet."

Igor shrugs. "Da." Igor likes taking Pavel along with him to the clubs because none of the clubs challenge anything that Igor does, fearful of Pavel's size. He chuckles to himself. And rightfully so, because if they step out of line, Pavel rip their fuckin' head off.

"What?" Pavel asks. "What so funny?"

"Nada," he says a Mexican whore having taught him a little Spanish. "Stop at liquor store. Buy something for club." Igor checks his left pocket, then his right, making sure he brought along some party favors: some little bags of heroin in one pocket and cocaine in the other. The heroin is the most lucrative. Some get addicted after only one bump. And just like that, he snaps his fingers figuratively, they're customers for life.

They stop at a liquor store as planned and purchase a case of Budweiser. Igor likes the red, white and blue cans, but not so much the beer. Too watered down, he thinks.

The XTC is off 290 East just east of I-35. They park in the mostly empty lot, the regulars yet to arrive. The building's not much to look at from the outside, but the inside's decent and dark. And the girls are okay, too. Igor peels off a wad of twenties and passes them over to Pavel. Igor has found that if you tip the girls nicely, your return will be tenfold.

Pavel opens the door for Igor and follows him in. Igor misses the smokiness of the Russian joints, but in America it would seem that the masses cower to the few. Fucking pussies, that's what they are.

Igor chooses a table near the main stage and smiles at the girl working the pole to an AC/DC song. Her name is Mercedes and she's one of his favorites—always willing to please. He smiles up at her and she sticks her tongue out at him and laughs. He sends Pavel to the stage to tip her. Maybe he'll take her home with him, a home that he keeps, one among many in Austin, in addition to his warehouse. From the homes, he runs his higher-end whores—many of which he's found in places such as XTC.

A waitress brings him a tub of ice to keep the beer cool. Igor slips her a little baggie. The night's young and life is good.

~~~

Eddie lays a hand on the man's shoulder. "I said hold on there a sec, pardner."

The man shakes his shoulder loose and attempts to continue on. Eddie grabs him again with a little more force. "I said hold on there, pardner. Don't make me say it again."

The woman lifts and hugs the girl to her as the man's forced to face Eddie. The man's an older gentleman and his eyes are fearful.

"You must have me mistaken for someone else," he says as his eyes scan for a way out.

"It's not you that I recognize, it's the little girl with you. Who is she? And where does she come from?"

"I... I don't know what you're talking about." He turns toward the woman with him. "Honey, go on, I'll catch up with you."

"Yesterday, in front of the GAP at the Arboretum, this same little girl walked up to us unescorted and the next thing I know I'm fighting a Russian to keep him from taking her until I found out what was going on. The next thing I know, I get whacked in the back of the head by a second Russian. Then the pair car-jacked an old lady's Buick and escaped. That makes me want answers."

"You're mistaken. This is our daughter."

"It's the same girl. And look, she's again intrigued with my dog. I'm not fucking crazy."

"It's her alright," Amy says, "and somehow I suspect she doesn't speak English."

The woman tries to move around Amy, but Amy blocks her path. "We need some answers, like who the hell are you?" Amy cocks her head, strains to place the woman. She looks familiar. She's seen the woman before, she's sure of it. The woman's eyes turn frantic, she begins waving her free arm.

"Officer, officer. Please help us!" she yells after an Austin police officer trying to encourage the continued flow of concert-goers to leave the park and using a long black Mag-light to do so. He trots on over, eyes the small group.

"Ma'am, what seems to be the problem here?"

The woman points at Eddie and Amy. "These two are harassing us—trying to stop us from leaving. I want you to arrest them. I know my rights."

Eddie raises both hands. "It's not like that, officer. If you'd give me a minute to explain."

The officer points his Mag-light. "If you mind stepping back sir." He keys the mic on his collar. "May need some assistance here. I'm just north of Barton Springs—above the entrance."

The woman again tries to leave with the child. Amy again blocks her path. "Officer," Amy says, "do you know who I am?"

The cop shines the light in her bloodshot eyes causing her to block the beam with her hand. "A stoned hippie if I had to guess."

"Hold on there, officer." Eddie steps forward.

The officer spins toward him. "I said step back!"

"They have no right to stop us, officer," the man says. "They've obviously mistaken us."

Amy sucks in her bottom lip and counts to five. "Officer, if you give us a chance to explain. Yesterday at the..."

"You shut up too before you go to jail for disturbing the peace. You two carry on. I'm sorry these folks disturbed you."

"Thank you, officer," the pair say in unison.

Eddie bites his tongue, metaphorically. He feels like wringing the fucker's neck. Of all the cops in Austin, the majority decent, they had to have this idiot arrive on the scene. Another cop jogs up the hill. Eddie attempts to follow the retreating pair with his eyes, but they soon disappear from view.

"What's the problem here, Jimmy?" the second cop asks. "Possible PI, possible possession. We'll need a female officer to search ex-Detective Foster here."

"Bastard," Amy says under her breath. The bastard knew who she was the whole time. "If you knew who I was, why didn't you let me finish explaining what was going on? The little girl is a possible kidnap victim."

Jimmy snorts "Right. They sure didn't look like kidnappers to me. And you," he points at Amy with the butt of his flashlight. "You're a traitor to the men in blue. And look how you're dressed."

"Oh, give me a fucking break. You're ridiculous."

"You recognize this pair, don't you Nick? What kinda partner shoots her own partner?"

"Yeah, I recognize them. And they don't look like they're doing anything wrong to me."

"Hell, I can smell the weed on them."

"Everybody in this park smokes weed. Did you see them smoking any weed?"

"No, I didn't, but you can smell it on them and they were harassing an older couple."

"Mrs. Foster, what was that all about?"

"Yesterday, at the Arboretum, the little girl that was just with the couple, who Jimmy just let walk off, was snatched off the sidewalk in front of the Gap by some Russian characters."

"Uh-oh," Nick says. "That made the news. I think you might have fucked up, Jimmy."

Jimmy slaps his thigh with his flashlight—looks to the stars. "Shit."

Chapter Ten

Johnson coughs as the gorge rises to the back of his throat and threatens to spew. He swallows it back and coughs. His throat burns from the acid and the booze. His eyes water. He blinks them clear and focuses on his TV. The weather's on. He reckons it must be going on 10:30 or so. His crotch is soaked and he wonders how that happened. Surely, he didn't piss himself. He ain't done that but once and he was pretty fucked up at the time. Must be the pills he's taking. The doc told him to not take them on an empty stomach, but what the fuck does a doctor know. Seems like Willie has a theory on that: "There're a lot more drunks than there are doctors," or something fucking like that. Or is it: "Old drunks than old doctors?" Hell, who cares. It ain't apt no how.

What to do about Eddie Boy and the slut? That's what he should be thinking about. He was supposed to get rid of his guns as a condition of his bond, but of course, he didn't. Johnson thinks about a bumper sticker he once had that read: "You can have my guns when you pry them off my cold, dead fingers." He chuckles. He liked the shit out of that bumper sticker. Wishes he had another. Johnson wonders where he got it. Oh yeah, off of some young punk he arrested. The punk had no right to that bumper sticker with his long, greasy hair and all. What's the world coming to? Now the kids wear all these baggy-ass pants that are near falling down. He chuckles again. Makes the little bastards easier to catch though.

Now as for food, it may be a good idea if he ate at least something today. Johnson pushes his recliner forward and lifts himself out of his chair. His eyes cloud—his legs give out from under him.

Johnson crumbles toppling to his right. His chin catches the corner of the coffee table with a whack. The whiskey bottle skitters across its top. The heavy table doesn't give. Johnson's chin does. The first of the blood precedes a snore.

~~~

The thump of the music reminds Igor of the discos in Russia. But the American women don't seem to be as long-legged, he thinks, as he watches Mercedes saunter on over. She may not be as long-legged, but she sure goes out of her way to please. She leans in to whisper in his ear—a firm breast pressed against him.

"Igor, one of our girls came in late. She's in bad shape. If she can't dance, they'll likely fire her."

Igor shrugs, takes a sip of his weak beer. "What's it to Igor?"

"It's Jodi, she's a good girl and she's got a little girl of her own that she's taking care of."

"How old's the little girl?"

What the hell does that matter? Mercedes thinks, drawing back for a second. She leans back in. "I don't know, young, but anyway she needs a bump bad. She's shaking and sweating."

"I don't know this Jodi you speak of."

"Do it for me please, Igor."

Igor enjoys the game. What's a $20 bag mean to him?

Nothing, that's what. He shrugs again and digs into his pocket. Drops the packet into Mercedes's hand. Closes his fist around hers.

"You tell this Jodi she owes me. Arrange for her to meet me in the VIP lounge after she gets her first dance in."

"Sure, Igor I can do that." She licks his ear. "Or I can join you in the VIP lounge myself."

Igor laughs, pushes her away. "Why, I can have you anytime. Now do as you're told."

Mercedes stumbles in her high heels before gaining her balance. Pig, she thinks. Why do you let them do you like that, Kim? Because you're hooked on the man's dope and, quite frankly, because you're scared of the man, that's why. It doesn't take a rocket scientist to figure that out, but what can you do? Nothing, that's what. She suddenly   feels the urge to cry, but she doesn't let herself. Not for him, not for any man.

Mercedes has to help Jodi hit a vein fearing if she doesn't help, Jodi will needlessly stick herself trying to find a vein. Though she doesn't shoot herself, in her previous life she did study to be a nurse. She finds a vein easily enough and injects the heroin. Jodi's relief is instantaneous. Her eyes roll back in her head momentarily. She sighs in earnest. Mercedes tells her the bad news. She's being summoned to meet with Igor in the VIP lounge. Jodi knows of Igor and she too is scared of him, but what can she do? She thinks exactly as Jodi does—nothing, that's what.

Jodi hears her introduction. She takes a deep breath and lets the heroin calming effect wash over her. She steps from behind the curtain, rolls up on the stage ending in a split. There's a smattering of applause. Jodi places her hands in tight near her crotch and adjusts her legs to form a spread eagle, leans over her hands and slowly presses herself into a handstand. She does a slow circle on her hands, drops and rolls out to stand before the pole. The clapping is a little more enthusiastic. Jodi scans the crowd not stopping on anyone but spotting Igor. Dread fills her heart as she begins her first routine.

Igor likes what he sees. Jodi's petite with naturally pert titties that have yet to come under a knife. He bets she has a tight little pye-LOT-ku nye-BRI-ta-ya. How do the American's say it, he thinks? Da, "shaved pussy," he says to himself. He passes Pavel a $20 to put into her G-string before she comes out of it. He smiles up at Jodi catching her glance. His beady eyes and smirk roil Jodi's stomach. God, did she fuck up.

~~~

"I may be stoned, Eddie, but I'm sure that was the same little girl," Amy says as they near Eddie's truck. "And I've seen that woman before. I'm sure of that, as well."

"Maybe it will come to you. But stoned or not, that was the same kid." Eddie stops, halts their progress. "What's the population of Greater Austin these days? And what are the odds of spotting the same kid?" They continue on.

"Couple million, I'd guess. And about the same odds, I'd guess." Eddie hits unlock on his fob. His truck twerps and the lights flash.

He opens the back door for Bobo to load, hoists the cooler into the back and digs out a couple of beers for them. He opens Amy's door, helps her in and hands her the beers. Eddie circles around and hops in.

"It looks like this may be our first case," he says inserting his key and cranking the truck. "But where do we start?"

She pulls the tab of Eddie's beer and passes it to him. "You alright to drive?"

Eddie pats her bare leg—backs out of the parking spot. "I can't see us leaving this alone, Amy."

"Think, Amy... Think, Amy," she says out loud. She recalls the woman's face and her words, "I know my rights."

"Excuse me?"

"No, the woman, she said, 'I know my rights.' She sounded like a lawyer. Amy smacks her forehead with an open hand. She shakes a finger at Eddie. "I may just know where I've seen her. Go by my house. Hopefully, I haven't thrown it out."

"Thrown what out?"

"The Texas Monthly with all the lawyers in it. Super lawyers or something like that. Not all of them have photos, but I always like to see if I recognize any of them."

Eddie turns toward South Lamar, takes a sip of his beer, turns the opening away from him and places the can between his legs.

"You have cup holders, Eddie," Amy says admiring his strong jawline. Eddie squeezes her above the knee.

"Yes, Honey."

Amy laughs. "Fucker."

Bobo rests his head between them on top of the console—his front paws dangling. They both laugh, both thinking that can't be comfortable. They ride the rest of the way listening to the radio. It's a short drive. Eddie pulls into the driveway.

"You should at least leave one light on," he says.

"I know, but what are they going to steal?"

"They might rummage through your lingerie drawer."

Amy laughs. "Right. I threw all that stuff out long ago. Who needs to dress up for a vibrator?"

"Vibrator?" Eddie says a little too quickly. Amy swats at him.

"Don't get ideas, Big Boy. You're its replacement."

"I'm not sure I like being objectified."

Amy smiles. Pats him on the shoulder. "Well, get used to it. You coming in?"

Eddie opens his door. "Absolutely, I want to meet your latest ex."

Amy blushes slightly—pushes her own door open. "I don't think so." Bobo follows the laughing pair into the house.

~~~

The bleeding's stopped. Johnson snores on.

~~~

Igor snatches a bottle of vodka off the table and proceeds to the VIP lounge. He's looking forward to seeing just how grateful the little slut Jodi is. Pavel trails behind carrying the iced-down beer.

He's made it a habit to never let Igor get too far out of his sight because Igor's been known to upset people from time to time and he needs to be there to make sure things don't get too far out of hand.

The VIP lounge is empty but for a couple of Mexicans that have dope written all over them. They eye Igor and especially Pavel, cautiously. The girls attending them hasten the entertainment for their Mexican customers, ready to get out of there and back to the safety of dancing and working the tables. Igor's nod is barely discernible and he picks himself a place toward the back to sit, his back to the wall. He smiles as Jodi enters the room. Somehow, she looks smaller than she did on the stage—more diminutive and fragile. Igor likes the transformation. She's clad in a bikini with

114

bowtie strings on the bottoms and what Igor expects is a bowtie securing her bra.

He takes a pull from his bottle as Jodi approaches him. She stops before him and if he's not mistaken, she shivers a bit. Perfect, Igor thinks. One must know their position in life. That's the way of the world.

"Come let Igor look at you. Da, nice." He pulls both bowties securing her bikini bottom and it falls away. He licks his lips. Perhaps the prettiest pussy he's ever seen, he thinks. But he shall not let her know that. He wets a finger and runs it through her slit.

Jodi tenses. Igor laughs.

"What, you no like Igor?" he asks.

"Uhm, I could get in trouble, fired. You're not actually supposed to touch us."

Igor puts his finger to his lip. Smells it, tastes it. He stands. Pulls Jodi in closer. He reaches around her and pulls the string on her top. Works it from her shoulders—pulls it free. Igor snaps his fingers. Pavel stands and indicates to the Mexicans it's time to leave. They offer no resistance.

"Jodi, da?" Igor reaches behind her once more. Clutches the

hair at the nape of her neck. He sits forcing her to kneel before him. He looks down at his crotch. Jodi nods her head no. Wrong answer. Igor takes a nipple between thumb and finger and gives it a twist. Jodi cries out in pain. Igor cups her mouth quelling her squeal. He leans in, his breath hot on her face. He grips her nape more firmly. He takes his hand from her mouth and grabs her by a wrist.

"You owe Igor," he says directing her hand to his zipper.

"I can't," she says feebly.

Igor's ire rises. He could care less about the bitch, but principle is principle. She owes and now it's time to pay the piper. He likes the expression even if he doesn't know what it means. Igor tightens his grip on Jodi's nape, pulls her within inches of his crotch.

"Last time Igor asks," he says in a voice that strikes renewed fear in Jodi. With a shaky hand, she unbuttons and unzips him. He helps her free his uncircumcised cock from his boxers. Tears form in Jodi's eyes as she takes his cock into her mouth.

~~~

"Found it!" Amy says exiting the bathroom and joining Eddie in the living room. "Let's hope I'm not imagining things."

"You made Texas Monthly your bathroom reader?" Eddie asks, playing with her.

"Yes, what's wrong with that?"

"I'd rather not picture you sitting on the toilet reading Texas Monthly."

"Oh, yeah. And what do you read?"

"I drink Bud Light. I don't spend a whole lot of time in the bathroom."

It takes a second to register. She smiles. "That's why we'll maintain his and her bathrooms."

"Got it all figured out, Detective Amy Foster, do you?"

Amy thinks about it a second. "Well, if you think you're going to scare me off, you've got another thing coming. We're in this for the long haul. Follow me, we'll look together."

Eddie shakes his head. He knows when he's been whipped and he can't say he's upset about the situation. In fact, Amy's a damn good woman and not to mention one damn hot woman.

"That smile better mean you agree, mister," Amy says.

"Okay, let's see what you have there, woman."

Amy slaps the Texas Monthly down on the dining room table and takes a seat. "That's better. Pull up a chair."

Eddie does and watches as Amy begins flipping pages. It's starting to look doubtful when she suddenly stops and stabs the photo with an index finger. "That's her."

Eddie leans in a bit closer. "By God, you're right. A corporate lawyer, at that." He leans back and takes a sip from his beer. "Ellen Downey-Smith. What in the world's going on with you?"

"I bet the man with her is her husband and he's likely a lawyer, too."

"Go a little slower and let's see if we can find his picture or perhaps his name."

"Smith's a pretty common name, though."

Eddie nods in agreement. They spend the next 20 minutes going through the pages more slowly. Though there's not a photo of the man, there's a number of Smiths listed and any of them could be the man.

"Now what?" Eddie asks. "Go to the authorities with what we know?"

Amy sucks in her lower lip. Cups her chin. Shakes her head slowly. "Not yet. Let's do a little more digging. Find out what we can about the pair."

~~~

Igor forces Jodi to look up at him while she sucks him off. He likes to look into their eyes when he comes and he's getting close to coming. Igor's Galaxy lights up on the table beside him and begins to vibrate. With annoyance, he glances over at it. The caller ID reads "Pedophile," the name he stored in his phone for the sleaze-bag lawyer, Dorbandt. He doesn't know for sure if he's a pedophile, but he has his suspicions and there's no denying his sleazebag assessment. Igor wonders what the dumb shit wants? Especially at this hour. Maybe he has the rest of Igor's money. Not likely, but he better answer anyhow. With a sigh, he pushes Jodi's head aside.

"Leave, Igor," he says. He digs in his pocket and retrieves two, $20 bags and tosses them on the floor beside Jodi. "Now!" he shouts, retrieving his phone from the table. Jodi snatches the bags off the floor and wastes no time getting gone.

"Igor, here. What fuck you want? And it better be you have the rest of money."

"Umm... Uh... We have a problem."

"You calling to tell me 'we' have problem. Debt is your problem. Figure it fuck out."

"It's the last girl... She was spotted earlier this evening by the man you fought with yesterday."

"What fuck you talking about?"

"... And that woman detective, Detective Foster. The adopters are panicking... They're afraid they'll get caught – arrested—go to prison."

"That's your fucking deal. Deal with it."

"These are respected people in the legal community."

Igor ponders the situation and he's not happy with the development. Maybe the answer is to take out Dorbandt. Cut his losses. But the sleazebag has generated some serious money for his crew. "You still there?" Dorbandt asks sheepishly. Just the sound of Dorbandt's voice makes Igor want to kill him.

"I'm still thinking. You and goddamn public exchange. You really fucked up. Give me name of the couple and address."

"Wha... Why?"

"Because we already know where you live. You would rather have Pavel visit you, da?"

Dorbandt can't spit the names and addresses out fast enough. If someone has to die, he'd rather it not be him. He still wonders if he'll be on a hit list. The phone goes dead against his ear. He nearly shits his pants in fear. Boy, did he fuck up, Dorbandt thinks. Why couldn't he have just been a better lawyer? Maybe it's time to buy a gun.

Pavel eyes Igor. "What is it, Boss?" Igor takes a pull from his vodka before breaking it down to Pavel. Though Igor always calls the shots at the end of the day, he trusts Pavel enough to defer to his judgment at times. They come to a decision. They got to do what they got to do.

Chapter Eleven

Johnson snores on.

~~~

"Alright Detective, if that's what you want to do," Eddie says.

"Complacent, are you?" Amy says pushing away from the table and standing. She turns toward Eddie.

"I wouldn't say complacent, necessarily."

Amy pulls the bow securing her bikini top, works it from her shoulders, lets it drop at her feet. "I'll just get out of this hippie garb and put something else on for the trip back. Want to watch?"

"If I'm not mistaken, Detective, your left breast seams to appear larger than the right."

"What?" Amy looks down to examine herself.

Eddie laughs. "I'm only kidding."

Amy laughs. "You had me going. For a minute there, I was afraid one was losing weight. You know it's quite common though, one being larger than the other. I'm more concerned with them sagging."

"If it makes you feel any better, for an old broad, you're holding up quite well."

Amy scowls. "Thanks. You know if you hit it from behind, you won't even have to look at me at all." They both laugh. Dutifully,

Eddie follows Amy into her bedroom. He smiles. Hell, he'll gladly take it any way she desires it.

Making it to the bedroom, Amy steps out of her cutoffs and climbs up on her bed and remains on all fours. It doesn't take Eddie long to shed his clothes and crawl in the bed behind Amy.

"You forgot to take off your panties, Amy," Eddie says hard and throbbing behind her. Amy turns her head to glance back at him. She smiles.

"Just push them to the side. This shouldn't take you long. Then we can get back on the road."

Eddie nods his head.

"Okay, but no looking," he says.

But, of course, the no-looking doesn't apply to him. Eddie pushes the panties to the side exposing a prominent mound and inviting lips accented by an engorged clitoris trying to shake its hood. He swallows. Jesus! Eddie thinks. Amy might just be right.

Eddie shakes the thought. The alcohol is on his side and it's always prolonged things for him without sacrificing any of the pleasure. He enters her without preamble and is surprised to find her as wet as she is. He drives his cock home causing Amy to gasp. Instinctively, Eddie knows this is what Amy wants and if this what she wants, that's what she will get.

Eddie pounds the pussy incrementally inching Amy closer and closer to the headboard until at first her head then shoulder makes contact with the headboard and there's nowhere else for her to go.

Amy moans increase. She's never been fucked with such intensity and she's loving it. She suspected Eddie would be good from the first time she spotted him, but never in her wildest imagination would she have believed such pleasure was possible.

An orgasm wracks her body. She cries out, but yet Eddie continues to drive into her. Amy bites a knuckle and squeezes her eyes shut. Oh, God, another. Amy's legs quiver. She arcs her back even more.

Sweat drips from Eddie's chin, splashes on the crack of Amy's ass, comingles with Amy's own juices. Amy's ass is slick with perspiration—Eddie's grip on it tenuous. He's getting close. He blinks the sweat from his eye. "Jesus," he says pounding on.

Her third is on the way. She never knew it was possible. Amy loses the knuckle. Fuck the not looking. She strains to look over her shoulder. Pleads with her eyes for Eddie to come with her. His eyes find hers.

"Now, Eddie. Please!" Amy cries out. It's all Eddie needs to hear. Jesus, what a hot woman, Eddie thinks, driving into Amy one last time. His own moan matches Amy's and Amy gets her wish. She comes with her new man.

Panting, Eddie withdraws and falls to his side. Amy's ass still hovers in the air for a few more seconds until she too falls to her opposite side facing Eddie. Amy takes another 30 seconds to catch her breath. She pushes the damp hair from her face.

"I think I've died and gone to heaven," she says.

"And to think I didn't even have to kiss you."

Amy hits him with her pillow. "And so much for my theory," she says. Eddie closes the gap between them and plants a hard kiss on her.

"But it was a close call," Eddie says causing them both to laugh. He's amazed at how comfortable they are with each other considering the short duration of their relationship. Suddenly, Eddie hopes it's a long relationship. Unbeknownst to Eddie, Amy's thinking the exact same thing.

"Want to just crash here tonight?" Amy asks. Eddie nods. "I'll grab the cooler," he says.

~~~

Igor and Pavel take their time walking the short distance back to where their car is parked. Igor pulls the stocking that disguises his face. Pavel does the same. They're not worried about cameras. The homes mostly sit off the road and there are dense cedar and scrub that protect the homes from spying eyes. Thus, they worry not about cameras.

But they have other worries. Things did not go exactly according to plan.

"What now?" Pavel asks pulling the driver-side door closed and looking across at Igor in the dim light. The overhead light slowly fades and goes dark.

"Back to warehouse. Call it a night. Nothing we can do about it now."

Pavel shakes his head as he cranks the car. "This is not good, Igor," he says. Igor runs fingers through his hair, part in frustration and in part out of vanity—the stocking having mussed his hair.

Igor punches the dash with his good hand. "Fuck! Drive, da. Let Igor think." And think he does. What mess the fuckin' sleazebag Dorbandt has caused. Stupid fuck! At least Dorbandt didn't lie about the address.

Igor pulls out a fresh cigar and bites off the end. He spits the tip onto the floorboard. Tonight changes everything. Everything!

Threatens everything Igor has worked so hard to build. Fuck, he thinks once more as they encounter zero traffic before entering Austin proper.

One thing Igor is sure of though, as the Americans like to say, "the shit's fixing to hit the fan" sometime tomorrow.

~~~

The sun's streaking through Johnson's living room window heating the side of his face. Johnson moans and stirs. He's surprised to find himself on his living room floor. His head's pounding and his jaw aches. He attempts to lift his head, but the fibers of his carpet tug at his chin. It takes a few seconds to register. He's somehow busted his chin and the carpet's stuck in the dried blood. Shit. He pictures yanking a large, well-adhered Band-Aide and doesn't relish the thought of freeing himself. Johnson opts for a less painful and slower route to freeing himself. He pulls individual strands of yarn loose from his chin.

It takes a few minutes but Johnson finally frees himself.

He pushes himself into a sitting position—his injured knee stiff and straight before him. The blood once again has soaked through the bandaging. He strains to recall what if anything he did the previous day but draws a blank. Fucking Oxies. It has to be the fucking Oxies, he reckons.

Johnson tries to swallow and can't. His mouth is so cottony and so parched he thinks he could possibly be dying from dehydration. Well, there's beer in the fridge, he's pretty sure of that. Johnson uses the edge of the coffee table to get his good leg under him and pushes himself to stand. He puts some tentative weight on his bad leg and winces at the pain. There's a knock at the door. Shit! It can't be anything good. He'll ignore it and perhaps whoever it is will go away.

Johnson lowers himself back to the carpet and begins the long arduous scoot on his butt toward the kitchen and refrigerator. The knock on the door turns more persistent. Too bad, he ain't answering it. Can't. Not until he's fortified and cleaned up a bit. God only knows what he did last night.

~~~

Amy yawns widely. Eddie sticks his finger in but yanks it out before Amy can bite down. She adds a stretch to her next yawn and smiles at Eddie who's every bit as handsome in the morning. He winks at her.

"Good morning, Sunshine. Did you sleep well?" Eddie asks.

"God, did I. Think it's the best I've slept in as long as I can remember. You?"

"Actually, I slept pretty well myself. Bobo seldom lets me sleep in. Speaking of, I wonder where he is."

"I let him out in the middle of the night sometime and left the sliding back door and porch door open for him. I'm sure he's fine."

"So, what are the plans, Detective?"

"We're going to find out what in the hell's going on. Get some answers."

Eddie studies Amy. Her hair is nice and messy this morning, but I can't say she's not a looker.

"What?"

"You're just as pretty in the morning, Detective Amy Foster."

Amy blushes slightly. She's not used to compliments and especially compliments in the morning. Her blush deepens at the thought of the previous night. God, she can't believe she acted with such abandon...

"Thanks," she finally musters. She tosses the sheet off and kicks it free. "Nothing in the house to eat, so my suggestion is we take a quick shower and then hit the road. Figure out a game plan when we get to your place."

"Sounds like a plan."

Amy rolls from the bed. "Give me a couple of minutes head start, would you," she says and disappears into the bathroom. Eddie smiles as the door shuts behind Amy. He'll take the opportunity to check on Bobo and relieve himself in the second bathroom.

Eddie finds Bobo in the backyard sitting by a sizeable hole. "Uh-oh," Eddie says. Bobo looks over at him and gives him the "I just ate the cord off the vacuum cleaner" or "I just ate all the cushions on the couch" look. Eddie can't help but shake his head and laugh. Man, he loves his dog.

Eddie joins Amy in the shower. She hands him the soap so he can wash her back for her. She blushes again, a blush that Eddie can't see as she recalls her fantasy involving Eddie that took place within this very same shower. Her knees grow weak at the thought. She turns in Eddie's arms and rises up on tiptoes to kiss him. She feels him grow hard against her. In her fantasy, Eddie knelt before her, but at the moment his good and stiff cock will do. Amy, you're shameless, she thinks and stifles a giggle.

At Eddie's suggestion, they finish their shower and Eddie lifts her from the tub and carries her to the edge of the sink. Yet, another new one for Amy. As she comes, she silently prays the honeymoon never ends.

Amy gathers up some clothes and essentials and packs them in a large suitcase to take to Eddie's. Eddie watches without comment from the end of her bed, an amused smile upon his lips. Though they haven't actually talked about living together, there seems to be a tacit understanding between them and Amy's not about to rock the boat by broaching the subject. A tacit understanding works fine for her, thank you.

Eddie carries the suitcase to the truck and returns for the cooler while Amy searches the house for something she may have missed. She grabs up her I-pad and follows Eddie and Bobo out to the truck locking her door behind her. The interior of the truck still smells of smoke and burned rubber and now there's the added smell of mildew. Eddie cranks the truck and rolls down the windows.

The beauty of Amy's I-phone is that it can work as a hot spot, a WI-FI, for up to five devices. Amy opens her computer, logs on to the web through her I-phone and opens Safari, her I-pad's browser.

After a quick ZabaSearch, an address pops up for Ellen Downey-Smith along with a map and an "x" depicting the address location.

"West Lake Hills," Amy says. Eddie looks over at her. "Ellen Downey-Smith," she adds. "It looks like they live in West Lake on top of the mountain overlooking Town Lake."

"Above Red Bud Trail?"

"Yeah."

"I believe it's called 'Nob Hill'," Eddie says. "Very nice. Very expensive. A friend's mother has a house up there. Spent many a mischievous   day up there in my teens."

"Mischievous, you? Say it ain't so."

"I cannot telleth a lie."

Amy smiles. "And I was born 30 years ago."

"Speaking of," Eddie says. "I read an article in the Men's Journal. It was a case study on aging. There's actual age, neuro age, cardio age, pulmonary age, telomere age and of course your metabolism. It's a new manner of determining how you're actually holding up." Eddie smiles. "Based upon my experience, I'd have to give your pussy a chronological age of 20."

"Experience, huh? I'm not going to ask compared to whom, but thanks. And the rest of me?"

Eddie fiddles with the radio. Amy smacks his arm with the back of her hand. They both laugh.

"So, you want to go take a look?" Amy asks.

"At what?"

"Their residence."

"Oh, I thought we were talking about your pussy again."

"As if you didn't get a good enough look at it last night. Anyway, their house. You want to take a look at it?"

"And what do we hope to discover?"

"Some kid toys in the yard. I don't know."

"Why not. See if you can find the husband's name."

Amy nods. She begins her search with a general Google search.

There's a number of results, but none pan out. Amy logs onto Refdesk and from there the Austin American Statesman. At the Statesman, Amy finds an article about a local breast cancer awareness benefit attended by Mr. and Mrs. John Smith and an accompanying photo of the smiling pair.

"Got him," Amy says. "She married the very prestigious John Smith."

Eddie turns left onto Lake Austin Blvd. "Must be millions of them," Eddie muses.

"Despite his name, he's distinguished looking enough. It says here he's also a lawyer and a partner in one of the bigger downtown firms. Corporate."

"Spells money."

They pass the University of Texas' Lions Municipal Golf Course on their right. They ride on in silence as Amy continues searching the web for additional information on the pair. Amy saves her search results and snaps her computer shut.

"Let's see if Ellen's in her office, shall we?" Amy doesn't wait for or expect an answer. Eddie turns left on Red Bud trail. They cross below the dam and spillway and start the climb into the Hill Country.

Amy ends her call. "Not in the office today. Don't know when she'll be back in."

"Try John Smith. See if he's in. They may be circling the wagons today."

Amy makes the call. Shakes her head. "Not in either. Huh. Strange, or not so strange." They start up the mountain.

Chapter Twelve

The buzz of saws wake Igor. Blindly, he reaches for his cigarettes. Must be chopping up last night's ride as he ordered. It's a shame. He hates chopping up perfectly fine automobiles, but what can one do? The car's not valuable enough to ship—thus expendable.

The smoke expands Igor's lungs. He reflects back on the previous night. Now it's all about damage control. He chunked his phone into the lake and with it his only traceable link to Dorbandt. Dorbandt, just the thought of him raises Igor's blood pressure. He stubs out his cigarette and reaches for his bottle of vodka. A shiver runs through him as the vodka hits his gut. The calming effect is immediate.

Igor sits up and swings his legs over the side of his bed. He steps into his boots. Zips them up. Stands. Stretches. He sighs. One thing he's good at is cleaning up messes. Igor flexes his sore hand. The knuckles blue, the hand noticeably swollen. He sighs again. He'll have to work on his anger issues. Nyet. Igor sets off to make his rounds around the warehouse. He loves his men, in his own special way, but sometimes he wonders where they were when the brains were being passed out. Fortunately, he's a good strong decisive leader.

Pavel spots him. Waves him over. Lays a big hand on Igor's shoulder. "Found a white Caddy on Craig's List. Sent Erik to buy it."

"Buy?" Igor says in an amused tone. "When does Igor ever buy anything?"

Pavel shrugs. "I figure with the heat, maybe we should lay low a bit."

Igor pinches Pavel's cheek. Pats him on the shoulder. "Da, good. You a good man, Pavel."

Pavel frowns at the retreating figure. He's never known Igor to be the least sentimental. Maybe Pavel better keep an eye on Igor. Maybe Igor up to something. Maybe leave with all the cash. Nyet, Igor never do Pavel like that. He hurries after Igor anyhow.

~~~

Johnson sits at his kitchen table and nurses another beer. Twice already this morning his door's been pounded on and there's not a doubt in Johnson's mind it's law enforcement related, be it Fire Marshall or otherwise. Somehow, he needs to stay sober today. No doubt the next time they come by it will be with a warrant of some kind. Though on exactly what grounds, he hasn't a clue. Maybe some camera picked him up on Eddie's street prior to the explosion. And how and the hell will he explain that? Why couldn't pretty boy and the slut have been killed in the blast? Is that asking too much? He fights the urge to down his beer. Hell, no, it's not asking too much. But they didn't die in the blast, meaning he has to come up with another plan. He'll be damned if they'll cart him off to prison and the two that caused him all the trouble will remain alive and well to continue their fornicating ways. His resolve wanes. He angrily downs his beer.

Johnson crushes his beer can in his fist and throws it across the kitchen. Think of a plan, Johnson. Think of a fucking plan. Slowly, a plan begins to formulate. It's not much of a plan, but it's a plan nevertheless. Perhaps one more beer won't hurt, Johnson decides.

~~~

"Used to ride my motorcycle up this hill most every day," Eddie says.

"I've never been up here before. It's definitely nice."

"Nice, but the taxes would eat you up. They have the best of everything in this community. Westlake High makes it to the state almost every year."

"Westlake's mostly white though, isn't it?"

"Yeah, but it really has to do with the fact that they have the best coaches, equipment and nutritionists."

"I can see that making a difference."

They come to the top of the small mountain. "This is essentially a big circle up here at the top, the houses overlooking Lake Austin commanding the highest prices."

"Slow down," Amy says. "Their property should be up here on the right... Hey, stop. Back up. I think you passed the entrance. See the mailbox back there?"

Eddie doesn't spot it in his rearview. He looks over his shoulder "Yeah, I see it. Well hidden." He throws the truck into reverse and backs up beyond the entrance and the mostly obscure gate. "Talk about privacy. I can barely see the house from here. There's a call box but the gate's open. Should we announce our presence."

Amy smiles. "And ruin the surprise. I should hope not."

Eddie chuckles. "Devious woman." He turns into the drive. There are several vehicles in the drive including a sparkling grey Mercedes 560 SL. "Looks like someone's home," Eddie adds. He parks behind the Mercedes. They step from the truck to the recently tarred drive. Bobo jumps from his window before Eddie can command him to stay.

The house before them is a 50's era ranch featuring a modern, double-door entrance of ornately carved oak and etched glass. Two giant yuccas flank the short walk to the front door. Off to the left of the house sets a large glass greenhouse. Eddie whistles in appreciation. Bobo waters one of the yuccas. Eddie and Amy both shake their head.

"Ring or knock?" Amy asks.

"You ring and I'll knock." A push of the doorbells sets of a series of chimes. They wait. Amy pushes the doorbell once more. Nothing. The sound of a meowing cat reaches them at the silencing of the chimes.

"Shit!" they say together... At the realization, they left the kitten back at Amy's house.

"Dammit," Amy says. "I felt like I was forgetting something. The little thing must have found it a comfortable place to sleep."

Eddie pats Amy on the back. "Obviously, you had other things on our minds"

"Hey! You forgot the kitten, too," Amy blurts out. They both laugh. Eddie leans in to knock on the door. To his surprise, the door cracks open at the first knock and the cat shoots through the gap its tail stiff and pointed straight in the air. It loves against Bobo's front legs before detouring to Amy's legs.

"Friendly cat," Eddie says nudging the door open a bit more.

An unseen breeze draws the door open wider. Their eyes are immediately drawn to hundreds of cat prints going to-and-fro in the foyer.

Dark paw prints in sharp contrast with the light-colored wooden flooring. Prints that vary in coloring from a light burgundy to an almost black the deeper into the foyer they go.

Eddie and Amy look at each other. The cat darts past them and back into the house. It disappears around a corner. No words are necessary, the implication of the prints is clear. Amy stabs 911 on her phone's screen and puts the phone to her ear.

Eddie's sure there's no reason to investigate the source of all the blood. Whoever or whomever bled that much is long dead. Not to mention the blood appears long dried. Eddie frowns, grabs Bobo by the collar to assure he doesn't go into the house. Eddie leads him to a spot in the shade to await the cops and what will likely be hours of interrogation. Amy sits down beside him—rests her head against him.

"What in the world have we gotten ourselves involved in, Eddie?"

Eddie sighs. "A world I know nothing about."

<center>~~~</center>

"Igor! Come quick!" Pavel yells out not knowing exactly where Igor is. "Erik! You know where Igor is... Get now!"

Erik nods and jogs off in the direction of the warehouse office.

Pavel turns up the news to the "BREAKING NEWS ALERT!" He's surprised the murders have been discovered so quickly. The quick discovery, however, pales in comparison as to the identity of the discoverers. Pavel attempts several times to close his mouth but it keeps dropping back open as he looks on. He gives up, closing it occasionally only too swallow.

Panting, Igor and Erik come to a stop next to Pavel. Igor can't believe his eyes or his ears. He's incredulous. How? How can this be possible? Maybe followed little girl to family home?

"Turn up more," Igor says though he can hear it fine. Pavel does and they watch and listen. Igor moves to his recliner and plops down in it, his eyes never leaving the screen. These same two, again. What does it mean? It can't be coincidence. But why? What the fuck? How is it possible? Dorbandt? Nyet. Too chicken shit.

Igor reaches for his vodka bottle that's not there. He left it in the office. He shakes out a Marlboro, instead, his mind inundated with possibilities and none of the scenarios playing out in his mind are good. He takes a hard drag on his cigarette and flicks it toward the TV.

"YOB tvo-YU mat!" Fuck your mother, he says to the image of Eddie. The story ends. Moves onto another. Igor runs both hands throw his hair. Drums with his fingertips on the end tables on either side of his recliner. Pavel and Erik wait him out, knowing better to interrupt Igor when he's deep in thought. Without a word Igor pushes to his feet and starts back to the office needing a shot of vodka to help him focus. Pavel and Erik trail after him.

Igor yanks open the office door banging it off the wall. Pavel stops it from banging shut on the rebound. He and Erik follow   Igor. Erik pulls the door shut behind him. Igor takes a long pull from his vodka.

"Maybe we shoulda wacked Dorbandt instead," he says beginning to pace the room. He throws up his hand and spins to face his men. "This man and this cop woman give Igor big headache. And always, the same, in the news. What the fuck? Igor think maybe personal."

Pavel doesn't remind Igor that Igor's already made it personal when they tried to blow up the two. But, of course, they couldn't have known it was them that tried to blow the two up. Or could they? Nyet.

At most, they suspect there is a couple of Russians involved, but not know who. Pavel breaks the silence.

"You know Igor, the woman was detective after all."

Igor eyes him. His eyes half-masked. "You think Igor not know this? You think Igor stupid?"

"No boss. But maybe she's investigating on her own."

Igor takes a pull from his vodka. Wipes his mouth with the back of his hand. "Tonight. Tonight, we kill them both. Maybe Dorbandt, too."

Pavel nods. Sounds reasonable enough. Like bad tooth, one must pull it before it gets abscessed. Or in this case, bad teeth. "Okay, tonight it is done."

~~~

On another channel, a NEWS ALERT gets Johnson's attention. Something about a double murder. He turns up the volume.

"A gruesome discovery was made this morning in this normally quiet and crime-free Westlake neighborhood overlooking Town Lake. In this ranch style house behind me, the bodies of two victims, a man and woman, believed to be husband and wife, were discovered by former Travis County Detective Amy Foster and one-time murder suspect Eddie Winston. The names of the victims are being withheld at this time pending notification of relatives. It is believed, however, that the victims are prominent Austin lawyers known for their philanthropy and community activism.

"According to police sources close to the investigation not authorized to comment at this time, a handgun was recovered at the scene and murder/suicide has not been ruled out at the present.

"No other information is available at this time. Please stay tuned throughout the day for additional coverage as this story continues to unfold."

"Mary Robinson reporting live from Westlake Hills. Back to you Jeffery..."

Johnson downs his beer. "Pretty boy Eddie and his slut. Can't even watch the FUCKING NEWS! without hearing their FUCKING NAMES! and seeing their FUCKING PICTURES!'' Probably killed the old couple themselves and planted the gun to make it look like a murder/suicide. Well, by God, they won't get away with it. Not if he has anything to do with it.

Johnson picks his Remington 30-06 and oil can and rag off his coffee table and begins to clean it once more. Hell, he hasn't shot the damn thing in 20 years, but it looks almost as new as the day he bought it. It's not the ideal firearm in most situations, but for what he has planned, it will serve the purpose. Johnson's pretty much resigned himself to the fact he's going to prison, so what the fuck does he have to lose? Nothing. If he gets killed trying to kill a pretty boy and his slut, so be it. At least he'll have gone out trying to stand up for the good guys. He chuckles. "Where did it go so wrong?" It seems like he heard a song something like that recently, but he can't remember where or when. He ain't into music much no how.

Johnson examines the clip. The damn thing only holds five rounds. Not many, but what the fuck, it is a bolt action after all. Johnson snaps the clip into place—takes pleasure in the mechanical sound. He works the bolt feeding a round into the chamber. He ejects it, removes the clip and feeds the bullet back into the clip. All's well as he knew it would be. He reinserts the clip.

Johnson considers taking a Sharpie and writing their names on the bullets but decides it's not worth the effort on account of his freshly bandaged leg. But, by God, another beer surely is. How many does that make? He chuckles. Not enough, that's for sure.

A loud bang on the door causes Johnson to jump. Shit, he can't keep on ignoring it. He hastily works the rifle under his couch and calls out in the soberest voice me can muster, "Hold your horses! I'm coming!"

~~~

"Well, at least we didn't have to go downtown," Amy says as they pass the Austin City Limits sign.

"Not yet, anyhow. Thank God the little girl wasn't among the dead."

"Yeah, but where is she? What happened to her? This all revolves around the girl. You know that don't you?"

Eddie looks over at Amy. "Give me a little credit."

"Sorry."

"And I think there's going to be a major investigation based on the murders alone. I think we convinced them that there's a small girl involved meaning it no longer involves us."

"But the detective said there weren't signs of a small kid in the house."

"Meaning, we likely spooked them yesterday evening. Still, we've done our part."

Amy pulls her leg up under her and turns in her seat to face Eddie. "I think we should keep digging."

"How about lunch at the Hula Hut? My treat."

"I've never eaten there. But you didn't answer me."

Eddie turns into the Hula Hut parking lot. He doesn't know what more they can do, though he does share Amy's concern for the girl. "If that's what you want to do, Amy, that's what we'll do."

Amy leans in and kisses Eddie on the cheek.

"Though you don't need my permission," Eddie says.

"I know, but we're a team. Hey, there isn't a car in this lot under $30,000."

''If there is, it's an employee. This is Doc Martins without socks, ladies in capris territory.

"It doesn't sound upscale."

"Still a very rich crowd. Folks from Tarrytown mostly. You'll like it. The ambiance and the food are excellent.

"What about Bobo?"

"I have a spare vest and leash in the dash. Plus, we can eat on the pier section overlooking the boats and the lake. They probably wouldn't care anyway."

Yuppie, is more like it, Amy thinks and she loves it though she wonders if the patrons actually have real jobs. They're just too casually dressed and everyone is drinking beer or mixed drinks. All-in-all, Amy looks forward to eating there.

Lunch over, they head back toward Amy's house to fetch the kitty. They find the kitten very much alive, very hungry and quite verbal. Amy gathers him up and gives him a kiss between the eyes.

"Smoky, did you miss us?" she asks. Amy carries him into the kitchen and locates a can of tuna in the cupboard. The kitten meows even louder. Amy sets Smoky and the can of tuna on the counter and has to hold the can in place to keep him from pushing it off the counter. "God, look at the little fellow go."

Eddie chuckles. "He reminds me of Bobo." Bobo perks up at the sound of his name, sits up a little straighter and licks his snout. "You just ate not 30 minutes ago, Bobo," Eddie adds.

Smoky chases the empty can to the sink before Amy rinses the can and drops it in the trash below the sink. She plucks Smoky from the edge of the sink and sets him on her shoulder.

"Let's roll, partner," she says.

Eddie opens the door for his new family.

Chapter Thirteen

The chains on the overhead door rattle as the garage door opens and Mikhail drives through in a large early 90's Sedan. "Now that's a car. Igor like," he says walking over to it and running his hand down the fender. "32 valve Northstar. Very good. Very strong, good motor."

Mikhail steps from the car and holds the door open for Igor to inspect the red leather interior. Igor slaps the roof and gives the thumbs up. "How much?" Igor asks.

"Three grand, boss."

Igor raises a brow—digs into his inner pocket for a cigarette and awaits Mikhail to light it. Lit, he exhales a rich plume of smoke. He pats Mikhail on the cheek. "You did good," Igor says looking beyond him. "Go get Pavel. Let's make rounds, da?" Igor watches Mikhail wander off and wonders if it might be time to move on. "Nyet," he tells himself. "Igor not run. Fuck cops. And fuck American and his ex-cop woman."

"Huh?" Pavel asks walking up on Igor.

"Da, tonight we kill the pesky American and his ex-cop woman."

Pavel shrugs. "Sure, boss. We kill." He sighs. Enough already.

"Good, let's make rounds."

~~~

Johnson collapses on a chair at his kitchen table. Exhales loudly. Relief washes over him. His meeting with the Fire Marshal went better than he could have possibly hoped, it becoming evident after the first few questions that the Fire Marshal didn't have shit on him. Meaning, too, that the cops don't have shit on him either. He giggles like a schoolgirl. Makes the effort to stand.

"That calls for a little drink," he tells himself as he takes the few steps necessary to reach his refrigerator. Johnson digs one of the vodka bottles from the freezer—breaks the seal and takes a good, long pull before recapping. He sighs, feeling the satisfying burn. He's amazed, at times, that his ulcers don't seem to be getting any worse. Like an old fucking workhorse that refuses to die. He likes that thought, old fucking workhorse, that's what the fuck he is.

Johnson replaces the vodka and retrieves a ring of three remaining 16-ounce Miller High Life beers. He carries them into the living room where he can sit before his TV and think a mite.

Johnson turns on the TV. It's a soap. He's done gone and missed the news thanks to the Fire Marshal. Too bad he doesn't have cable. He pops the tab on a beer. So, it would appear there are no cameras in or around Eddie Boy's house. That seems odd, with cameras everywhere these days. Johnson takes a drink from his beer. No cameras, that's a good omen, he thinks. Someone up there is looking out for the good guys for a change.

"So, well, what you going to do about it then, Johnson?" he asks himself. "Why, post up and draw them out somehow and then shoot them at a distance." He giggles again. "Tonight, yessiree."

But first, he needs another vehicle and preferably another pickup truck. And he knows just where he might locate one—at the H.E.B. in South Austin on Slaughter Lane where the Mexicans always have trucks and cars parked for sale. But getting there will be a bitch, he thinks. The city bus stops at the end of the block, but he doesn't have a clue in hell which bus goes where. Riding the city bus—has it come to that? Well, a man's got to do what he's got to do. Anything less just wouldn't be right.

Johnson downs the rest of his beer. He'll, by God, figure it out and do so discretely. Well, as discretely as one can with a busted knee and recent pictures on the TV.

Johnson limps to his bedroom and his concealed wall safe. He has it set for the last turn on the dial in case he has to get to the contents in a hurry. He turns the dial and pulls down on the handle. Several bundles of cash fall from the safe as he opens it. In fact, his safe has little room for anything else with all the cash that's crammed in it. One of the perks of being a detective is shaking down the dopers. Johnson's come to learn early the dopers rarely complain. He snickers. God the good times that he's had.

Johnson removes his spare Taurus 9mm from the safe and crams all but one of the bundles back. He fans the bundle with his thumb. Reckons there's at least five thousand in varying but mostly larger bills. That should buy him something decent. Hell, reliable is all he really cares about. And perhaps something nondescript. He selects himself a ball cap from the top shelf of his closet and a dark pair of shades off his dresser top. He studies himself in the mirror. Winks a wink that can't be seen because of the dark lenses.

"Time to catch a bus, Johnson," he says to his reflection. "Yep, time to catch a fucking bus, Johnson old boy."

~~~

"You'll probably have to refinish this floor," Amy says rubbing a burned spot in the living room floor with the toe of her boot. "And of course, buy new curtains," she adds.

"I'm sure you have some new color scheme in mind," Eddie says leaning against the door jamb that separates the living room and kitchen. Amy smirks.

"Maybe."

"Well, just in case someone is actually trying to kill one of us, I wouldn't spend too much time in front of that bare window."

"Oh, right. There is that."

Eddie smiles. "Now you're beginning to sound like me."

Amy meets Eddie in the doorway. Wraps her arms around his waist. "And in these boots, I can almost kiss you."

"And there is that," Eddie says tilting his head to meet Amy's lips. The kiss is short and sweet to both of them. They step into the kitchen where Amy's placed her Mac across from Eddie's Surface Pro. She takes a seat before her computer.

"Let's see if there's anything new on the murders." She logs onto Austin360.com to see if there's anything to be found there. Though the site's mostly to promote Austin events, there's already a short piece on the murders. Not the murders per se, but the victims. Amy begins to read.

Eddie takes a seat before his computer. There are plenty of other sites to visit including the websites for the local television stations. Eddie starts with a favorite local station—a Fox affiliate. He peers over the top of his screen and wonders what news Amy watches. Amy's absorbed in her screen and doesn't notice Eddie watching her.

She sure is beautiful. Eddie decides he wouldn't care if Amy voted for Bernie Sanders, God forbid. Amy finally feels his smile and looks up.

"What?"

"Just thinking how pretty you are."

Amy blushes slightly. "Thanks," she manages, not sure if she'll be able to concentrate with Eddie sitting across from her. But it's something she'll happily get used to, she decides. Amy sighs and attempts to get back to the article she's reading. She feels like the luckiest woman alive—"alive" being the optimum word. She rereads the paragraphs she's just finished reading as Eddie turns his focus back to his own screen.

~~~

The day begins to wane. The rounds have gone well. No more heat on the eastside than usual. The cops seemingly not pushing too hard to find the killer of a known druggie. Hell, it barely even made the news. Speaking of the news, Igor thinks, he wants to catch the evening news.

"Get us back to warehouse in time for news, Pavel," he says. Pavel nods while always keeping his eye on the rearview mirror, ever watchful for the cops. Pavel's still worried about yesterday's killing, but nothing he can do about that. If they all get busted tomorrow, it wouldn't surprise him. He keeps his thoughts to himself. Turns down the street on which their warehouse is located. The Caddy's clock says they have five minutes to spare.

Pavel pulls into the warehouse and kills the engine. The large warehouse is void of activity. The doors shut disturbing the silence. Igor hurries over to take his spot before his TV. The others gather around and await the news. As expected, the murders are still top of the news. Igor gleans nothing new and shuts off the TV. Eyes the men around him. Shrugs.

"Igor too smart for fuckin' cops. No have a clue."

"And what of little Syrian?" Erik asks.

"They must hide girl, of course," Igor says reaching for his new phone. He dials his man keeping an eye on Dorbandt. Nods as he receives his latest update.

"Dorbandt no go nowhere," Igor says. He snickers. "I think punk scared."

"What's that American saying?" Pavel asks. "Loose lips sink ships?"

Igor grunts. "Da, something like that. But what does Dorbandt really know? He don't know gav-NO! He don't know shit!"

Erik frowns. He believes Dorbandt's a weak link needing to be removed like a weed that sprouts in the middle of your lawn. But his brother-in-law is the boss. At least for now. "So, what we do about this Dorbandt?" he asks.

Igor slaps the armrests of his recliner. Winces at the stab of pain in his right hand. "We have little talk with Dorbandt. Make sure he knows what is good for him. Also, we let shit know we want our money." Igor pushes himself up to stand. "Da, we go now."

"ya nye mo-GU DU-mat na-to-SCHAK. I can't think on an empty stomach," Erik says.

Igor eyes Erik with contempt. "ya go-lod-NA." I'm hungry he whines in feminine Russian. "We get food on way," he adds thinking, for what seems to be a daily occurrence, someday I put bullet in stupid fuck. Erik, he don't even fuck sister no more. Maybe he put bullet in her, too. The thought brings on an unexpected smile. He leads his men back to the Caddy.

~~~

Johnson stashes his walker in the bushes on the corner and sits on the bus-stop bench. He's the only one present besides a plump fiftyish Mexican woman that he suspects is someone's maid. He smiles at her. "Where does the next bus go to?" he asks.

"No hablo English," she says meekly.

Johnson turns hot at the temples and thinks they need to send all the non-English speaking wet-backs back to wherever they came from. He'd bet his left nut the hag doesn't have a green card. Too bad he's temporarily on suspension or he'd find a reason to roust her, take her in.

The roar of the diesel precedes the bus. The brakes squeal followed by a hiss of air as the bus comes to a stop before them. Johnson coughs on the fumes before loading. He doesn't know what the fare is or where the bus is going and is not inclined to ask at this point. He drops a handful of coins into the counter. It rattles and clicks as it sorts out and totals the change. It spits out a ticket which the driver hands him. Johnson takes a seat behind the driver, reaches for his flask, but thinks twice about it. The last thing he wants to do is be remembered. He looks around him. Not many people on this bus and he's one of only two whites present. The other looking like he hadn't bathed in a month. What the fuck has his life come to? In legal pleadings, it'd be "but for pretty boy Eddie and the slut, he wouldn't be in his situation today." Well, killing the two will go a long way to righting the injustice, he thinks. He might even celebrate by getting him a little free head from one of the whores he routinely shakes down. Maybe, some pussy, too.

Johnson stares out the window as the bus continues to weave south. He turns—spots the map and route for his bus. It gets him all the way downtown before circling back. Perfect. Once he gets downtown, he'll be able to figure it out. Shit-loads of buses travel downtown. Johnson works his way toward the rear and the back exit. He takes a seat behind it and continues to stare out the window though he actually doesn't see any of it beyond the window. Forgetting his resolve, he uncaps his flask and takes a pull from the Beam. Damn fine whiskey, he thinks. Made in America with pride.

Johnson takes another pull from his flask as the bus rolls into downtown.

~~~

"Interesting pair," Amy says folding the lid to her Mac. She rubs her eyes. She's tired of reading. She looks at her watch. It's 6:46 p.m. "You know, we missed the evening news."

"Getting hungry again?" Eddie asks.

"I could fix us something healthy for a change. I feel like eating a big old chef salad."

"With tons of salad dressing."

"Don't worry, I'll run an extra mile. You could join me, you know..."

"It's hard to jog in boots..."

"...and keep me safe."

"Perhaps we'd both be safer if you were just fat."

"Right. I don't think so. I'm not genetically predisposed to be fat, I'll have you know. Come on, let's make a quick run to H.E.B. Plus, you're almost out of beer. I'm not sure how you'd act if you ran out of beer."

"Only because we need kitten food and milk, as well. I almost hate to disturb him. He's been asleep on my lap for the past two hours."

"He's so cute."

"Okay, let's go. I am getting kind of hungry."

"And with me around you need to keep your energy level up, too."

Eddie smiles. "There is that. Stay, Bobo. We'll be right back."

They pull out of the drive and head toward Burnet. Pass the apartment complex on the left. A dirty white Ford Explorer pulls out of the road fronting the backside of the complex and turns in behind Eddie's GMC. Eddie takes a right on the red. So does the Ford.

"Let's see where they go, da," Grigori, one of Igor's underlings, says to the other.

"I don't know, Grigori. Igor say only call if they left house," says Sergei, the other man.

"Grig, you always worry too much. This simple. We follow. Maybe take out, nyet."

Grigori doesn't like the plan, but shrugs. "Okay."

The pair follow the short distance to the H.E.B., watch as Eddie's truck turns in. They keep on going, take a right at the next light and circle back around.

"New plan," Sergei says. Grigori moans... Not like. "We go back to house. You drop me off. I go in and wait. Kill when get home."

"But Igor..."

"But Igor. But Igor. Fuck Igor. We be hero if we kill two, nyet."

Grigori moans once more. "I don't ..."

"Good. All settled. To house. Hurry!"

Reluctantly, Grigori speeds back toward Eddie's as Sergei screws a silencer on his Russian-made revolver. "Suppressor" is more like it, thinks Sergei, because it only takes the sharp edge off the gun's report.

"Not so good as in movie, Nyet." he says. Grigori nods, takes a quick look around him before pulling to the curb beyond Eddie's drive. "You go back and keep watch. Come get five minutes after return." Sergei grins revealing tobacco-stained teeth. "Both be dead." He tucks the pistol into his waistband, hops out. He whistles as he enters the garage from where he saw the two exit. Maybe door no locked, too, Sergei thinks. If not, he pick... No problem.

He reaches for the knob. It turns and clicks.

Bobo's ears perk. He scrambles to his feet.

Sergei eases the door open a crack. Opens it farther.

Bobo barks his deep bark and comes sliding into Sergei's sight. Bangs off the jamb. Barks again.

Sergei yanks the door shut and nearly trips over his own feet as Bobo makes contact with the door. "Shit!" he says. He feels like his heart just jumped out of his chest. Bobo continues to bark and bounce off the door. Sergei high-steps it out of the garage. Bobo's tail thumps on either side of him. He stops, sits, and wonders why the man didn't come on in and perhaps play.

Sergei curses under his breath as he walks back up the block toward the apartment complex. He forgot all about the big dog of the American. He decides for Grigori that they won't mention it to Igor. He slams the truck's door after getting in—slouches in his seat.

Fifteen minutes later they watch Eddie's GMC pass and pull back into the drive. "Probably in for the night," Sergei surmises.

"Da, probably so," Grigori concurs. At least Igor will never know they defied him, he thinks.

Foster Cares

154

Chapter Fourteen

Igor taps the screen on his phone ending the call. "Dorbandt no leave house," he says and chuckles. "Unless pedophile sneak out backdoor and hide." They pull into the drive of a reasonably nice North Austin stone house, park next to Dorbandt's aging Mercedes and all exit at the same time. Though the house is nice enough, the yard is scruffy. And on closer inspection, the eaves are flaking and in need of paint. Mikhail reaches the front door first and rings the bell. After a long moment, he follows up with his fist. Nothing. Despite the pounding, no answer to the knock is forthcoming.

Igor nods in Pavel's direction. No words are necessary—they've been down this road too many times. Pavel steps back, raises a heavy boot and kicks the door near the knob.

The wooden door splinters—bangs off the inner wall. The four men step across the threshold and pull their pieces while doing so.

"Spread out and find fuck," Igor orders. It doesn't take long to locate Dorbandt cowering under a bed.

"In here," Erik calls out from a spare bedroom. Igor, Pavel, and Mikhail join Erik in the bedroom. "He's under the bed."

Igor bends, peers under the bed and shakes his head. He wiggles his gun. "Dorbandt, come out from under there before you piss Igor off."

Dorbandt shakes his head no, moves closer to the center of the bed. If it weren't so pathetic, it'd be funny, Igor thinks. On second thought, it is pretty fucking funny, he decides. His crew joins him in laughter.

Igor hops up on the bed and begins bouncing up and down reminding him of his youth. Dorbandt's cries only add to his pleasure. He hears the first of the slats crack. The bed drops a few inches on one end. Winded, Igor hops to the carpet. He can't remember the last time he had so much fun. He bends and grabs his knees. Catches his breath.

"Get fuck from out under," he finally orders.

Pavel yanks the mattress from the bed and then the box spring from its frame. Pavel and Mikhail step within the framing and pull Dorbandt to his feet. They lift him from within the framing and hold him upright before Igor. Dorbandt wets his pants. Igor looks on with disgust. Real men don't wet themselves. Never. Igor die before he wet himself.

Igor backhands Dorbandt across the face with a resounding slap.

Dorbandt faints. Pavel and Mikhail have to hold him upright. "Is this guy for real?" Erik asks no one in particular.

"Get some water Erik—wake pussy up," Igor orders. Erik gets a glass of water from the kitchen, douses Dorbandt with it. Dorbandt moans, stirs, reluctantly opens his eyes.

Igor pulls a cigar from within his light jacket. Allows Erik to light it for him. Dorbandt's eyes never leave the glowing end of the cigar. Intuitively, Dorbandt knows what time it is. He might not be the sharpest tack, but he watches plenty of TV. Igor pinches his cheek.

"Look at me. Pay attention. You pass out again, I kill you." Dorbandt blinks. At least he's paying attention. "Now you answer Igor and you not lie. Where is little girl?"

"I... I... I don't know."

"Where's the rest of my money?"

"I'll get it. I swear. Need a little time."

"You thinking about calling police?"

Dorbandt shakes his head vigorously from side to side.

"Nyet. No. Good." Igor eyes each of his men in turn. "What Igor should do with this pussy?"

"Maybe should kill," Pavel offers. Dorbandt moans. Grows weak at the knees. Mikhail and Pavel lift him to stand straight again.

"And kill our investment. Not yet," Igor says. "But…"

Dorbandt's eyes remain glued to the tip of Igor's cigar. "I'll get your money. I promise."

"Let me see your hand."

Dorbandt vigorously shakes his head once more.

"What you think Igor burn your hand? How do you Americans say it, 'so cliché.' Or is that French? Whatever, no matter. Igor not burn you. Give me your hand NOW!"

Dorbandt offers a shaky hand. Pictures being burned by the cigar despite Igor's assurances. Igor grasps Dorbandt's hand and pulls it against his chest. He separates Dorbandt's left little finger from the rest. The snap of the finger is audible. Dorbandt's screams more so and faints again. This time they allow him to collapse to the carpet. Igor and his men laugh at the stricken man.

"Such pussy," Igor says. "Wake once more, then we go."

Erik rouses him once more with a cup of water. Dorbandt moans—clutches his hand to him. Tears streak down his face. The sight is enough to make Igor second guess his decision to allow

Dorbandt to live. Dorbandt, weak like little child, he thinks. After another moments thought, Igor decides to allow him to live and hopes decision doesn't come back to bite him in ass. Igor chuckles. He's been in America long enough to even begin to think like them.

Igor turns his attention back to Dorbandt. Shakes his head in disgust. "You call cops and you die. Understand?"

Dorbandt nods. He's a believer. Especially after seeing today's headlines, there's not a doubt in Dorbandt's mind that Igor and his crew killed the Smiths. And there's not a doubt in his mind it's because he gave them up. Better them than me Dorbandt thinks for the hundredth time. Better to be a coward than dead.

"Or you try to run and hide, you're dead. Igor find and cut throat himself. And you get Igor's money. One week. No extensions. New shipment coming in, too. Like Igor mention. Beautiful, blue-eyed Syrian boy. Sorry, can't show picture again. One week. Sell boy, too. Understand?"

Dorbandt sniffles, wipes the snot from his upper lip. "But it might be too soon..."

Igor kicks him in the gut. "One week. Sell boy, too. And have all Igor's money."

Dorbandt's nod is barely discernible. "Okay," he says in a voice so soft but for the movement of his lips he might not have been heard. Igor draws his foot back. Dorbandt curls into a fetal position. Igor and his men laugh. Leave Dorbandt where he lies.

The sky is clear and the stars are bright as they step back into the night. Igor takes a deep breath of the fresh air. He still has trouble believing that the air can be so fresh in a city of its size. He feels good about the meeting with Dorbandt. He looks to the sky and opens his arms expansively. God is good to Igor. He turns to face his men.

"Yellow Rose, nyet and maybe check with Dorbandt again tomorrow."

His crew smiles. The women at the Yellow Rose are some of the prettiest women in town. And Igor and his men love pretty women.

Igor and his crew begin to sing an old Russian drinking song as Pavel steers the Caddy south and toward the Yellow Rose.

~~~

Riding the bus sucks, Johnson decides as he finally gets off at the stop fronting the H.E.B. on Slaughter. Of all fucking things, he got on the wrong bus and before he knew it the bus was traveling north again. Johnson pulls his flask from his back pocket only to discover it's empty. He feels like throwing it to the ground and stomping it, but that wouldn't bring near the satisfaction of slapping around or kicking a suspect or detainee. Johnson pines for the good old days that preceded smartphones and the ability for anyone to video.   Even worse, the fuckers sell their videos to the media, so the media can exploit the videos and make the boys-in-blue out to be the bad guys. What the fuck is the world coming to?

Johnson starts out across the near-full parking lot. Sure enough, there's a cluster of cars and trucks for sale. He hones in on a 90's-era teal Chevy extended cab pickup with $3,000 written on the windshield. The truck looks relatively clean for its age and the wheels are a bit nicer than Johnson would care, but all-in-all it will meet his needs. Most of all, he likes the fact that it has a sliding rear window meaning he can shoot from the front seat with only the tip of his rifle extended beyond the window.

Johnson whips out his phone and dials the number. He's in luck—a Mexican answers the phone. A Mexican who can speak little English. God must truly be shining down on him tonight. Well, except for getting on the wrong fucking bus and running out of whiskey, but shining down on him nevertheless, sending him a Mexican who's probably an illegal too. One thing Johnson's learned is illegals tend to never call the police, even when robbed.

Johnson's wait is a short one. A faded maroon Dodge Dart pulls into a spot several spaces over. Johnson frowns at the sight. It looks like the Mexican brought his entire family with him including his mother-in-law. Sure enough, the owner speaks very little English, but he's quick to grin. He hands over a lone door key and stands aside as Johnson unlocks the door, slides inside and cranks the truck. The truck fires right up. Johnson revs the engine a couple of times and goes to pop the hood and decides, fuck it, the truck's fine. He counts out the $3,000 and hands it to the Mexican plus an additional $20. Johnson holds onto the $20 for a second before releasing it. Johnson takes the offered title and points to the $20.

"Go into the store and buy me an 18-pack of Budweiser, Si?" The Mexican's all grins as he hurries off to buy the beer. Johnson backs out of the spot and drives to the front of the store to wait on his beer. He's surprised to find that even the AC works. He turns it on high and directs the closest vents on him. He notes too that the truck's stickers are good. And here comes his beer. Does it get any better than this, he thinks as the Mexican passes the beer through the window?

Johnson finds himself grinning as he pulls away from the curb. "Ready or not, pretty boy and your slut, here I come," he says.

~~~

"Kitten!" Amy says. "He won't stay off my keyboard,"

"He's just trying to help you."

"Well, it's not helping," Amy says pushing her chair away from the table. "I'm not finding out anything useful anyway. I'm not sure what I'm looking for, either."

Eddie moves in behind her and begins to massage her neck and shoulders. "Ah," she says. "Now that helps. So, what are we missing?"

"You're the Detective."

"Ex. Well, at least for now. You know that's a nice house up there. You would think they would have a maid, but we haven't heard anything about a maid yet."

"Perhaps they just haven't made that information available yet."

Amy twists in her chair so she can look up at Eddie. "Eddie, until we figure out what's going on, perhaps you ought to keep that cannon of yours close at hand."

"Cannon, so you've already named it."

"Right. No, not that silly. I'm talking about your Colt. I'm sure it was Johnson who tried to blow us up, but what if it wasn't? I mean think about it a minute. Why would Johnson rig a car that he doesn't know anything about when your truck is in the drive, too?"

"Good question. Maybe he assumed it was your car. He knew yours was totaled out."

"That's giving Johnson a lot of credit. He's probably been deep in his bottle ever since he got out on bond."

"Wouldn't that be in violation of the terms of his bond?"

"Yeah, but in his case, it won't make any difference. He's been in law enforcement too long and's too well connected. Hey, that's starting to feel a little bit too good. You're going to put me to sleep if you keep it up."

Eddie moves to the side of the chair, leans in and gives Amy a kiss. "I didn't put you to sleep the last time I kept it up."

Amy blushes despite herself. "No, you didn't," she finally manages. She can't believe she's been as brazen as she's been. Talk about coming out of one's shell. "Thanks for reminding me," she adds, causing them both to laugh.

"How about popping some popcorn and I'll put up some makeshift curtains in the living room and we can stream or order up a video."

"Okay, I'll just slip into something more comfortable first. Say a T-shirt?"

"You're incorrigible," Eddie says causing them both to laugh. On a more serious note, Eddie thinks they should be perfectly safe in the living room with the windows covered. Surely, they will.

~~~

Igor and crew laugh and slap each other on the back as they exit the Yellow Rose. Drinking and women always put him and his men in a good mood. Things turn a little more somber as the four doors to the Caddy slam shut. It's getting late and there's still one important thing to do, namely, kill the American and his bitch.

Igor turns toward Pavel as Pavel cranks the Caddy. "Yes, tonight, Pavel, we kill American and ex-cop." Igor bangs a closed fist against his chest. "You, Pavel and Igor, we handle."

Pavel studies Igor in the dim light before putting the car into reverse. Igor's eyes look manic, a look that sometimes scares Pavel. Well, maybe not so much scare, as worry. And he has to admit to himself, that the vodka's talking to him, too, somewhat and he wouldn't mind killing the cocky American and maybe kidnapping the woman.

Pavel puts the car into drive and allows his rational mind to kick in. "Let's send boys. We stay back, talk business," he says.

He senses Igor's intense eyes scrutinizing him.

"Talk business." Igor mimics. He flexes his injured hand. Finds the pain pleasurable. He wonders if Pavel grows soft. He shakes his head. Not Pavel. Never Pavel. A smile threatens, he holds it at bay as he pictures the worst-case scenario of sending others instead and the American killing his brother-in-law.

"Sure, we talk business." Igor turns to look over his shoulder.

"Erik, you take soldier and kill them, da."

Erik scowls back at Igor. Fucking Pavel. Erik liked the thought of Igor going and perhaps getting killed and him assuming control. Erik shrugs. He has no choice but to save face.

"Sure, why the fuck not."

Igor does smile this time. He'll send him along with his worst fuckup. Someone capable of fucking up a wet dream. "Good, we drop off. You and Sergei, you kill American and bitch."

"Sergei?" the name almost gets stuck in Erik's throat. Igor's eyes turn to a squint.

"You have problem with Sergei?"

"Well, no..."

"Good, it is then settled," Igor says turning back in his seat. "Pavel, swing south. Drop off brave brother-in-law."

Erik's hand snakes inside his sports jacket and finds the grip on his automatic. Mikhail tenses beside him. Erik counts to ten. Not today but soon, he thinks. His hand drops back to his side. Mikhail exhales. At times, he too would like to put a bullet into the back of Igor's head. Someday, too, he too thinks.

~~~

Johnson kills the lights. Pulls to the curb to retrieve his walker. He leaves the lights off as he continues down the street. He's been driving around for the past couple hours drinking beer and envisioning himself putting a bullet between pretty boy's eyes. He'll turn him into a fucking cyclops, he thinks with a broadening grin. Johnson pulls into his driveway. He'll just fetch his rifle and be on his way, yes sirree.

Johnson snatches his walker out of the back of the truck and slowly makes his way into the house. He finds his rifle where he left it, under the couch. For an insane second there, he had the perverse thought that the rifle would be missing. But there she is, shining like new. Johnson hastily wraps it in a blanket. Only one thing else he needs from the house and he has a number of them never used, a Trac Phone, an untraceable one. Ain't they all, he thinks. While he's at it, he flips through his relic of a phone book until his finger stops on Eddie's home phone number. He stores the number in his phone and drops it into his front pocket.

All set, Johnson abandons his walker at the door. Hell, he doesn't really need it, no how, now that the pain's mostly gone. He eyes his pill bottle one last time and thinks better of it. He needs to stay on top of his game. Keep his wits about him. He chuckles. Keep his shooting eye open and his trigger finger steady. Yep, that's the. ticket. "Enough with the platitudes, Johnson. Get on with it," he mumbles stepping out into the night. He takes no notice in just how beautiful the night is. He's just happy to have something worthwhile to do.

His used Chevy fires right up. Two blocks away he hits the lights. He foregoes the AC and opts for rolling down the windows. Mostly, because he needs a bit sobering up. Not that he needs much sobering up, mind you, but just enough to give him that needed edge. If truth be known, he purdy near has drunk himself sober since switching to beer only. He pulls another warming beer from the carton—pops the tab. It foams, spills over his fingers and wets his crotch. Johnson could give a shit less. He's on a mission, by God, from God, by God.

~~~

The buttery aroma of the freshly popped popcorn precedes Amy into the living room. Bobo beats her to the couch. Jumps up to claim the center of the couch. Somehow, his eyes manage to never lose sight of the popcorn.

"Bobo, you've got my spot," Amy complains good-naturedly. Eddie chuckles.

"Toss one kernel to the floor and he'll move," Eddie says taking the offered beer from Amy. Amy tosses one across the room. Bobo clears the coffee table getting to it. Eddie and Amy laugh. Bobo posts up and awaits another kernel.

Amy smiles. "If only all men were so easy to please," she says setting her beer on the table and removing the kitten from Eddie's lap and placing him on her own lap. "Nice curtains. I see I've hooked up with a regular Martha Stewart."

Eddie lifts his 45 caliber Colt 1911 off the table. He points it at the ceiling. "Does this look like something Martha carries around in her purse?"

Amy purses her lips. "No. Hey, no spare clip?"

"Good shot. Don't need one. You know, technically it's a magazine and not a clip."

"You know, I actually knew that. Learned that in firearms training, but you know, the term clip is so much more economical—easier to say."

"What do you want to watch?"

"Have you seen the newest Road Warrior movie? I hear it's pretty good."

"Road Warriors it is. Give me a minute to find it." Eddie finds it on Netflix. Lays his arm across Amy's shoulder. Kisses the top of her head. Amy snuggles in close as the movie begins. She feeds Eddie a couple kernels of popcorn. Amy feels safe like never before tucked in the nook of Eddie's arm. Yes, safe like never before.

Chapter Fifteen

Pavel pulls in beside the Explorer. Rolls down his window. Sergei does the same. "Still at home, I hope," Pavel says. Sergei's surprised at their arrival—does his best not to show it.

"Yeah, they just went to the store and back. It looks like they've settled in for the night," he says.

Grigori catches the gaffe, tenses up.

"Oh yeah and how did you know they went to store?" Igor asks leaning in so that he can be seen from the passenger seat. "I ordered you to stay put—watch house only."

"Just... Just a guess, boss. What I meant is they weren't gone long. You got something else you want us to do? We do. No problem."

Igor turns in his seat to face Erik. "Get out. Take care of problems. Meet you back at warehouse. No fuckups, da."

Reluctantly, Erik exits the Caddy. Fucking Igor. Someday. For now, though, he resigns himself to the fact that he needs to kill the two Americans. Oh well, not so hard. It won't be his first kills and, god willing, it won't be his last.

Erik climbs into the back of the Explorer as the Caddy pulls away. He leans in between the pair. "Your lucky day, Sergei. Today, me you, we kill the Americans. Something Igor bragged he'd do."

"Um, you know American have big dog. Probably bark," Sergei says. Erik slaps him playfully in the back of the head. "So, we kill fucking dog, too. Nyet."

~~~

Johnson traverses the darkened neighborhoods to approach Eddie's house from the east only to realize his error. "Shit, Johnson, the truck will be facing the wrong direction." He slaps himself. No problem, he thinks, killing the lights and making a U-turn. He pulls to the curb a block shy of Eddie's house. And as God and luck would have it, in front of a house that looks dead to the world.

Johnson stretches over the back and works the sliding window open. From his location, it will be a long shot or hopefully two long shots. His plan suddenly seems lacking. He's not so much worried about the distance. It ain't but maybe 60 yards or so. But what can he say to draw them both out? Think Johnson—fucking think.

He pops the tab on a warm   beer and downs about half the can before setting the can in the cupholder. He lifts the rifle from the floorboard and unwraps it from within its blanket. Johnson's heartbeat ticks up notch. If God willing and the creek don't rise, he's fixing to purge the earth of one and possibly two evils. And Johnson won't be wrong in his beliefs.

~~~

"Pause the movie and I'll get us another beer," Amy says though reluctant to move from her comfortable spot. Eddie hits the pause and briefly admires Amy's backside before she disappears from the room. He smiles as he thinks how lucky he is to be given another chance at life and love. There's no denying he's getting fonder of Amy by the minute. What's not to love, he thinks. Amy catches him smiling.

"Whatcha smiling about?" she asks before plopping back down on the couch and reclaiming her spot nestled beside Eddie.

"Just glad to have you here," he says. Amy turns her head and offers Eddie a kiss. It's an offer too good to refuse. Their lips meet. Amy's lips are so soft. Eddie can't help but feel a stirring. His hand slips under the hem of the T-shirt and finds her hot and wet. Amy parts her legs slightly and kisses Eddie harder. Fuck the movie they both think. It's time to unfold the sleeper.

~~~

"What's the layout?" Erik asks.

Sergei turns in his seat. "The garage seems to always be open," he says. "They always come and go through garage."

Erik thinks about that for a moment. Likely has a flimsy door that opens to the kitchen or a utility room then the kitchen. Seems like logical place to breach the house. "What else, Grigori?"

"I think until just now they were watching TV in the front room. They got windows covered but I see flickers of light. But no more now." Grigori chuckles. "Maybe watch porn and hit pause." Erik and Sergei chuckle as well.

"Maybe catch with pants down, da," Sergei says. "We better hurry then. Maybe have only minutes to catch Americans fuck."

"It's 'fucking'," Erik corrects. "It's catch 'fucking' you moron. Anyway, you stay in car. We go now and you be ready to pick up in hurry. You understand?"

"Da, da," Grigori says. He doesn't like being called a moron, though he's not exactly sure what a moron is. It just sounds bad.

"We walk from here. When we get to house. I go in garage. You count to five and put half dozen rounds in front room and I kick door in. You understand, Sergei? No problem, nyet?"

"Da, Da. Sergei no dummy."

Erik pushes his door open. Steps out into the night. If all goes well, he'll be in and out in seconds. He unholsters his piece, works the slide and chambers a round. Sergei joins him outside the Explorer, draws his revolver. Erik shakes his head at the sight of the revolver. Sergei shrugs. Erik lowers his pistol to rest against his leg. Sergei follows suit. They start toward Eddie's at a brisk pace.

~~~

Johnson slings the rifle across the seat. Rests the tip of the rifle on the window's lip. It's a little more awkward then he planned. He can't straighten his bum knee. He tries several positions and settles on the least restrictive, yet still awkward position. He'll sight through the rifle once and then make the call. Hell, he'll tell pretty boy there's someone lurking around his house. That should get him out and perhaps the cop in Amy will bring her out as well.

Erik reaches Eddie's   fence line. Drops to a crouch for the last 50 feet. Sergei follows suit. The light on Eddie's back stoop is out and Eddie's garage is open and dark. The Americans apparently unconcerned about crime. He motions Sergei to hold up a sec. He wants to slow his breathing: Still his nerves. Prepare himself for the assault.

Eddie allows the sleeper's last third to fall into place. A giggling Amy sheds her T and beats Eddie atop the thin mattress. "Tramp," Eddie says slipping in beside her.

"Position yourself behind truck and begin count," Erik whispers, pointing toward the back of the truck and preparing to dart the last 20 feet to the open garage.

Johnson chambers a round, uncaps the end, caps on his scope and leans in to sight through the scope wishing he had a night scope.

"What the fuck!" He laughs. God provides for the righteous. Eddie's looking at something at the back of his truck.

Johnson holds his breath. Lines up the crosshairs.

Erik signals he's going in.

The boom of the rifle is deafening in the confines of the truck. The recoil rocks Johnson.

The rifle flash is like a flashbulb going off.

Sergei's knocked off his feet. Goes down hard.

Erik stops in his tracks... Drops to a knee. "gav-NO! Fucking trap."

Bobo barks.

Eddie pushes Amy from the sleeper. Rolls the opposite direction. Drops to the floor. Snatches his 1911 off the end table. "Stay Down, Amy!"

Amy peers at him from just above the mattress. "Sounded like it's a ways off Eddie."

"Stay down, dammit!"

Johnson laughs. He saw his man go down. He works the bolt. Chambers another round.

Sergei pushes himself up. His left arm lay dead at his side.

The pain causes a moan to escape his lips. Stepped right into a trap. Damn sure didn't see that coming, he thinks. He locates the source of the gunshot. A lone truck a block and a quarter up. He raises his pistol.

The rifle kicks his shoulder like a mule. The boom disturbing the still of the night once more.

The taillight explodes near Sergei's head. Shards of plastic and glass pepper the side of his face. He screams and begins pulling the trigger.

The back window implodes. Johnson's windshield spiders. The rearview falls from its spot, bounces off the dash, lands in Johnson's lap. "Shit! Fucker's shooting back!"

Johnson hastily chambers another round.

Eddie kills the living room lights. It sounds like a gun battle taking place right outside his house. What the hell is going on?

"Stay down!" Eddie once more admonishes. "Shut up Bobo, I can't hear!" He grabs his blue jeans.

A third boom disturbs the night. Sergei's sent sprawling. The top of his head goes missing. Erik's seen enough. He takes off in a sprint toward the Explorer.

Lights in neighboring houses begin to come on. Johnson lets the rifle fall to the rear floorboard. Time to make himself scarce. His laugh fills the cab as he straightens out ever mindful of his bum knee.

Johnson turns the key. The starter clicks. Sweat begins to form at his temples. "Uh-oh!"

"The shooting seems to have stopped, Eddie," Amy whispers from her prone position on the carpet.

"Just stay put, please. Someone will call the police."

Johnson wipes the sweat from his eyes. More lights are coming on. He pats the truck's dash. "Please girl, you can do it," he tells the truck sounding contrite for once.

Johnson turns the key. The truck fires to life and he quickly drops her into drive and squeals off, takes the next left, then the next right. He digs a warm beer out of the carton. His last.

"Hell yeah!" His scream fills the truck. He laughs. "How do you like that, fucking pretty boy? You stupid fuck. Now, look at you. And your cunt is next!"

Beer spills down Johnson's chin. Man, what a night! Does it get any better than this? Hell no. Man! Now what? Where do you park the truck? How do you get back to the house? And, what was Eddie doing at the rear of his truck? It's the last question that sticks in his craw. What was he doing?

~~~

Erik hops into the front seat and slams the door. "Go! Go!"

"Where's Sergei? What the fuck happened?"

"Go! Go! Get fuck out of here!"

Grigori reluctantly cranks the Explorer, pulls out and turns toward Burnet. He looks over at Erik who's still panting and trying to catch his breath. Grigori clearly heard the rifle shots. He doesn't like leaving Sergei behind. He's always liked Sergei, as silly as he is. At least leaving Sergei behind is not his fault. Igor's going to be as mad as an old Russian bear, he suspects. A pair of cop cars speed by going in the opposite direction—lights flashing, sirens blaring. The cops pay them no attention. Grigori exhales audibly.

"Tell Grigori what happen, Erik."

"Trap. American set trap. Sniper. He wait for us."

"But how can this be, Erik. I ask you?"

"Perhaps they spot you and Sergei, da."

"No way. They no spot."

"Well, then you explain, da."

Grigori's grip tightens on the steering wheel. Erik's already looking to shift blame. Shift the blame on Grigori. Bullshit. That's what it is. Too bad Erik didn't catch a bullet, too. Someday if Igor doesn't kill first, perhaps Grigori kill Erik himself. Shut Igor's brother-in-law up for good.

They continue on toward the warehouse. Neither of them in much of a hurry to get there.

~~~

Cop cars slide to a stop outside Eddie's house. Park at all angles. Eddie sets his pistol on the end table. Offers Amy a hand.

"You might want to put something on, honey."

"Jealous?"

Eddie smiles. "Suit yourself."

Amy returns the smile. "Okay, but I'm going to play hard to get later."

"We'll see." They both laugh. Surviving always works to lift one's spirits, it would seem. And they both know Amy's not going to play that hard to get. The phone in the kitchen rings.

"I'll get it," Eddie volunteers. It's a representative of the hordes of cops outside. And quite naturally, they want everyone inside to exit the house unarmed and with their hands up.

"Well?" asks Amy. wiggling into a tight pair of blue jeans.

"Seems we have a dead fellow in our driveway and they want us to make an appearance."

"Hands raised, huh?"

"You got it. Said you had a penchant for shooting cops."

"Seems unfair. Shoot one dirty cop and it gives a girl a bad rap."

"Put that way, it does seem unfair." They both laugh. Amy motions she's ready. Eddie gathers one of Bobo's longer leashes and hooks him up. He's sure not going to give the cops an excuse for killing the world's friendliest dog.

Together they exit the front door into what appears to be a sea of piranhas—piranhas with their pistols drawn.

"Why can't we just all get along," Eddie jokes. The cops don't find things so amusing. They cuff them both, hands in front, assured that it's for their own safety. Their hands are bagged in anticipation of forensic testing for gunshot residue. "Paraffin" test, Eddie believes it's called.

"Always the suspect, Eddie," Amy says. From where they're standing, only the bottom of the dead man's feet can be seen.

"Wonder who our lucky visitor is?" Eddie asks nodding in the direction of the recently deceased.

"I'm more interested in who killed him and why?"

"There is that," Eddie says. "Everything seems to come back to the little girl. I think she's the key to all of this. And we've put ourselves right in the middle of it."

"Because it's the right thing to do."

"Agreed. But still, how would... Scratch that. Once they knew our names, or my name, finding us would be easy enough. I guess someone feels like we pose a threat."

"And I hope we do. That girl's got a family somewhere. Hey, look, Eddie, here comes the ME's van."

"And maybe they'll uncuff us then."

"Here come the detectives, too."

"Recognize them?"

"Yes and no. Can't put a name to them."

Eddie and Amy spend the next 20 minutes adding little to the investigation. The test for residue comes back negative and they're finally uncuffed.

"When they're finished processing the scene, I want you two to take a look at the victim and see if you can identify him," the lead detective says.

"Sure," they say in unison. The house is swept and cleared allowing Eddie to put Bobo back inside.

One of the detectives waves them over. "Careful not to step in the blood," he says. There's a significant amount of blood pooled under the deceased. Eddie gets as close as possible. Looks down on the man. He doesn't recognize him and says so. The dead man does have a distinctive Slavic look to him, though.

"I'll bet money he's Russian," Eddie says.

The detective nods. "But then who killed this character?"

Eddie shrugs, steps back and allows Amy to take a look. She, too, doesn't recognize the man. She shakes her head no. "Nope."

"Hmm, okay, well thank you for your cooperation. If something comes up, we'll be in touch."

"Good enough," Eddie says.

"Night Detective," Amy adds.

They cut through the garage and back into the house happy to be alive.

Foster Cares

Chapter Sixteen

Grigori honks the horn lacking an opener for the warehouse garage doors. His stomach grows weak as the door rattles open. He pulls in and parks next to the Cadillac. Expecting the worst, he steps from the Explorer. Erik does the same. Pavel towers over the pair. Igor is thankfully kicked back in his recliner and snoring loudly.

"Been listening to police scanner," Pavel says. He crosses his arms in front of him. "Tell Pavel what happened..." He looks over at the snoring Igor. "... And maybe I can talk to Igor. Keep Igor from killing you."

"What's to say," Erik begins. "Trap. Had man watching house with rifle."

"And you no see nothing, Grigori?"

"The man was over a block up in other direction," Erik answers for him. "And truck look like just parked at curb. No way to see if someone inside."

Grigori adds his nod of assent. "Too far for Grigori to see," he says his nerves beginning to calm. He was all but sure Erik would lay the blame on him.

"So be it," Pavel says. "Sergei not sharpest tack. nu, a mnye kaKOI khryen? What the hell do I care?"

"Then you talk to Igor?" Grigori asks hopefully.

"Yeah, I talk. But you two owe, Pavel, da?"

Relief washes over Erik and Grigori. If anyone can keep Igor under control, it's Pavel. Pavel shakes a Marlboro out for each of them. Yes, things will be alright. Left unsaid, the Americans will surely have to die now. Eye for eye. Man for man. That's Igor's rule. Well, in this case, two for one shall die. So be it, he thinks.

~~~

The morning sun streaks through the spidered window casting an eerie pattern across Johnson's face. A loud rap on his driver's side window stirs him. He's momentarily confused. Then it all comes flooding back. He killed Eddie and he's sure the urgent rap on his window is the cops. Reluctantly, Johnson wills his eyes open. His relief is palatable as he spots a Mexican outside his truck. The Mexican says something that's not discernible to Johnson's muddled mind. He feebly waves indicating he's okay. Johnson pushes himself into a sitting position. He's surprised to find himself back in the H.E.B. parking lot on Slaughter. He has absolutely no recollection as to how he got there. His throat's parched and his head and knee are throbbing. Well, at least he managed not to get arrested.

Johnson looks over his shoulder to check on his rifle. It's where he dropped it and he hadn't even bothered to cover it up with the blanket. Not too fucking smart. The back seat's covered in square pieces of safety glass. He faintly remembers a bullet missing his head. Hell, maybe two bullets. At least the for-sale sign is no longer in the back window, that portion of the window now ceasing to exist. Another bonehead move, not bothering to scrape the for-sale sign-off. But, all things considered, he came out smelling like roses. Johnson chuckles. Divine intervention—that's what it is.

Johnson licks his chapped lips. A beer sure would work right about now, he thinks. He checks his leg. A little blood has seeped through his slacks, but not all that much. He reaches over the seat and covers up the rifle. If he can find a spot close enough to the front of H.E.B., he can use one of their electric carts and fetch his own beer. Maybe pick something up at the deli, too. Man can't live on beer alone, some wise fucker once said.

Johnson goes to check himself in the rearview mirror only to discover it missing. Shit. He forgot. The damn bullet knocked it off before punching a hole through his windshield. He chuckles again. Better the fucking windshield than his head.

Fuck it, Johnson decides, he'll park in the fire lane in front of the grocery store. If anybody doesn't like it, he'll flash his spare badge and hope like hell they don't recognize him.

The truck fires up. The day's going to be a beauty.

~~~

The kitten's kneading on Eddie's neck and its little motor is purring away. Eddie plucks him from his neck and nuzzles him against Amy's throat. Amy yawns wide. "Thanks," she says somehow knowing Eddie turned the kitten's affections on her.

"You're welcome," Eddies says hardly containing his mirth.

"No pussy for you," Amy says in response.

"And suddenly you're the 'Pussy' Nazi?"

Amy laughs. "Well, maybe nothing quite that drastic. I take it you've seen the episode?"

"Perhaps a dozen times. Seinfeld is probably my favorite all-time show."

"Married with Children probably being a close second, huh?"

"How could one not love Al Bundy? And Christina Applegate sure turned out fine."

"I suspected you might like her. Speaking of, isn't she in the movie Bad Moms?"

"Her and Mila. Those are the only two that I recognize."

"Might be fun to watch."

"So, what's on the agenda, Detective?"

"Whew. After last night's development, I don't know what to think. Keep digging, I guess. Make a few calls. See if there is anything new happening."

"Well then, since you decided it would be impractical, plus unrealistic to cut me off, I'll make us breakfast."

"A win-win situation for a gal with a healthy libido."

"And understanding as well."

Eddie rolls from the bed—beats Amy to the bathroom. "Unfair," she calls after him. Eddie pulls the door shut and hollers back at her, "I can't hear you."

Amy nods. Good one. "Come on kitten and Bobo. I'll feed you while I wait, seeing how my toothbrush and accessories are in that bathroom."

Bobo happily shadows Amy. After last night's events, they've decided it might be safer to sleep in the bedroom as opposed to remaining in the living room.

Amy dishes out a can of Alpo and fills a bowl of milk for the kitten. She sits down before her computer to check if there have been any developments in the murders. Nothing new, but she and Eddie made the news once again. According to the reports, the deceased had yet to be identified and the police received no hits on the prints.

"Unusual," Amy says to herself. The guy appeared to be in his late 40s or early 50s. If he was involved in criminal activity, which she assumes he was based upon the fact he got himself shot, he should have had some kind of brush with the law by now.

"Your turn," Eddie says entering the kitchen. "What are you looking at?"

"Oh, just checking my Austin news aggregate. It seems our dead man from last night is a ghost."

"Hmm," Eddie says scratching the stubble on his chin.

"Fingerprints came back negative, then."

"You got it." Amy stands. Goes on her tip-toes to kiss Eddie. "Give me ten and let Bobo out."

"Yes, ma'am." Eddie smiles at the retreating figure. Shakes his head. He never imagined he could be domesticated so quickly, but it's beginning to appear more and more so to be the case. Eddie steps to the cabinets, opens the one over to stove and retrieves a cast-iron skillet. His kitchen phone rings. Eddie frowns. He has an old-fashion recorder which he likes because you can listen to the caller and decide whether to pick up or not. Can't do that with call notes, Eddie thinks, reaching into the refrigerator for eggs, butter and bacon.

"Eddie, it's me. Wanted to see how you're doing, say hello..." Eddie snatches the phone up, punches talk. "Lori? You okay?" There's a long pause then a sigh. "Yes and no. Physically, I'm mending, but mentally I'm struggling."

"That's understandable. It will take some time. Have you been to counseling?"

"Eddie, it's not so much that..."

"Oh."

"Right. As far as the kidnapping goes, I'm doing okay. The kidnapper is dead, so he's no longer a threat to me or anyone. It's just... It's just that I think I screwed up leaving Austin. My mother's a mess and frankly, I miss you."

"Oh."

"Ouch. I know I gave you both my blessings. I've been following the news, so I take it that you two hooked up."

Eddie's at a loss for words. The last thing he wants to do is hurt Lori. He settles on the truth. "Yes, she's here now, Lori."

"Okay."

"But I need to qualify that some. I was on a long downhill spiral when we ran into each other at Little Ginny's. Meeting you that evening, I'm mean I knew who you were, but hooking up with you that evening was the catalyst... Was the wakeup call there's a life for me after losing Holly. You saved me, Lori."

"I'm not sure that makes me feel any better," Lori says and laughs softly.

"I'm not sure I know what else to say."

"I put you on a spot, didn't I?"

Eddie pictures Lori smiling and for some reason, he knows she is. "Yes, but that's okay. Our night together will always be the best of memories."

"Thanks. How's the mutt?"

"He's outside doing his morning constitutional."

"And Amy? How's she doing?"

"Other than somebody's trying to kill either one or both of us, she's doing good."

"You think it's that dirty cop? The one that Amy capped in the knee?"

"'Capped?' You been watching gangster movies, or what?"

Lori laughs. "Actually, I've been watching lots of TV here at mother's. God, she's a mess. I think I'm cramping her style. She's in a mood to find that next husband, or better said, 'hook' that next husband."

Eddie chuckles picturing the mother he met. "Somehow, I think she'll do just that."

"So, what's the skinny on the little girl?"

"We haven't put that together yet."

"Well, I want to be the first to know."

"Deal."

"Um, Eddie. I decided I'm ready to come back to Austin. Go back to work as soon as my black eyes go away."

"You'll be sure and come by, won't you? Once I'm convinced it's safe around here again."

"Of course. Give my regards to Amy." She giggles. "Remember I still owe you for saving me."

"That leaves a lot unsaid," Eddie says feeling Lori's smile over the phone line.

"That it does, Eddie Winston. See you around."

"Later, Lori. Take care." Eddie hangs up. Turns to find Amy standing in the doorway. "Been standing there long?" he asks.

"Only long enough to know you're a great guy."

"I think she'll be alright. She's a survivor."

"How about I cook breakfast?"

"Jealous?"

"Hell, yeah." They both laugh as Amy pushes past Eddie and sets the skillet on the burner.

~~~

"Fucking dead!" Igor screams. "Fucking dead! Where is that no good brother-in-law? Send him to kill two, lousy fucking Americans and he gets our man killed!"

Pavel holds up both hands, palms out. "Take it easy, Igor."

Igor kicks the coffee table sending everything flying and hurting his foot in the process. "I should kill Erik myself."

"It was a trap, Igor. They had sniper up road guarding house. This time not Erik's fault."

"Where are fucking cigarettes?"

Pavel shakes out one of his own. Offers a light.

"So, they made our crew?"

Pavel shrugs. "Pavel not know. But possibly."

"I guess Igor have to kill Americans himself after all."

"Why not leave Americans be?"

Igor slaps his chest. "Fuck Americans. This personal now."

Aren't they all, Pavel thinks? He exhales audibly. "Let be, Igor."

"You think Igor pussy?"

"No, Igor. Course not."

"So, I kill, da?"

"If must, kill."

A horn outside the garage door sounds. The monitor shows it to be the expected box van. Igor grinds his cigarette out with the toe of his boot. He watches the door rattle open. At least something is going right. The van rolls to a stop, the clattering diesel stills and the forklift comes to life. His men quickly unload the pallets and remove the fake backing. The new arrivals huddle together. Igor grins up at them. Motions them to disembark. As usual, it takes some encouragement from his men. So be it, Igor thinks. Best to establish authority from get-go.

Igor eyes the blue-eyed, blond-haired Syrian boy. He's much prettier than the cell-phone photos depicted. Yes, this one will bring top dollar. Perhaps five thousand more.

Igor's mind turns to thoughts of Dorbandt. His best and mostly only outlet for the children. What to do about Dorbandt? Dorbandt, worse than woman, Igor thinks. His face involuntarily reveals his thoughts. The boy clings to the woman beside him. Igor looks the women over, not too happy with the quality. Fuckable, but not much better than that. In fact, he's not inclined to fuck any of them.

Igor spits on the floor. Instructs his interpreter to take them to the container. Clean one of them up in case he changes his mind. Hell, he don't necessarily have to look at 'em to fuck 'em, Igor thinks. The thought causes him to shake his head and chuckle. In a year's time, they won't be so modest. Just whores that know their place in life.

Igor's thoughts turn to his brother-in-law who's no doubt hiding from him. "Pavel, go find Erik. We take ride, da," he says.

~~~

In his haste to down his first beer, it sloshes from the can and drips off his chin. Johnson absently wipes his chin and tosses the can out his missing rear window. Man, was that fucking beer good, he thinks. Johnson digs another beer from the carton and wonders what he should do next—ditch the truck? Not yet, he decides. Might still come in useful. I mean, he still has a bitch to kill. One down—one to go. He may have to give that a day or two. With pretty-boy gone though, fucking Foster will be forced to go back to her own house—a house he knows well and a house to which he has a spare key. The bitch probably doesn't even remember giving him the key years back—back when they first became partners. He drops the truck into drive and pulls away from the curb. He turns the AC on max and punches the power button on the radio. Switches it to AM in search of a news station. Comes up with nothing but country music and static. He punches the power button killing the radio. Just another distraction.

First things first, Johnson. Get the fucking windows fixed. He pulls out of the lot and merges with the traffic heading east. There's a number of junkyards on South Congress and he seems to recall that at least one of them installs glass.

Johnson works his way through the ever-increasing traffic. He's in a good mood. The beer's cold and he's scored one for the good guys. It just doesn't get much better than this, he thinks as comes upon the first of the junkyards on his right. Johnson pulls into the dirt entrance and parks before the ramshackle of an office. He's amazed that junkyards even exist anymore. The land itself is worth a fortune. These fucking grease-monkeys will be millionaires one day. He shakes his head and steps from the truck.

The office is at least air-conditioned. Johnson steps to the grimy counter and interrupts an attendant almost as grimy who seems intent on making an old part look new. The power of the badge never ceases to amuse him. Sure enough, they have the used glass in stock and though Johnson could give a shit less about the cost, he negotiates a favorable price anyhow.

The TV on the counter draws his attention. The 11:00 news is just airing. He reaches over and turns up the volume. Johnson's smile broadens as the top story is last night's shooting.

...and sources close to the investigation that are not authorized to speak, tell News 36 that the victim of last night's shooting has yet to be identified ...

Johnson's vision blurs. He pulls at the hair at the side of his head. "Son of a bitch!" he wails startling the attendant and causing him to step back from the counter.

Johnson rakes the old TV from the counter sending it crashing to the floor. Sparks shoot out the back and the screen goes dark.

"Sir, are you okay?" the startled attendant asks from his frozen position.

"Huh?... Um, yeah. Migraine set in." He digs in his pocket. Peels a hundred from the wad and tosses it on the counter. "Um, sorry about the TV. This should more than cover it."

The attendant says nothing. Probably couldn't get ten dollars for it at a yard sale. He continues to polish the windshield wiper motor in his hand and keep his safe distance. The cop seems familiar to him. And, in addition, scary and unstable.

Johnson smooths his hair back in place. He feels the blood pounding at his temples. Way to go dumbass. You shot the wrong fucker. Not to mention, you should have listened to the rest of the story. Hell, for all he knows, they're looking for a Chevy truck right about now—his Chevy truck.

Johnson steps outside, finds him a place in the shade to watch the progress being made on his truck. He pulls his personal cell phone from his front pocket and calls a veteran in blue and fellow detective. Johnson still considers himself a member of the boys-in-blue and rightfully so, considering he's still in the game to do good.

"Yeah, this is Detective Johnson," he says to the voice on the other end.

"What's up with last night's shooting?"

Chapter Seventeen

Eddie sets the plates on the floor to be licked squeaky clean by Bobo prior to going into the dishwasher.

"When you volunteered to do the dishes, I should have known," Amy says booting up her computer again.

Eddie smiles. "You would think. Hey, did you know that the protein in a dog's saliva promotes healing twice as fast?"

"No, but that probably explains why a dog licks his wounds. Check this out, Eddie," Amy says pointing to the screen. "Wonder who this is?"

Eddie leans over to peer over her shoulder. "It doesn't say?"

"No. It lists everyone but her."

"Where was the photo taken?"

"At a fundraiser at their Westlake home."

"You think maybe she's their maid or hired help?"

"Or maybe she's one of their mothers."

Eddie straightens, puts his hands on his hips and leans back to stretch his back muscles. He does a couple of twists. "I doubt it or she'd likely be named. But, she's old enough though."

"Crick in your back?"

"Yeah."

"Probably from doing the dishes."

"Ha, good one Detective Amy Foster. What if she's part of the catering crew or something?"

"I wish we could see more of her face. Can you blow it up and print it for me?"

"Email it to me or I can load the printer driver on a USB stick and you can add it to your I-pad as the default printer. I mean I don't see you venturing too far from home."

Amy smirks. "And it's for your own good."

Eddie kisses the top of her head. "There you have it."

The doorbell rings and Bobo barks and goes skittering from the kitchen.

"He only barks when there's no danger," Eddie says. "I'll get it." Probably a reporter, Eddie thinks, catching up with Bobo at the front door. He answers the door. Finds a 20-something black man in faded blue jeans and a Black Lives Matter T-shirt on his stoop.

"Can I help you?" Eddie asks.

"Mr. Winston," he offers his hand, "James from the apartment building up the block."

Eddie shakes the offered hand. "Nice to meet you. How can I help you?"

"Well, it may not be anything but I thought I'd bring it to your attention. For the past couple of days, there's been a Ford Explorer parked at the side of our apartments. Parked nose out. And there's been a couple of guys in it. White guys. Looked to me like a stakeout. Like they were watching somebody on this block. And your house, of course, is the closest to the apartments."

"Hmm. You think they were cops?"

"I didn't get the impression they were cops. I was thinking more along the line of private detectives."

"And you think they were watching my house?" Eddie asks, opening the door wider and motioning the man into the living room.

James steps into the living room. Bends to pet Bobo. "Hope your dog don't bite."

"Not likely."

"He's a pretty dog. Looks like he's got some brindle pit in him. Anyway, like I was saying, I thought they might be PIs until I learned about last night's shooting. And this morning, no Ford Explorer."

Eddie notices for the first time that James has something enclosed in his fist. "Whatcha got?"

"Oh, yeah." He unclasps his hand to reveal a Ziplock baggie. "They did a lot of smoking while they were there. Cigarette butts everywhere."

"Meaning DNA left behind."

"Not hardly. Meaning they smoked a lot of filter-less cigarettes.

They were tearing the butts off before smoking them."

"And the matchbook?"

"You might get a print off of it. But I think you'll find the logo more informative. XTC. Ever heard of it?"

"Yeah, the nude joint off 290."

"Exactly. Somehow, they ended up with XTC matches."

"And I take it you didn't share this information with the police."

James smiles and points to his T-shirt. "Not hardly," he says handing over the baggie.

Eddie takes the baggie. Flips it one way than the other. "The cops that bad here in Austin?"

"Not too bad. They used to harass the brothers on the eastside. But people began filming all the encounters and now that the black community is slowly being squeezed out, there are a whole lot fewer brothers to harass."

"I hear you. Property taxes are fucking a whole lot of folks these days."

"Amen. I hope you figure out who's trying to blow you up or whatever they're trying to do."

Eddie tosses the baggie up and down. "Thanks for the info James. I owe you one. Stop by and have a beer with us some time."

"You hooked up with that female detective?"

"Ex detective."

"In that case, hell, why not. See you around Mr. Winston."

"It's Eddie. Thanks again. Take care."

Eddie rejoins Amy in the kitchen. "Interesting," Amy says. She smiles. "I was listening in."

"Why didn't you introduce yourself?"

"In only a T-shirt? I don't think so. Though you'd probably get a kick out of it."

"Probably. You speak volumes as to the efficiency of the AC."

Amy checks herself out. "They are pretty perky, aren't they?"

"Yep, not bad for an older gal."

"Thanks... I guess," Amy says causing them both to laugh. She taps the screen. "We need to find out who this woman is."

Eddie tosses the baggie on the table. "And follow up on this lead."

"It would have to be a totally nude joint, wouldn't it?"

"And I hope that won't be a distraction for you."

"Right." Amy pokes Eddie in the chest. "Nor you."

"Anything for the cause."

"And I suppose we're looking for the Russians?"

"Exactly."

"Which still leaves the $64,000 question. Who shot the man in the drive last night?"

"You know, I thought about it off and on all night and I just can't figure it out."

"Strange. Someone was obviously watching the house. And it would appear more than one party from opposite directions." Amy shakes her head. "Somebody was protecting us but who? I'll call Howard. See if he knows anything new."

"And I'm going to get dressed while you do that. We need some kitty litter."

"And quite a few other things for the house. Give me a few minutes and I'll go with you."

~~~

Igor's stare is like daggers at times. Erik feels the beady eyes boring into him as he approaches. He's sure Igor is going to blame him for Sergei's death. He looks at Pavel for an indication that he's spoken with Igor, but Pavel's face is dead-pan. If he has, Pavel's not giving it up. Erik sighs and comes to stand before the small group.

"Maybe Igor should have sent whores to do job," Igor says in a voice that's nothing but pure venom.

Erik sighs for a second time. "It was trap. Sniper up road. How was I to know? Maybe American and cop lady figured you'd send someone. And figured right."

Igor's face turns beet red. The veins at his temples throb. He reaches for his pistol. Erik is quicker on the draw. The warehouse is silent but for the double-click of Erik's pistol.

"Don't make me kill you, Igor," Erik says. The tension's palatable. Erik's pistol trembles slightly. He can't believe he got the drop on Igor, but thank God he did or he'd be dead right now. Hell, he may well be dead anyway, having crossed a bridge from which there is no return. He swallows. "I mean it, Igor. Put gun away."

Igor shrugs. "Igor only fucking with you. Sure, I put gun away." He chuckles. "You, me, we family, da. Let's take ride, yes," Igor says holstering his piece. There's a collective exhalation of breaths. Erik's slow to holster his piece.

"You ride shotgun," Erik says. The room laughs. Igor reaches over and pinches Erik's cheek. He chuckles.

"Sure, Igor ride shotgun."

They move toward the Cadillac. All knowing that one of the pair will die soon. Pavel puts his money on Erik. If he didn't owe Igor his life, he wouldn't mind a change at the top. But if Igor should die, it will be him, Pavel, who will take control and he'll kill anyone who attempts to stand in his way.

Pavel opens the driver's side door to the Caddy and drops in. He keeps his smile to himself. Hell, he wouldn't mind giving the orders for a change. If Igor should die, so be it. But for now, he'll continue to cover Igor's back.

"Where to, Igor?" Pavel asks.

"Check eastside operation. Then go talk to pedophile. Put little more squeeze on."

Pavel cranks the Caddy and puts her into gear as the garage door rattles open. Yep, Pavel will make fine boss someday, he thinks.

~~~

Relief washes over Johnson as he ends the call. The detectives assigned to investigate the shooting have little to go on. They have grainy images of a dark-colored Chevy pickup in the area that's of interest but nothing beyond that. Shit, that ought to be worth celebrating, Johnson thinks. And what better way to celebrate than with a good old bottle or two of Jim Beam. Just the thought wakes up his saliva glands. Now what to do with the truck? Park it at an H.E.B. closer to home, Johnson. Don't take a rocket scientist to figure that out. And now that his windshield and rear window have been repaired, he can lock it up. His right eye tics, but Johnson doesn't notice. He pulls out on South Congress and heads north.

Johnson crosses Ben White and continues on. This stretch of road brings back good memories. Memories from back in the day when the white hookers worked this section of town. Boy did he love to shake the white girls down. Not to mention, some of them were even fuckable back then. Then came crack and everything went downhill from there. Every dollar going to the next hit—the next high. No such thing as money in the purse any longer. Now, usually nothing but a cracked-up glass stem, glass dick, wrapped in toilet paper. What's the world coming to? Johnson wonders. Now even the good cops, such as he, are endangered.

Johnson passes Allens Boots on the left, The Continental Club on the right and in the distance looms the Texas State Capitol. Few things resemble Austin anymore, Johnson thinks. The changes not for the good. He crosses Colorado and works his way over to North Mopac and the fastest way to traverse Austin. Johnson lays on his horn and forces a spot to merge with the northbound traffic. He's catching the beginning of the lunch-hour traffic and the bastards just don't want to let you in.

Johnson eyes the fucker behind him in his reattached rearview and shoots her the bird. He chuckles. "Do something about it, bitch," he dares the driver behind him. A soccer mom no doubt hauling a car full of snot-nosed brats somewhere. Stupid cunts need to learn that's what you get when you keep spreading your fucking legs. Stupid cunts. He takes the Koeing Lane exit, way short of where he should, but there are no liquor stores on Mopac. He was so lost in thought that he'd passed the liquor store on South Congress. Johnson's tempted to do a drive-by past Eddie's, but why tempt fate? He's not fucking stupid. He rubs his face. Shit, he needs a drink. The warm beer no longer doing it for him.

Johnson turns left on Burnet Road, the liquor store just up on his right. Probably the same liquor store pretty boy uses. Owned by some Pakistani fucker that only knows how to say, "Good day. Come again." They need to learn to speak the fucking language, that's what he thinks. Probably has ten fucking kids, too, wearing sandals with used-tire tread on them for soles. Stupid fucks. Johnson's eye tics as he turns into the entrance of the small strip mall that houses the liquor store. He stops in the fire lane. Fuck 'em if they can't take a joke. Johnson enters the liquor store and is momentarily taken back by the attendant's beauty. A white woman in her early 40s of all people. He's momentarily at a loss for words—loses his train of thought. He hates it when he loses his train of thought, but it seems to happen more and more lately, not to mention the blackouts. He can't delude himself into believing the episodes are anything but blackouts. It seems that he has Beam at home but can't remember. Oh, well.

The woman looks at him oddly as he sets the two bottles of Jim Beam on the counter. He wonders what the fuck that's all about. Johnson shakes it off and pays in cash for his liquor.

The woman watches Johnson exit and enter his still running truck and pull away. She leans over the counter to get a better look, but the windows are too obscured by posters and signs for her to get a decent look. But she knows the man. Seen him on the news often enough. And the truck could be the truck that was parked outside her house last night prior to the shooting.

The woman reaches for her phone. Changes her mind. She knows Eddie from his living down the block and from his regular stops at her store but decides it's best to stay out of it. That the detective is just too dangerous to get involved. Perhaps if she had, she'd have saved a life.

~~~

"I think Smoky believes it's a sandbox. Something to play in," Amy says.

"He'll figure it out. Give him time," Eddie says watching Amy hover over the kitten and the litter box.

"Maybe we should train him to use the toilet," Amy says.

"And train Bobo to flush. Tie a milk bone to the lever."

"You'd get exactly one flush per milk bone out of him. Hey, look, I think he's fixing to use the bathroom." "

It might help if you give him some privacy."

Amy stands and straightens. "You think?"

Eddie shrugs. "I'm just saying."

"Yeah, probably. Hey, I'm going to go for a jog. Want to go with me?"

"Keep in mind, someone's trying to kill one or both of us."

"It's the middle of the day. It'll be safe enough."

"Take Bobo. He wants to go."

Amy unconsciously rubs her hip. "I haven't completely healed from the last time I took him jogging."

"It did leave quite an unsightly bruise."

Amy smirks causing Eddie to laugh. "Thanks for reminding me," she says.

"So, I take it you don't want to go."

"I'm thinking about dusting off the old bench press. Suggestion: don't wrap the end of Bobo's leash around your hand. That way if he decides to take a detour, he won't take you with him."

Bobo's not sure what they're talking about, but he's sure it involves him. His tail thumps from side to side. He licks his snout.

"Okay, you both win. I'll take him with me," Amy says leaving the kitchen to change while Eddie realizes he might not dust off the bench just yet. Instead, he cuts through the living room to the front door where he retrieves two days' worth of The Austin American Statesman and The Wall Street Journal. Eddie carries them back into the kitchen where he opens today's American Statesman to the metro state section and finds the latest article on the double murder. The article adds nothing to what they already know—basically nothing.

Amy joins them back in the kitchen. She leans over Eddie's shoulder to see what he's reading. "Anything new?" she asks.

"Nope, but the funerals are already scheduled for the day after tomorrow. The memorial and viewing are going to be held at Saint Ignatius on Oltorf and they're to be buried at a private cemetery."

"And we should go."

"Why?"

"To see who shows up, of course. Don't you watch any TV? There's always a cop or two at the funeral of the murdered. Never know who might show up."

"And we'll recognize what we're looking for?"

It's Amy's turn to shrug and she does. She leans in to kiss Eddie on the cheek. "Got to run, literally. Keep this ass nice and firm so your eyes, mister, won't roam."

"Good plan," Eddie says turning his attention back to the paper.

Amy smacks him playfully in the back of the head opposite the lump. "Starting tonight at the XTC."

"Like any man would find nude dancers entertaining," Eddie says not turning back from his paper. Amy leans in to kiss him again.

"Back in an hour," she says.

Eddie smiles to himself. He sure loves Amy's sense of humor. For that matter, he can't think of anything that he doesn't love about her. She's truly a lifesaver. The development with Lori's a little uncomfortable, though. The last person he wants to hurt is Lori, though she did give her blessing at the time. Awkward, Eddie thinks again. Maybe he shouldn't have jumped into a relationship with Amy so quickly, for that's exactly what it is, a relationship. Eddie sighs. Equally, he'd never want to hurt Amy either.

~~~

This time Dorbandt doesn't bother to pretend he's not home and he looks like shit. Igor grins—pushes past him.

"pri-VYET, du-ZHI-schel," he says stepping into the mess of a living room—a room littered with empty beer cans and overflowing ashtrays.

"Huh," Dorbandt says dully. Pavel slaps him in the back.

"He said, 'Hey buddy,'" Pavel says causing Igor and crew to laugh. "You don't look so good," he adds. Igor invades Dorbandt's space.

"You smell like shit, too... So, you got Igor's money?"

Dorbandt moans—grows weak at the knees. He should have fled, but he was too scared that they were watching the house.

"Well?"

"It's... It's only been a day," Dorbandt whines. Igor doesn't like whiners—pussies. He slaps Dorbandt hard across the face with his good hand. Disgusted, he wipes the resulting oil from his hand on Dorbandt's shirt. He turns toward Pavel.

"Clean this pussy up. Then we talk business, nyet."

Laughing, Pavel and Mikhail grab Dorbandt under his arms and drag the sobbing Dorbandt toward the bathroom leaving Erik and Igor alone in the living room.

Igor and Erik eye each other cautiously. They've yet to speak to each other since leaving the warehouse. Igor retrieves his pack of Marlboro. Shakes one out for himself. Doesn't offer Erik one. Erik accepts it for what it is—the ultimate insult. So be it, no love lost. As far as he's concerned, Igor's days are numbered. Be it him or someone else, someone's bound to punch his ticket.

Igor tears off the filter and tucks the cigarette into the corner of his mouth. He lights it with his BIC. Blows out at thick plume of smoke. He's still pissed about letting Erik get the draw on him. But for that, Erik would be one dead fucker right about now. Well, it ain't over, not by a long shot. He continues to eye Erik wearily. The only thing thicker than the tension in the room is the next plume of smoke Igor exhales.

"Truce, brother-in-law," Igor finally says. Not that he means it, but perhaps so Erik will let his guard down. Then no more Erik. He catches himself almost smiling. He changes his expression to more of a contrite look. A look that Erik doesn't buy for a second. Erik shrugs. Then nods.

"Sure, why not. We're family."

Pavel leads a still dressed and soaked Dorbandt back into the room. Igor shakes his head and snubs out his cigarette.

"Dorbandt, Dorbandt. What Igor to do? You tell Igor. What Igor to do?"

"I... I... I need more time. Pleeeeaaasse!"

Igor draws back as if to slap Dorbandt again. Chuckles instead. Pinches Dorbandt on the cheek. As much as he despises Dorbandt, the sad truth is he still needs Dorbandt to move some of his merchandise. The young ones. The ones that bring instant profit. Igor extracts his phone. Brings up the blue-eyed Syrian boy's picture and turns the screen for Dorbandt to see.

"The one I told you about has arrived. Fresh. Untouched. Virgin."

Dorbandt swallows. Pictures a way out. Perhaps he can get an extra $10,000 out of this one from one of his clients—a child pornographer that's recently been released. So, the future life of the kid won't be so rosy. That's not his fault. If anything, it's the fault of his own people. Always warring. Always causing refugees. He braves a look into Igor's beady and menacing eyes.

"I... I think I have a buyer for this one."

Igor smiles. Pats Dorbandt on the cheek. "That's better. Now listen good. Don't damage goods before you sale, nyet. Last chance. Two days you have Igor's money. I call you later. Tell you where to pick up boy." Igor snaps his fingers. "Let's go."

Chapter Eighteen

Johnson hastily twists the cap from the bottle and takes a healthy pull on the Jim Beam. "Ah, now that's some good shit," he says to himself as the whiskey does a slow burn in his gut. He grins at his reflection in the rearview. "So, you shot the wrong fucker. You're still a handsome bastard," he says. Talk about a pick-me-up. Good whiskey will brighten any day, he thinks. Unfortunately, it's back to two needing killing, but what the fuck. He's still free, ain't he? He chuckles. And he still has a few good buddies on the force and leverage on a few others. Hell, now that he thinks about it, things ain't so bad after all. He takes another long pull from the bottle. At this rate, maybe he should have bought three bottles. What the hell, he'll stop and get another bottle and some more beer while he's at it. Then he can head back to the house, fuck parking at the H.E.B., and give himself a chance to regroup, think. Yep, think and plot. That's the ticket. That's the answer.

A honk of a horn jerks Johnson back into this lane. He shoots the fucker a bird. A world of inconsiderate bastards is what it is. He shoots the fucker another bird for good measure and chuckles once more. He's feeling his oats, he is. Whatever that means. Yep, time to regroup. Plot. That's what fucking time it is.

Johnson continues on. A shit-eating grin plastered on his face. I coming for you, Eddie boy. You and your slut. You can count on it.

~~~

Bobo precedes Amy through the door. He's worked up a lather and heads straight for his bowl. Amy's worked up a good sweat herself. She stops before Eddie, hands on hips and bending at the waist. Her sports bra is a darker shade of blue with perspiration. Her shorts are plastered to skin. Eddie takes a sip of beer and admires her as she catches her breath. He smiles.

"Have a good run?"

Amy straightens, offers her smirk and lifts her damp hair from her nape. "How'd your workout go?" she counters.

Eddie takes another sip of beer. "Can't complain," he says causing them both to laugh.

"Actually, I got in a pretty good run," Amy says. "I can really tell the difference when I've missed a few too many days."

"And Bobo didn't get you killed. That's also good."

"That dog of yours, Eddie, strained at his leash the entire run. I don't think he'd ever run out of energy."

"Kinda like me in bed," Eddie offers.

"Right," Amy says a little too fast. They both laugh. "I guess I better go shower. Want to wash my back for me?"

"Oh yeah and what's in for me?"

"I might accidentally drop the soap."

"Deal!" Eddie says.

"I said, 'might.'"

"Oh."

"Don't look so dejected," Amy says. "I'm just kidding."

Eddie smiles. Finishes his beer. "I know."

Amy studies Eddie a long minute. He's got me figured out, she thinks. And, she couldn't be any happier about it. But she just may have him figured out as well. Time to test her theory. She shucks her sports bra, drops it as his feet and stretches languishingly. Amy turns, slowly works her shorts down her long legs and steps out of them. She saunters out of the room with a knowing smile that Eddie can't see. She too, can't see his reaction, but there's no mistaking the scrape of Eddie's chair against the kitchen's tile.

Her smile widens, turns to a giggle as she streaks down the hall with Eddie on her tail. A foot stops her from being able to shut the bathroom door. Eddie pushes it on open. Enters the bathroom with her. He lifts her off her feet. Amy wraps her legs around Eddie's waist, her arms around his neck.

"I didn't think you'd be able to resist," Amy whispers in Eddie's ear. She nips him on the ear for the hell of it. Eddie carries her to the tub, bends with her to reach the cold nozzle and turns the cold water to wide open. He flips the lever diverting the water to the showerhead.

"Eddie! Don't even think about it. Eddie!... Oh, shit, that's cold!" Amy screams as Eddie steps into the shower and the water hits Amy dead center in her back. Her struggles for naught. She quits struggling. Resigns herself to the cold spray.

"Don't you know I owe you one now," she says as her feet settle on the tub's surface and her teeth begin to chatter and Eddie's laughter fills the room. Amy beats Eddie feebly on the chest and joins in the laughter.

Eddie's lips find hers. Her hand snakes inside his shorts where she finds him growing hard. Amy wraps her small hand around him and strokes him a couple of times.

"Uh-huh. Just what I thought Mr. Winston. You find me irresistible." She stops and starts back. "Well?".

"Um, what was the question again?"

Amy squeezes him one good time. Offers her knowing smile. "Just what I thought." They both laugh. Two peas in a pod it would seem.

Eddie kisses the side of her neck, begins working his way down, her skin still salty from her run. He takes one breast in his mouth and then the other. Elicits a moan from her. He continues on down the flat of her belly where he encounters the cutest of bellybuttons. He kisses it and continues down. Stops just inside the beginning of Amy's thigh. Her knees grow weak with anticipation. Eddie grips a cheek in one hand and reaches for the warm water nozzle with the other.

"Um, Eddie," Amy says. Eddie looks up from where he's kneeling.

"Yes."

"Good try," she says stepping out of the way and letting the cold water rain down on him.

The cold water takes his breath. He falls back on his ass and bangs his head on the wall. "Shit, that's cold!" he yells.

"Ain't it," Amy says struggling to control her laughter. She drops to her knees with the effort. And to think he thought he had her fooled for a second. But dammit, it was a close call.

She reaches forward and unzips Eddie's shorts freeing him. He's at half-mast. Dammit! She failed to take the cold into consideration. They both laugh. Amy reaches behind her to add warm water. She has a solution to their problem. It's a two-part solution beginning with adding some warm water to the mix. She smacks her lips. Part two coming right up. Amy smiles at the prostrate Eddie.

"Now whatever you do, don't come in my mouth," she says.

"Deal!" he says. They're both pretty sure he's lying.

Igor's panting hard. He withdraws, pushes the whore to her side. He reaches for his bottle of vodka. He doesn't know what prompted him to fuck his ten-dollar whore, but he did. He eyes her with contempt. Thinks she'd look better in a fucking burkini. Speaking of, at least the French are trying to do the right thing and ban the crap from their beaches. Who wants to see a bitch dressed looking like a fucking orca? Not fucking him. He wipes himself off on the shirt and casts it to the floor.

He feels Pavel's eyes on him.

"What?"

"Receipts are down again, boss."

Igor turns on one of his two house men. He's starting to believe there may be some skimming going on. "Tell Igor what's happening. Why so little cash?"

The man shrugs. Wrong answer. Igor pulls his piece and cocks the hammer. He pokes the man between the eyes with the barrel. He has good mind to kill his man to set an example.

"Shrug again, bitch, then Igor kill you," he says leaving not a shred of doubt in the man's mind that he'll do just that. He trembles slightly instead, while Igor's hand remains rock steady.

"It's been slow, Igor. What can I say," the man says softly.

Pavel steps between them and gently pushes Igor's pistol to the side. At the moment, they can't afford to lose another man. Not to mention, sometimes gunshots bring the law even in this part of town where gunshots sometimes go unreported. "Igor, let's go. We check back tomorrow," Pavel says. He eyes the man he just saved. "And maybe tomorrow's receipts will be much better, da?"

The man eagerly nods. Crisis averted for now. A bead of sweat rolls from his temple. Maybe it's time to roll on. Take his stash of cash and a couple of the better whores and set out on his own.

He stands there until the door closes behind the last of Igor and his crew. Let's out a long-held breath and moves over to the bed where Igor's discarded whore sits. He slaps the smirk off her face.

"Go get cleaned up. Get ready for customers."

She looks up at him with eyes mostly dead. Fucking coward, she thinks in Arabic. She'll cut his fucking head off if she ever gets the chance. It's thoughts like this that sustain her. Passive only in their eyes, she gets up and does what she's told. She smiles as she steps into the bathroom. She has a secret. She knows where the money's stashed. And she has another secret. She's learning to speak English.

~~~

Amy tucks her wet hair behind both ears and takes Eddie back in her mouth. She wants him to watch and gets a thrill out of being watched. One hand grips the base of him and the other cups Eddie's balls and gently massages them. She can feel him pulse in her mouth as she bobs and strokes him at the same time. And it's having the desired effect if Eddie's moans are any indication. God, she loves the feel of his cock in her mouth, she thinks, as her pussy gets hotter and wetter. She wonders if she'll come with him even without being penetrated or stimulated and she's inclined to believe she can and will, yet another first for her. Damn, where has this man been her entire life? All this time, she had no clue what she was missing and there's nothing she won't do for this man, she realizes. If he wants a whore in the bedroom, so be it. Amy can't believe her own thoughts or how horny this man makes her.

Eddie's toes curl, the pleasure too intense. "I'm about to break my promise, honey, if you don't stop."

Amy stops on the upstroke, her tongue circling the head. "And," she says before threatening with her eyes to take him back in her mouth again.

Eddie struggles to get his legs under him—kicks his shorts free. He lifts Amy as if she was weightless and sets her before him. He clears his throat. "I want you in the bedroom and on the bed," he manages. A typical Eddie answer surfaces in Amy's mind.

"Deal!" she says. They both laugh. Amy turns and bends to shut off the water all the while watching Eddie over her shoulder. Whatever Eddie has in mind is keeping him hard and erect. Water off, Amy stands and turns back to face him. "Just point the way and I'm right behind you," she says pun intended. They both laugh.

God, aren't we having fun, she thinks, snatching up a pair of bath towels that Eddie neglected to do in his haste. She tosses him a towel as she steps into the bedroom. Eddie ruffles his hair with it and drops it to the floor. He takes Amy's towel from her and drops it to the floor, as well. He wants her and wants her now. But he has full intention of tasting her first. Damn, this woman is hot, he thinks for the hundredth time. He picks the giggling Amy up and tosses her on top of the bed and drives in beside her. Rolls atop her and kisses her hard. Amy attempts to work a hand between them to guide him in. Eddie breaks the kiss, shakes his head. He kisses her behind the ear.

"Not yet," he says his breath hot against her neck.

Eddie pins Amy's arms above her head for a long moment and trails a series of kisses down the side of Amy's neck. Kisses her once more, harder and hotter on the mouth, before starting downward.

Amy's heart flutters recalling again her fantasy of Eddie and her masturbating in the shower to the thought of his lips and tongue finding her center. She shudders as Eddie takes a breast in his mouth. Amy's thoughts again drift back to the fantasy and just how hard she came that day. She flushes—God did she come!

Eddie tastes the other breast, nips the nipple gently and continues his downward trail of kisses. Amy runs her fingers through his still wet hair and encourages his descent. She's ready for him.

Eddie's lips find the inside of one thigh, then the other. His tongue teases her as it ever nears the point of her desire. Amy's breathing becomes irregular—ragged.

Eddie's tongue and lips find their mark and it does more than just curl Amy's toes. She burns up more calories than she did on her earlier run. God, does she come and come hard!

~~~

Fuck it, Johnson thinks. He stopped and picked up another bottle and a case of beer and is finally turning down his driveway. He's going to park in his own garage, by God. His garage openers are inside his real truck. He steps from the Chevy and takes a look up and down his block. No one's out and about or paying him or his house any attention. He reaches inside his truck and snatches the remote from the visor. Johnson depresses the remote and watches as the double doors slowly open. His garage is quite cluttered. He hasn't parked in it for years, but he ain't planning on straightening it out now. Hell, the truck will fit. Might run over a thing or two but he'll make the truck fit. Johnson pulls on in and runs over a couple of boxes on his right. Pushes his riding mower until it's jammed against the far wall. He chuckles. He knew the fucking thing would fit and best yet, with a little effort, he manages to get his door open far enough to get out.

Johnson gathers up his purchases. Leans into the door to get it to shut. His vision clouds for a second, but after a few more, it clears. He wonders if his blood pressure is up. Probably, but it ain't killed him yet. With some effort, he manages to get the kitchen door open without setting his purchases down. He doesn't bother with shutting it back. All in all, he's feeling pretty good. He makes it as far as the kitchen table and plops down. Johnson picks up his prescription. Hell, one little ol' pill won't hurt. He struggles to remove the cap. He gives the cap another hard twist and good yank sending pills everywhere.

"Shit! God damn cap!" Johnson picks up one of the pills and pops it into his mouth. He chases it with a good pull from his Jim Beam. Hell, he'll just rest here for a minute, he decides.

Johnson lowers his head to the table. "Yep, a little rest and then I'll make plans," he mumbles. His mouth falls open and he begins to snore. He dreams about killing Eddie and his ex-partner.

~~~

"bra-TAN," bro, "I go fetch us something to eat." Boris chuckles. "You watch whores, da."

"Use phone. Call Jimmy Johns," Peter says.

Boris chuckles again. "Fuck Jimmy Johns."

Peter laughs as well. "You buy for whores, too."

"YOB tvo-YU mat."

"No, fuck your mother," Peter says. He slaps Boris on the back. "Hurry. Many customers arrive soon."

"Yeah, yeah. Boris hurry," he says stepping from the apartment.

The recently slapped Dawao watches the exchange from where she sits on the unmade bed. She pats the bedding beside her and takes comfort in the fact that Igor's Uncle Henry knife, open Uncle Henry knife, is still where she stashed it. She managed to pinch it from Igor, the dirty pig, while his pants were dropped. Stupid Russian pig, she thinks. Dawao feels the urge to laugh at the irony of it, the fact that she'll kill Igor's man with his knife. Too bad it won't be Igor's throat she'll be slitting, but   at least it will be Igor's money she'll be taking. Maybe someday she get the chance to kill Igor, but that is very unlikely seeing how she plans to get as far away as possible, as fast as possible.

Dawao inches her hand under the covers and retrieves the knife. She slips it into her robe's pocket but keeps it tightly clasped in her hand. She gets up and moves to the front window and pushes the curtain aside a bit to peek out. She stares at the dead parking lot beyond. She smiles to herself.

"Hey, what you doing at window?" Peter asks.

"Cops."

"Cops, shit! Get away from window!"

Dawao shushes him. Continues to peek from behind the curtain, stares out at the empty parking lot beyond.

Peter jumps up, hurries over. "I said get fuck away from window!" He grabs Dawao by the collar of the robe and pulls her from the window. He moves to where she was standing. Inches the curtain back.

Dawao removes the knife. Steps in behind Peter. "Hey, there're no fucking cops...

Dawao draws the knife across Peter's neck.

214

Blood sprays the curtain.

Peter's hands go to his neck. He turns to face Dawao. His face registers fear. Registers that he'll soon be dead.

Dawao smiles. "I know," she says. She drives the knife into his chest. Steps back and watches him crumble at her feet. She spits on the felled man and laughs. "Made you look," she says.

The three other women in the room look on in shock. She addresses them rapidly in Arabic. Tells them that she's out of here and she'll share the money with whoever wants to leave. There are no takers.

Dawao frowns, but can relate to their fear. The other women speak no English. She shrugs, helpless to do anything about it. It is what it is she thinks in Arabic.

Dawao hurries to dress in the only clothes she has, slutty clothing common in the Western World and high heels. It will do until she can buy something else. She retrieves the satchel of cash. She doesn't know how much is there but it looks to be a bunch. Dawao kicks the dead Peter once before letting herself from the apartment. She turns toward busy Caesar Chavez and begins walking. On the corner is a Metro bus stop. She reaches it just as a bus comes to a stop before the small crowd. The bus hisses and the door opens. Dawao climbs aboard. Her smallest bill is a $20. The black driver waves her in. It's the first nice thing that's happened to her since arriving in America. She smiles back at the man and thinks maybe she'll head to California.

Chapter Nineteen

Amy laughs. "Sorry about the hair. I guess I got a little carried away."

"You think?" Eddie says and turns serious. "Amy, it's not the hair I'm worried about. It's my ears. I can't feel my ears."

Amy hits him with her pillow. "Right," she says. "So, what's the plan until tonight?"

Eddie clears his throat and points down at his erection. "There is that," Amy says. She rolls to her back and spreads her legs. "Men," she adds in a faux-exasperated tone. She checks her non-existent watch—yawns.

Eddie nods his head. "Good one, Detective Amy Foster," he says as he moves in between Amy's legs. It will take a lot more than that to discourage him, he thinks as he enters her.

Amy can't believe she has yet another one in her but she does.

She wraps her legs around Eddie and comes with him. Spent, Eddie falls to his side.

"And, let that be a lesson to you," he says. They both laugh. Not only is the sex good to both of them, but they have a hell of a lot of fun in the process.

Amy finishes catching her breath and poses the same question. "So, what's the plan?"

Eddie rolls to the edge of the bed and drops his feet to the cool hardwood floor. He stands and stretches. He turns back to look down on Amy. "I think I'll put on another pair of shorts and work out on the heavy bag. It's been over three years since I messed with the thing."

"I haven't seen a heavy bag. You have one here at the house?"

He reaches for her hand. "Get up. It's in the garage. I need you to help me hang it."

Amy takes his hand, stands and hops to the floor. "Sure, I can do that." They take a minute to make their selections and dress. Eddie opts for sweatpants instead of shorts and Amy, a fresh T-shirt and panties.

Eddie digs out the heavy bag from a cluttered corner of his garage. The thing's covered in dust and cobwebs. He dusts it off the best he can and moves it to the center of the garage. He points to the hook in the ceiling.

"Pull up a chair and hook it for me when I lift it." Amy does and Eddie hoists it up high enough for her to attach the bag to the hook. She hops down and pulls the chair out of the way.

"This I have to see," she says planting her hands on her hips and offering Eddie a smile. Eddie finds his pair of light gloves. Gloves with the fingers cut out and padding across the knuckles. He slaps them against his leg before putting them on. He takes a deep breath and attacks the bag with gusto, adding the occasional knee, high kick and spinning backhands and kicks, followed by flurries of combinations. It doesn't take long for Eddie to get winded and break out in a sweat. He adds one last knee and stills the bag. Amy claps.

"Impressive," she says in earnest. "Martial arts. Where in the world did you learn that?"

"UFC."

"Wow, UFC. You fought UFC?"

"No, I watch it on TV."

Amy smiles. "No doubt while drinking beer."

Eddie returns the smile. "Not just pretty, but smart, too."

"Thanks. Hey, how come you didn't use any of those fancy moves against the Russians?"

Eddie shrugs. He really doesn't have an answer to that. "I don't know. Perhaps it's been so long since I worked out it never crossed my mind. You know, I wasn't really expecting to be in a fight and it went down so fast."

"I can see that. Well, all-in-all, you did pretty well. I was proud of you."

"As was the young lady in the Gap."

Amy frowns. "Let's not forget you were knocked out." They both laugh. There is that.

Eddie finishes catching his breath. He didn't realize just how out of shape he is. Well, actually he realized but chose to ignore the fact. "We still have most of the day before us. Any suggestions, Amy?"

"You, take another shower as I do a little more research on the computer. Then, I don't know. We have to eat. Ever been to the Alligator Bar & Grill?"

"Sure, the one on South Lamar this side of Ben White."

"That's the only one I know of. Anyway, between two and four appetizers such as shrimp are like ten cents and oysters are 35 cents."

"You sound like an 80's gal, 'like, you know.'"

"I am an 80's gal. I graduated high school in the late '80s. Anyway, 'like' still creeps into my vocabulary from time to time."

"And what high school are we talking about?"

"Austin High, of course. They bussed us there. And you?"

"Travis High. You know, now that I think about it, I have a late 80's Austin High Year Book. An old girlfriend of mine left it behind." Eddie smiles. "Let's see what Amy looked like in high school."

Amy doesn't know if he's kidding or not, but the last thing she wants to do is look at her high school photos. "Ugh!" she says causing them both to laugh.

"Let's not."

Eddie follows Amy back into the kitchen. The kitten shoots out from under the table, almost trips Eddie up. He reaches down and picks up the kitten.

"Where's your sidekick, Smoky?" Eddie asks. Speaking of, Bobo comes bounding into the kitchen, paws at his empty bowl. He stares up at Eddie with soulful eyes, then turns his attention to Amy.

Amy laughs. She doesn't recall ever having laughed so much. "I'll feed him another can," she says. "He did get in a pretty good run." She reaches for the kitten. "Go shower."

Eddie shakes his head, takes his leave. What a family.

~~~

Boris paces the small apartment, reluctant to look down at the dead body of his comrade, Peter. He's been back for a couple of hours now, but has yet to make the call he's dreading. The food's gone untouched and long forgotten. Even the remaining whores are sullen. Boris feels like he might as well be dead himself. But worse, the whore Dawao took off with all the cash leaving him no viable options. And now to top things off, he's having to turn away customers because there's a dead body lying on the floor of the living room and he can't even answer the fucking door.

He lights yet another cigarette, the ashtray overflowing with smoked-to-the-filter butts. Boris runs his hands through his thinning hair. Plops down before the small table. Eyes the phone. Eyes the bottle of vodka. Boris finds himself once more opting for the vodka. He takes a long pull, thinks maybe later tonight he can dump the body somewhere, clean up the mess and tell Igor tomorrow that Peter ran off with the whore Dawao and the day's receipts. The more he thinks about it, the better he likes it. But what if the whores give him up? Igor would sure as hell kill him then.

"Shit," he moans. "Why fuck this happening to me?"

~~~

Johnson wakes with a start. His head's pounding, his mouth's cotton.

Somehow, he can't connect it to his recent excessive drinking. He was having a dream, a dream that he can't quite recall. He studies the bottle before him. Almost reaches for it. No, better stick with beer. He chuckles. He may have some killing to do later. Now, that's a pleasant thought. Johnson wonders what the fucking pair are up to?

Probably screwing their brains out. He can picture the pair together all sweaty and entwined. It's enough to make him sick. Now what to do about the fornicating pair? Why, kill them, of course. But how? Hell, he's already fucked up twice. One thing's likely for sure, the police have ramped up patrols in pretty boy's neighborhood and that limits his options. Not to mention his fucking bum knee.

A bum knee that he can thank his ex-partner for. What kind of cop shoots her partner? A no-good, back-stabbing cop. That's what kind. If that ain't, in and of itself, a reason to kill the bitch.

Johnson eyes the bottle again. One little ol' sip ain't going to hurt him none. Plus, his leg is throbbing some and a little Jim Beam will go a long way in helping him to reach the refrigerator and his cold beer, his most recent purchase having not made the fridge.

Johnson's sip turns into a long pull from the bottle. His eyes water as the whiskey does its slow burn in his gut. A smile creases his face. Fuck it, maybe his calling is to risk a bullet for the team. Go out in a blaze of glory.

Johnson takes another pull of whiskey and pictures himself taking the fight to the pair. Pulling up in pretty boy's driveway, honking the horn to draw both out and opening up on them and killing them deader than roadkill. Yep, that sounds like a plan. He shrugs. Not much of a plan, but a plan nevertheless. Maybe he won't even get shot in the process. Getting shot is downright hurtful and he can surely attest to that. "Well, Johnson? Hedge your bet and wear your old bulletproof vest," he mumbles to the room. "And maybe you'll even survive and escape. Wouldn't that be the shit?"

Johnson sighs. One can't shuck one's responsibilities, he thinks.

~~~

"Get the boy," Igor says as he checks out his nails. He can't for the life of him figure out how he gets dirt under his nails, but he does. He reaches for the knife at his side to find the case for his Uncle Henry empty. "Huh?"

"What, Igor, did you say something?" Pavel asks.

"Seen my knife?"

"Why would I have seen your knife?"

"'Cause it's fucking missing. That's why."

"No, Igor, I haven't seen it." Pavel smiles. "Probably whore stole it."

Igor doesn't find that a bit amusing, but lets it slide because it's Pavel. "Yes, and Igor wring bitch's neck. Where the fuck is Erik with boy?"

"He's coming."

"I phone again, pedophile. See if he got Igor's money." He turns towards the source of the commotion, Erik dragging the screaming, blue-eyed boy. "Feed him couple Valium. We need peaceful transaction."

"I had hard time separating from women," Erik says.

"Of course you did. They're women after all. Women always give you hard time." Igor sneers. "Why can't be man like Pavel?"

"How 'bout finishing hen party in car?" Erik says his hand at ready to snatch his gun if need be. Igor turns red. Jumps to his feet. He'll kill the bitch yet.

"If wasn't married to whore sister. No more Erik."

Pavel steps between the ever-increasing hostile men. It's only a matter of time, he thinks. "Let's take care of business, da."

Igor turns on his heals, stalks off in the direction of the Cadillac. Brother-in-law, your time is corning soon, he vows.

~~~

"At your age, I figured plenty of vitamin E couldn't hurt," Amy says. "That's why I ordered a third dozen oysters," she adds followed by a condescending smile.

Eddie returns the smile. "That and beer goggles. How can a man go wrong?"

Amy straddles Eddie on the couch. Tilts his chin up and plants a kiss on his lips. "Touché," she says. Amy kisses him again. "But it all works for me." She rolls off Eddie's lap and snuggles up against him. She plucks the sleeping Smoky off a throw pillow and sets him in her lap. His motor instantly begins to purr.

"I hope we find the Russian link to the missing girl this evening," Eddie says.

"It may go way beyond just one little girl. Could be she's a victim of human trafficking."

"That's definitely crossed my mind and that's kinda scary. If we get any indication that's the case, we're going to call the Feds."

"The Sheriff's Department is probably already looking at that angle," Amy says, "but we probably know more than them considering we've actually seen two Russians."

"True, true. And seeing how the mag to my 45 only holds seven rounds, I believe I'll go out to the garage and retrieve the second mag to my Colt."

And Eddie does just that, retrieves his spare clip from the garage while Amy scans the TV's menu for something to watch. She settles on a rerun of The Big Bang Theory as Eddie enters the room.

"Big Bang Theory," she says. Eddie takes his seat back on the couch.

"Actually, I like the show and I especially love…"

"Don't say it."

"… Penny."

Amy nods her head, makes a face. "Of course, what man doesn't? Though you know she had a tit job, don't you?"

"Which makes watching her ride a horse that much more enjoyable."

Amy nods again. "Of course. Being the equestrian and all, how could you not notice?"

"Posture and form are a big part of scoring in competition."

Amy smiles. "As it should be. Speaking of… Here's your girl now. Eddie, are you listening to me?" She pinches his inner thigh.

"Ouch!"

"That's better." They settle in to watch some TV. Both feeling as if they should be doing something other than watching TV.

Foster Cares

Chapter Twenty

Johnson runs his fingers through his greasy hair and unconsciously wipes his hand on the leg of his trousers. He eyes the clock on his microwave: 8:45 p.m. He must have zoned out for a while, he realizes. His life is unraveling at the seams, but he doesn't recognize it for what it is. He takes a drink of his hot beer and struggles to his feet. He has to lean on the table for a long second until the darkness around the edges in his mind clears. Better, he thinks as he pushes off in the direction of the fridge. He makes the few steps easy enough. His knee seeming to cooperate. Hell, it might even be healing, but in such a short period he can't see how. Fuck it. It must be a sign from above. God giving him the wherewithal to get 'er done.

Johnson pulls a six-pack from the fridge. "Time to saddle up and ride old boy," he says to himself. A smile creases his face as he plucks his 9mm of the table en route to the garage and his new pickup. Destiny calls and with God shining down on him, he might just come out of it unscathed. He makes his way around the clutter and squeezes himself into his truck. Johnson depresses the open button on his garage door opener and cranks his pickup.

Time to roll—rock-and-roll.

~~~

Only three thousand shy, Igor thinks. But, hell, it's more than Igor figured he'd get from the pedophile Dorbandt. He chuckles, he ain't sure, but he thinks Dorbandt might have wet his pants again. What a pussy. And speaking of pussy.

"Comrades, to XTC, da? Tonight, we celebrate."

There's a collective roar. Igor is in a good mood. They'll take it when it comes. Igor opens the small humidifier on his desk and offers everyone, brother-in-law included, one of his better Cubans. He takes one for himself, licks it up and down and reaches for his knife that's not there. He suppresses a grimace. Bites the tip off the cigar instead and spits it to the floor. Good old Pavel extends him a light. Igor takes a long drag of his cigar and blows out a thick plume of rich, blue smoke. He savors the flavor and aroma for a moment. He nods in satisfaction.

"Okay, we go. Pavel, you drive. Erik, you shotgun."

~~~

"Okay, I'm about TV'd out. You think it's too early to head to XTC?" Amy asks.

"Is it ever too early to view naked women?" Eddie counters.

Amy whacks him with a throw pillow.

"Technically, we're not actually going to view naked women. Our goal is to locate these Russian characters which will hopefully lead us to the little girl."

"And as to the origin of the little girl," Eddie adds.

"You don't think they took the girl back after killing the Smiths?"

"We don't know for sure whether the Russians killed them or not."

"Come on, Eddie. The Smiths are not the kind of people that tend to get murdered."

Eddie rubs the stubble on his chin. "True enough. But what purpose was served in killing them? To sever any link to them?"

"More than likely any ties to a middleman. The child's probably part of the bigger picture. Maybe they can't afford to lose the middleman. Not if other children are involved."

Eddie stands, stretches. He's stiffened up since his short workout on the bag. He reaches for Amy's hand and pulls her to her feet. They can speculate all night and it won't get them any closer to the truth, though their speculations are probably correct. "Well, let's go then. See where this thing goes if we can."

Eddie tells a disappointed Bobo that he can't go before pulling the door shut behind them. It's not often he leaves Bobo behind and he feels bad about it. He closes the garage door and opens Amy's door for her and gives her an unnecessary boost up and inside his truck.

Always the gentleman, Amy thinks, as Eddie closes the door after her. She sighs a contented sigh still amazed at how rapidly their relationship is developing. The only thing that gives her pause is the thought of Lori. Poor Lori and the ordeal she went through. And now she's coming back to Austin. Amy's not sure how that's going to play out but hopes no one gets hurt including herself. Eddie squeezes her above the knee before cranking the truck.

"Ready?"

"Sure."

"You okay?"

"Yeah, it's nothing. I'm ready," she says. And she is. She feels safe in Eddie's company. It's just something about him. An aura that's hard to explain. Eddie cracks the window to let some cool evening air in and to dissipate some of the lingering odor of burned rubber and an ever-increasing odor of mildew. Eddie backs out of the drive.

"I think it's time for a new truck," he says.

"Sorry about your truck."

"It's okay. Might as well shop for you a new car, as well, while we're at it."

Amy nods, fiddles with the stereo, lands on a Miley Cyrus song and leaves it there. They ride on in silence. Both absorbed by their own thoughts.

Eddie takes the 51st exit and on to Cameron Road. Amy turns in her seat and tucks a leg under her. She smiles.

"Know the back way in I take it?" she says. Eddie returns the smile.

"And then some," he says.

"Right," like I didn't see that coming, Amy thinks good-naturedly.

They turn into the lot, the gravel crunching under the truck's all-terrain tires. The lot is mostly empty. Eddie parks near the front entrance, rolls up the windows and kills the truck. He takes his big Colt and tucks it under his seat. Unfortunately, the law doesn't, as of yet in Texas, allow firearms in bars, though they should, he thinks with a trace of humor.

Amy wags her purse to emphasize she doesn't share his concern. She reminds Eddie she has a concealed carry license. Eddie suspects it doesn't extend the right to carry in a bar, but figures no harm will come of it considering their odds of encountering any Russians involved in human trafficking seems like an extremely long shot to him. He reaches beyond her and pushes her door open. He opens his own door and together they alight from the truck.

~~~

Pavel turns the Caddy into the XTC's parking lot, the headlights doing a lazy pan of the lot in the process. The lights momentarily illuminate Eddie and Amy in the process. Erik's jaw drops. He turns in his seat, watches the pair enter the strip joint. He shakes his head to clear it. It can't be.

"What? What is it?" Igor says from the back seat. Erik shakes his head. Surely, it can't be.

"I think I saw the American and the cop go into club." He points. "And look, that's the American's truck."

Igor leans halfway over into the front seat. He blinks, stares harder at the dimly lit truck. "cho E-to za bal-DA?" What is the deal? Igor says. "It can't be. What are two doing here?"

Confusion clouds Igor's face. His beady eyes seem to water. He feels the heat in his face. They fuck with Igor, he thinks. He pushes his door open as the Cadillac comes to a stop, begins to exit causing Pavel to reach across the back seat and grab a big fistful of Igor's jacket preventing him from exiting the car. Igor looks at Pavel, then Pavel's fist on his jacket and then Pavel again. For a second, he pictures drawing his piece and shooting Pavel in the back of the head. Nobody puts their hands on Igor. Nobody. He scowls and awaits an explanation.

"This is not good," Pavel says. "Why they here? We not know. We come to the club too much. Whatever Igor plan, not good in club, da?"

Igor allows his breathing to slow. Maybe Pavel right. Maybe Igor act too impulsively at times. He relaxes back in his seat, pulls the door closed. He looks back down at Pavel's big fist until his jacket is released. He readjusts his jacket. Smooths the imaginary wrinkles.

"These two. They fuck with Igor. What in fuck brings them here?"

Pavel shrugs. Puts the Caddy in park and lets the car idle. He does not know how the two ended up at XTC, but is smart enough to know it's no coincidence. "Pavel go in, keep an eye. See what's up. They not know Pavel," he says. Igor doesn't like the idea of sitting in the car, but at least he has vodka, beer and cigarettes. He nods his assent. Pavel snaps his fingers.

"Igor, give Pavel money." He grins. "Pavel don't want to stick out."

Like Pavel's size alone doesn't make him stick out, Igor thinks as he slaps a wad in Pavel's outstretched hand. Igor shoos him. "Go. Go. See what can find out."

The petite waitress in her Daisy Dukes and bikini top brings Eddie and Amy a tub of ice for the Bud Lights that they purchased en route to the club. Eddie scans the room as he peels off a $10 to tip their waitress. Less than a dozen other tables have customers at the present and several singularly occupied by elderly men nursing their whiskeys while longingly eyeing the young dancer currently gyrating on the center-stage pole. It's sad and Eddie silently hopes he never finds himself in such a desperate situation, especially now that he seems to be on the mend.

"Wave if I can get you anything else," the waitress says. Eddies smiles up at her.

"Perhaps some information if you have a minute," Eddie says not noticing a new customer has entered the club and has taken a seat at the table behind them.

"Are you guys cops or something?"

"No. No, nothing like that. PIs in fact," Amy offers adding her own smile.

"Oh... Well, I guess that's not the same thing."

"Exactly," Amy says. "Pull up a seat."

"Umm, I don't think so. This is my first day and I don't want to get in trouble. I need this job."

"Sure, honey," Amy says. "No big deal. Thanks." She turns toward Eddie. "Go tip the dancer. We'll have company before you know it."

"Been here before, Detective?"

Amy gnaws at her bottom lip for a second. "Not hardly."

Eddie laughs, Amy's expression being both funny and sexy at the same time.

"Go," Amy prompts again.

"But she won't be totally nude until her next dance."

"I think you misunderstand the nature of our mission, Mr. Winston," Amy says giving him a different look—one that provokes yet another laugh out of Eddie. He peels a ten from the fold in his front pocket and approaches the stage. The dancer dances her way over, turns her back to him, bends at the waist and smiles at him through her spread legs.

Eddie tucks the ten under the string of her bikini. She turns, bends at the knees and leans over to kiss Eddie on the cheek. "Thanks, handsome," she says.

Eddie turns and spots the new patron at the table beyond theirs.

Rather a big fellow, Eddie thinks. And, of all the tables, why did the guy pick the table next to theirs when so many others are available? Eddie shakes off the thought. Just being paranoid, he tells himself.

He takes his seat back next to Amy.

"What did she whisper?" Amy has to know despite not wanting to have to know.

"I think you misunderstand the nature of our mission, Ms. Foster."

"Good one, Eddie. Well?"

"Her phone number."

Amy elbows him. They both laugh.

A different dancer approaches their table. Pretty, Eddie thinks, but at the same time, he gets the impression of seasoned.

"Buy a lap dance for your man?" she asks Amy. "Only 20 bucks."

"No thank you. What's your name, honey?"

"Mercedes."

"But maybe you'd care for a beer? Pull up a seat. Maybe you can help us with a little information instead."

She eyes one then the other. Somehow, they look familiar, but she can't place them. "You ain't cops, are you?"

"Not hardly."

"Twenty bucks. Same as the dance."

Amy pats the seat beside her. Mercedes tentatively takes the offered seat. "Mercedes your stage name?"

"Yep. About that twenty." Eddie folds the twenty and slides the bill to rest in front of Mercedes.

"Get any Russian customers?" Amy asks.

Mercedes noticeably stiffens. She pulls a beer from the tub. Picks at the ice on its top. Eyes the bill. "I suppose," she finally says.

"Regulars?"

She shrugs. "Nah, not really."

Eddie leans in so that he can be heard over the music. "How about a beady-eyed guy? Say 45 or 50? Reminding you of Vladimir Putin?"

Mercedes nods her head no, too vigorously. Eddie and Amy look at each other, think the same thing—she's lying. Mercedes snatches up the $20 and leaves the unopened beer where it sets.

"I... Got to get going," she briefly looks over her shoulder before hurrying off.

Amy slides over to fill the empty seat next to Eddie. She leans in close. "Why do I feel eyes boring into me? Did you notice that big guy sitting at the table behind us?"

"He's got big Russian bear written all over him. Did you catch Mercedes glancing back before hightailing it?"

"Not to mention she was obviously lying," Amy adds. Eddie nods his assent.

"And I feel it, too," Eddie says. "He's eyeing the shit out of us for some reason." Eddie takes a pull from his beer. "But how in the fuck could that be possible? I've never seen the dude before."

"Nor me, but if he's part of the same group, he's no doubt seen us on the news."

Eddie takes another sip of beer. "There is that. What now?"

Amy shrugs. "Talk to some more of the dancers I guess." She looks around the joint. A few more tables are seated. "I think the place is going to be hopping here shortly."

Eddie pats her on the thigh. "Hold that thought. Be right back," he says. The girl on the main stage is now totally nude. Eddie smiles as he approaches the stage. He can't help but think the gal's bikini trim gives a whole new meaning to bikini trims. There's nowhere to tuck the bill. He peels off another ten spot and lays it at her feet.

The dancer bends at the knees and leans in to give Eddie another kiss on the cheek and to murmur in his ear thanks and the name's Jodi.

Amy pinches Eddie on his inner thigh as he retakes his seat. "Try not to enjoy yourself so much," she says with a good-natured smirk.

"I'll try," Eddie weakly manages. They both laugh despite the situation.

"Well, Eddie, what do you think?"

"I think in all probability, we found the Russians we're looking for. Which leaves us with the question, what are we going to do now? Give the information to the cops?"

Amy traces the rim of her beer can with a finger. Flicks off a small piece of ice. "Yeah, I'll call it in to the right person, but I don't believe it abrogates our responsibility to see this thing through. Only we know what the little girl looks like, well with the exception of the one cop at Zilker Park and he didn't pay the kid any attention, so I feel as if we are obligated to follow through with our investigation. Also, we know what at least two of the Russians look like."

"And the bruiser behind us," Eddie says before taking another pull from his beer. "Suggestions?"

"Yeah, go tip the dancer and try not to enjoy yourself," she repeats.

"Gotcha," Eddie says. They both laugh. Eddie makes it to the stage to tip the latest dancer on the center stage, gets his hug and kiss on his cheek and heads back to his table somewhat disturbed to discover the bruiser that sat at the table behind them is gone.

Eddie takes his seat back at their table.

"I'm not going to kiss that cheek for a month, you know," Amy says.

Eddie pats her on the thigh.

"Well, the bruiser seems to have left," Eddie says. "Strange, considering how early it is."

Amy turns to see for herself. Sure enough, the guy's gone. Hmm, she thinks. "Well, maybe our next visitor will speak a little more freely with him gone."

Eddie and Amy watch on as Jodi leaves the stage and another girl takes her place on the center stage. Eddie nudges Amy indicating for her to vacate the seat between them again.

"I think we're fixing to have company again," he says. Amy does so but only because it's for a good cause. God, why did all these dancers have to be so young and pretty and some even so naturally endowed? It almost doesn't seem fair. Having served as a detective for as many years as she's had, Amy's no stranger to the tittie-bar scene, but this is the first occasion in which she's actually set at a table and observed the dancers. Amy has to remind herself that she's got a damn nice body herself, thank you. And the looks and the personality, too, thank you.

"What are you smiling at, Eddie?" Amy asks realizing too that Eddie's watching her and not the dancers on the stage. For how long he's been watching her, she cannot say—but apparently long enough that her thoughts gave her away. Amy sticks her tongue out at Eddie before hiding behind a slow sip of beer. Eddie laughs. Points. Sure enough, here comes Jodi.

Jodi addresses Amy. "Care to buy your man a lap dance?" she asks then leans in to whisper in Amy's ear. "If you're going to ask questions, you've got to at least make it look good."

Amy nods. "A lap dance it shall be," she says not exactly too thrilled to give the go ahead. Amy turns her chair to watch, grows somewhat hot under the collar as the girl gyrates her ass in Eddie's face and turns to straddle him and continue her provocative dance. Maybe she should have told her "but keep your bikini bottoms on, though," Amy thinks. Too late. A tug at both bow ties and off they come, the bottoms. Well, Amy knows one thing for sure. When she gets Eddie home, she's going to fuck the shit out of him and make him forget all about his lap dance. And dammit, damn if he doesn't seem to be enjoying himself. Thankfully, the dance comes to an end and the girl takes a seat in between them. Amy slides her chair nearer. "I didn't get your name," Amy says.

"Jodi," Eddie answers for her. Amy scowls at him until she realizes her scowl is only adding to Eddie's enjoyment at her expense.

"You want to know about the Russians," Jodi says so softly she can barely be heard over the din. Mercedes told me. I suggest you be really careful. The big oaf that was sitting at the table behind you a few minutes ago is one of them. The guy you're interested in, I think, is a Russian named Igor. Very bad dude. And the big guy is one of his main men. Meaning the others are likely nearby." Jodi helps herself to a beer out of the tub, pops the tab and downs a good portion of it. "Anyway, I've got to move around," she says offering her open hand to Eddie. Eddie peels off a couple of 20s and places them in her hand.

"Thanks," she says and downs the last of her beer. She begins to rise. Amy lays a hand on her thigh keeping her temporarily in her seat.

"One more question," she says, "Please. What are they involved in?"

"They sling a lot of cash. Drugs, of course."

"What about kids. Any rumor about kids?"

"Look, I really got to go. I don't know anything about any kids." With that said, Jodi rises and scampers off. Amy slips back into the vacated chair to confer with Eddie.

"I take it you want to hang around a little longer then," Eddie says.

"Might as well. "

"Then I'm going to go and water the horse." Eddie smiles. "Try not to hit on any of the dancers while I'm gone."

Amy smirks. "Yeah, right. Don't get lost. Umm, Eddie, the bathroom is that way." Amy says pointing in the opposite direction.

"Oh, yeah. I often get the directions to the VIP lounge and bathrooms confused." Eddie stretches and takes a casual look around.

Still no sigh of the bruiser. Eddie shrugs, reckons the guy most be gone. He leans over and kisses Amy on the mouth. "Be right back," he says before heading this time in the right direction.

Eddie enters the restroom. He seems to be alone. Eddie glances at the condom machine as he steps past it to stop before the urinal. Who the fuck would want a blue condom with raised "pleasure" bumps? he wonders to himself.

Eddie unzips his jeans. Hears the creak of a nearby stall door opening. He doesn't recall seeing any feet in the stalls as he entered. Not good, he thinks as he hastens to rezip his jeans. He spins on his heels a split second too late.

The Russian bruiser is on him. Slams into him driving Eddie into the urinal. Eddie's lower back makes contact with the chrome flush mechanism.

The pain is excruciating. Eddie sings out, "Shit!" as part of the wind is knocked out of him.

Eddie attempts to shift his body—free himself from the Russian's powerful grip.

By the lapel, the big Russian lifts Eddie off his feet, slams him once more off the tile wall backing the urinal. Eddie grunts upon impact, but is thankful that he cleared the flush mechanism this time.

Eddie frees an arm. His left-hand finds the Russian's face. He gouges an eye with his thumb. Pictures ripping the eyeball from the socket. It's the Russian's turn to scream and he does.

"khu-ye-sos! Coksucker!" he screams – tossing Eddie to the side as if Eddie was weightless.

Eddie lands on his ass, bounces off the wall, and comes to rest below the condom machine. He shakes his head to clear it.

Pavel wipes the blood from the corner of his eye with the back of his hand. His eye is tearing, as well. Pavel sees nothing but a blur through it. He looks on as Eddie turns to eye the bathroom door and his hopeful escape. Though it may not be prudent, Pavel decides to kill the pesky American.

"YOB te-BYA! Fuck You!" He says and spits in Eddie's direction.

Though the distance to the door and escape is a mere 15 feet, it seems like an insurmountable distance to Eddie at the present. He shakes his head once more. Draws in a deep breath. Watches as the Russian moves between him and the door. Eddie reaches for a pull handle on the condom machine to slowly help hoist himself from the bathroom floor. Damn, he's a big fucker, Eddie thinks. Another thought crosses his mind – along with you fucked up. Where are the half-dozen bouncers when you need them?

Eddie rolls his neck and shoulders, eyes the big fucker with a healthy dose of trepidation. "I'm not sure what this is about pardner, but perhaps we can handle this in a more amicable manner."

Pavel's not sure of what all was said and the American's intention, but to Pavel, it spells "pussy." He blinks his injured eye and grins. Pavel will make quick work of the cocksucker.

Resigned to his fate, Eddie mumbles, "I didn't think so." He moves into a kickboxer style stance, squares off. It's going to hurt, but he's not going out without a good fight...

Amy checks her watch. How long does it take to water your horse, Eddie? She pushes her chair back sensing something is not quite right. She stands, snatches her clutch purse off the table and heads off in the direction of the men's room.

Eddie kicks at the Russian's head which the Russian blocks with a forearm seemingly as thick as a tree branch and with surprising agility for such a big fellow. Eddie follows up with a quick straight right to the jaw that would take a normal man down but barely rocks the Russian. Pavel counters with a right to Eddie's chest sending Eddie sprawling.

Clutching his chest, Eddie rolls to avoid a heavy stomp to his head. Christ that hurt. For a second, he thought his heart had stopped. He finally manages to groan as he scrambles to get his feet under him and avoids another kick. The big fellow's grin broadens.

"I know," Eddie says shaking his head and thinking the door is his only hope of survival.

Amy knocks on the bathroom door. "Eddie, you alright in there?"

Eddie feints to his left.

Pavel takes the bait.

Eddie spins as if he was a running back and shoots for the momentary opening.

Amy pulls open the bathroom door.

Time stops. Eddie watches in slow motion the bathroom door opening and Amy framed in the opening. He gets a second boot under him en route to freedom.

Pavel stretches out, hooks Eddie's boot with his own and watches in satisfaction as Eddie goes sprawling yet again.

"Freeze, police!" Amy screams as she struggles with the zipper on her clutch purse.

Pavel registers the threat posed by Amy's sudden appearance. "SU-ka!" Bitch, he yells as he closes the short distance leading with a shoulder. He runs slap over Eddie in the process.

"Shit!" Amy says finding the grip of her small automatic.

Pavel lowers his shoulder and barrels into Amy taking her off her feet and out the bathroom door. She hits the ground with a thud and groans. Her head bounces off the floor. Her clutch skitters away on the polished floor, her automatic along with it.

"Shit!" she screams at the fleeing Russian.

Eddie watches as the bathroom door swings shut. He took a boot dead center between the shoulder blades. Afraid for Amy, he peels himself from the floor—gets his feet under him. "Amy!" he screams, as he bursts through the door and stumbles to avoid Amy who is in the process of sitting up. "You all right?" he asks as a small crowd begins to gather.

"I think I got run over by the entire Dallas defensive line," she manages to say before smiling wanly. "You?"

"I'll live," Eddie says rubbing his chest. "That fucker kicks like a mule with his hands. Near stopped my heart." He chuckles, "dammit hurt."

Eddie takes the offered hand and pulls Amy to her feet.

Jodi passes over Amy's clutch. She shrugs. "I told you so."

Amy smirks. "Thanks."

The manager orders Jodi back to work. Shoos away the rest of the rubberneckers. He steps before Eddie and Amy. "Look, I don't know what the hell is going on here, but we can't have this kind of shit going down in the club. I'm going to have to ask you both nicely to leave. No, I'm going to insist that you both leave. Like right now."

Amy renews her smirk. "Right. So, I don't suppose you know who the big Russian that just fled is, do you?"

"Didn't see any Russian."

Eddie clears his throat. "I don't suppose you called the law either then, did you Hoss?"

"I watch the news. I know who you two clowns are." He nods in the direction of the exit. "Now get the fuck out of here."

Amy wraps her arm around Eddie's waist. Kisses him on the cheek. "Twice, shame on me. I'm going to buy myself a new clutch without a zipper." She rubs the back of her head. "Ready handsome?"

"Am I going to get lucky?"

"You know it sailor," Amy says. They both laugh their way to the exit, both happy to survive to live yet another day.

Chapter Twenty-One

The thought of Eddie and his slut draws in Johnson like a moth to a flame. All semblance of rationality flees him as his truck steers him mostly north and nearer and nearer to Eddie's residence. Johnson crushes his latest empty and tosses it out the truck's sliding rear window. The heft of the gun in Johnson's lap gives him comfort. He soon finds himself arriving at Eddie's street. He makes the left off of Burnet and onto Eddie's street. A Burnet south-bound cruiser turns in after him. Johnson spots the cop in his rearview and decelerates to exactly 30 mph. Sweat forms at his temples as his face and scalp grow hot.

"Stupid fuck," he mumbles to himself. Of course, the cops would increase their presence in Eddie's neighborhood after two attempts on Eddie and his slut's lives.

Johnson increases his grip on the steering wheel to keep his hands from shaking. The cop remains plastered to his bumper. If he has to, Johnson decides, he'll kill the cop. Not that he'd ever be a cop killer, mind you, but for the greater good—a world without Winston and Foster.

The siren whoops once and the grill's blues begin to oscillate.

"Shit! Motherfucker!" Johnson pulls to the curb as his hand feels for the grip of his 9mm. His eyes never leave the rearview.

The cop car shoots around him, does a U-turn that's illuminated by the truck's headlights. Johnson's relief manifests into a roar that fills the cab. Johnson has a good mind to do a U-turn himself and finish what needs to be finished. The cop not pulling him over reaffirms his righteousness. God has sent him a personal message. Has given him his blessings. Johnson's grin stretches the skin on his face. He truly is blessed to be tasked with such a noble mission. His truck steers its way home, but not to abort the mission but to regroup, formulate a new plan.

~~~

Igor studies his injured hand in the dim light cast from the car's dash. This American, this Eddie Winston, is a much more formidable opponent then first believed, Igor thinks. "So, Pavel. You catch American alone in bathroom and no beat shit out of?"

Pavel sighs. Turns the rearview to check his eye once more before straightening the mirror back. How to explain this for the hundredth time so Igor understand? Exacerbated, he tries again. "Igor, I had man down—fixing to snap neck. But woman yank open door—have gun." He shrugs, "What Pavel to do, Igor?" he adds though his recitation of facts not entirely true.

How is possible? Igor again thinks, Pavel being the baddest fucker in his crew. Hell, maybe baddest fucker Igor ever know. "Okay, Pavel. All good, but we burned XTC. No can go back. Maybe call law of Pavel."

"Yeah," says Erik from the back seat, "Maybe we should have waited on them to come out. Maybe have better chance in parking lot."

Igor could spit nails. He spins in his seat. Glares back at Erik. "Maybe, Erik, if aunt have balls, she be uncle. So, shut fuck up! Let us men think."

Erik blows out his cheeks and stares holes in the back of Igor's head as Igor turns back in his seat to face forward once more. He will kill bastard one day. One day soon, he vows.

The garage door rattles open. Pavel drives in and parks. They made it safely home, but things to Pavel appear to be slowly unraveling and some of the blame falling squarely on his shoulders. He has a premonition of doom. Something that's never happened to him before. A shiver runs through him for the first time in his life. Pavel hopes no one noticed.

~~~

"Down, Bobo," Amy says trying to get through the kitchen door. Eddie laughs, scoops up the kitten who's also at the door to welcome them home. What a family, he thinks. And, by the volume of the kitten's cries, Smoky intends on being fed.

"I've got it," Amy says picking the empty bowl off the floor and placing it on the counter. She retrieves milk from the fridge and fills Smoky's bowl. Eddie sets Smoky down who is so eager to get to his milk he lands a paw in his bowl. Eddie and Amy share a laugh.

Bobo paws at Eddie's leg. "Right, can't forget you, can we Big Boy," Eddie says. He grabs a can of Alpo out of the pantry and fills Bobo's bowl. The Alpo lasts all of 15 seconds. Eddie and Amy shake their heads in amusement.

"Well, we didn't learn a whole lot from visiting XTC, did we, Eddie?" Amy says as she takes a seat in front of her Mac.

"It was a good lead but I'm afraid we blew it. I doubt they'll be back if ever."

"I think I'll do a Google image search on the mysterious elderly woman in the group shot with the Smiths. You just never know. So, what did you think of the dancers?" Amy asks wondering why she asked.

"Not the prettiest dancers in Austin, but they were decent enough."

Amy isolates the woman by cropping out the others in the photo. "Anyone, in particular, catch your fancy?" Amy asks pretending to focus on the screen before her. She could kick herself for even asking.

"I liked the one with the Hitler 'stash for a bikini trim."

Well, you asked, Amy thinks. "I meant as a person."

Eddie moves in behind her, massages her shoulders. "If it makes you feel any better, you have the prettiest pussy in the world."

"Well, I'm not exactly sure if it does, but thanks." They share another laugh.

"Oh, that feels too good. Don't stop," Amy says leaning back into the massage. "Dammit, no hit on the woman. Maybe if she wasn't in profile."

"So, what's the plan now?"

"Let's see if we can find e-mails for the names we do know in the photo and see if one of them can identify the woman."

"Both smart and beautiful," Eddie says. Amy smiles inwardly sensing the sincerity of Eddie's words.

"Feel like a late snack? Hungry at all?"

Eddie kisses the top of Amy's head. "Carry on with what you're doing. I'll whip us up something. How does a BLT sound?"

Amy turns slightly to look up at Eddie and covers his hand with her own. "Add a fried egg to mine."

"Sounds like a winner. Coming right up." And he does just that as Amy continues on her Mac. It doesn't take her long to find individual e-mail addresses though some are work-related. She sends the same short e-mail to each with the photo as an attachment.

"How's it going?" Eddie asks bringing the sandwiches to the table and pulling up a seat next to Amy.

"Found e-mails on them all. As long as they're not afraid to click onto an attachment from a fired detective, we'll hopefully have an answer by morning."

"'Hero is more like it. The public views you as a hero, not as a fired cop," Eddie says. Amy closes the case on her Mac as Eddie slides her plate before her. Bobo squeezes his body between their chairs.

"Bobo," Eddie and Amy say in unison. Reluctantly, Bobo drops to the floor and rests his snout on his paws. He watches them with soulful eyes knowing there's at least a bite or two in for him. And he'll soon be proven right when both plates are placed on the floor for him to lick clean.

Amy smiles. "Can't say he's not efficient. It will still take me a little time to get used to your boy's dish-washing system, though."

"Understandably," Eddie says adding his own smile. "Well," he adds, "it's getting late. Ready to call it a night?"

"I think it's as good of a time as any to vanquish all thoughts of dancers from your mind," Amy says believing she's capable of doing just that. And after a quick shower, she does vanquish those thoughts. Eddie happily thinks of only one woman, the woman with whom he's sharing his bed.

~~~

A steady knock on the doors rouses Boris. His throat's parched from all the cigarettes he's smoked and Vodka he's drunk. His mind flashes back to the calamity of the previous day and the fact he never made the call. "Shit," he moans. Igor will kill him. He sits up surprised, but not too surprised, to see the remaining whores still present and eyeing him expectantly. For a second, he fears it's Igor outside wanting in but then realizes of course it's not him for Igor would never knock. He points at the door.

"Get fucking door," he yells. Stupid fucking whores.

What to do? What to do? Think Boris. He watches as the whore lets in a well-dressed elderly white man, a somewhat regular with money. He wonders what brings a man of apparent stature to bottom feed on his low-dollar whores. He shrugs as a plan formulates in his pounding head.

"Come in my friend," he says. "Welcome. Good to see, da."

The man pauses, offers a palsied hand. Boris shakes the offered hand, forces a smile that sets the old guy on his heels. Boris's breath is rank enough to part the Red Sea. "Da, da, take prettiest... prettiest in back, enjoy."

Boris moves to the windows as the old codger is guided to the rear of the apartment. He parts the curtains. Grins even broader. Yep, the old fucker's still driving an Escalade. He shakes his head in wonder and his new good fortune. Fuck Igor and fuck this place. He's fucking out of here and he's fucking out of here in style. He eyes his fake Russian-made Rolex, wills the old fucker to hurry up. He chuckles. Can't have Igor rolling up on him. That could be messy.

Boris scratches the stubble on his chin as he decides what to do with the old codger. Kill him for Igor to find in this dump? Or take him and his credit cards along? And what of the whores? The remaining whores, that is? Fuck it. He'll take them all along. But where? Florida sounds nice. He's never been to Florida. He shrugs. Florida it is then.

"You two, get your shit," Boris says to the remaining whores in the front room. He mimes gathering and packing and shoos them to hurry up leaving no doubt of his intentions. He walks in on the old guy and his whore. He's between the whore's legs eating up her furry muff. He winces. Almost chokes. Much too early to witness something like this. He clears his throat. The old man reluctantly looks back.

"It's your lucky day, comrade," Boris says. "You, whores and Boris take road trip, da. Then you eat all pussy you want." He chuckles. "On house." We'll not exactly. He motions for them to hurry, by clapping his hands together.

Boris lifts his shirt exposing his pistol and in a surprisingly short time, Boris and his group hit the open road.

~~~

The partially ajar door to the apartment sends an ominous message to Igor and his men as the Caddy comes to a stop. Mikhail throws the car into park and they all exit as one. Igor slips his piece from his waistband and holds it pressed against his leg. He nods at Pavel who in turn kicks the door open. They stare agape at the empty front room. Everything is gone. Even the furniture but for a seedy mattress and box spring. Igor's first to speak.

"chto za BLYAD-stvo, What the hell is going on?" he asks. He notes the big square missing from the carpet. "Fuckin' morons. Igor kill both when Igor catch." He waves his gun indicating he wants the rest of the apartment searched.

"Igor, you no like," Pavel calls out from the left-hand bedroom.

Igor and the rest join him in the room. Pavel points to the closet where a bundle that obviously contains a body is crammed into a corner. Igor wipes the sweat from his upper lip. He reaches for his knife that's not there. He curses under his breath as Mikhail pulls the body from the closet and uses his own knife to slit open the tape securing the bundle.

Mikhail exposes the face. Collectively, everyone shakes their heads. To all it appears, Boris killed Peter and hightailed it.

"You're a dead man," Igor vows.

~~~

"Good morning, sunshine," Amy says running her fingers through the hair on Eddie's chest.

"It's morning already?" Eddie says playfully facetious. He stretches feeling pretty good after sleeping much better than he expected considering someone or more is apparently set on killing them. He yawns despite feeling refreshed. "Sleep well?" he asks.

"Like a log. I only woke once to find Bobo asleep across my legs. God that must have been uncomfortable but it took a couple good pushes to get him to move."

"Speaking of, where is the big fellow?"

"He followed the kitten out the door. Probably suspected that Smoky was onto something, foodwise, that is. "

"What 's the plan for today, Detective?"

Amy props herself up on her elbow. Snakes the other hand under the sheet. Eddie smiles in response to the glint in Amy's eyes.

"You are incorrigible, Detective Amy Foster," Eddie says not for the first time.

"Not quite ready for this honeymoon to be over with, Big Boy," Amy says offering Eddie a mint. "In case I have to kiss you," she adds with a smirk.

"God forbid," Eddie says pushing Amy to her back. "Lucky for me you lost your panties last night."

"And you lost your boxers," Amy says guiding him in. They both laugh, both content in the knowledge that this honeymoon is far from over. It doesn't take either of them long to get to where they want to be.

"God, that was good," Amy says as Eddie falls from atop of her. She elbows Eddie. "Well?"

He takes a second to catch his breath. "Beautiful... And I only had to kiss you once."

"The longest kiss of my life," Amy says. "Nearly sucked the life out of me." She fans herself as they both laugh yet again. Two peas in a pod, it would seem they both think in their own ways.

Amy rolls from the bed. "And now we can officially start our day." She giggles, beating Eddie to the master bath. She just manages to slam the door shut and lock it before Eddie reaches it. He bangs on the door one good time.

"Woman!" he yells at Amy through the door. She giggles once more as she bends to adjust the water for her shower. Amy can't recall a time that's she's been so happy, notwithstanding their near brushes with death. She hugs herself one good time before stepping into the shower. As she reaches for the shampoo, she wonders what exactly she was thinking locking Eddie out. "Woman," she says repeating Eddie. "Live and learn, Amy," she adds.

Eddie stops at the guest bath long enough to relieve himself and brush his teeth. He finds Bobo and the kitten in the kitchen awaiting someone to feed them.

"Out first," Eddie says opening the backdoor for Bobo. He picks up Smoky and sets him in his litter box. Smoky leaps from the litter box and skitters across the tile floor scattering cat litter and vying for traction before rounding the corner and disappearing into the living room. Eddie smiles. Someone's on his side. What a family. A family he'll protect with his life if need be. And that ain't no joke. Eddie happily prepares breakfast for his family. Yep, his family.

~~~

Johnson's hand shakes so hard he has trouble opening the child-proof cap on his Oxies. Hell, he doesn't know what caused him to sleep so long but the sun's up. He strains to recall the previous evening. He seems to remember nearly getting pulled over in front of Eddie's but's not sure if he's remembering correctly. Fucking mess and fucking Foster. Ever since she shot him in the knee things have been going downhill for him.

The cap pops off with an audible pop and goes sailing. Fuck the cap, he thinks. He'll be damned if he'll go off chasing the thing again. Johnson pops an Oxy, washes it down with the remaining sip of a hot, stale beer from last night. He grimaces at the taste but's thankful that there wasn't a cigarette butt in the can. He always hates it when that happens. He rocks the recliner back into a sitting position. Winces as his feet make contact with the carpet. Fuck if his knee don't hurt this morning. Fucking Foster. He rubs his face - his hands turn oily from the sheen off his face. He wipes them dry on the worn armrests of his recliner.

Fuck it, Johnson thinks. He ain't getting nothing done just sitting here. With an effort and grunt, he pushes himself up to stand.

He's a little wobbly on his feet and his mind grows dark around the edges before clearing. Shit, you'll survive, Johnson. Now get your ass moving. A little fortification and you will be fine. At least you'll quit shaking. His plan to deal with the pair begins to take shape once more. It ain't much of a plan, he concedes to himself, but it's a plan by God and perhaps safer, too. Well, for him at least.

Johnson makes it to the kitchen. He chuckles at the sight of all the booze he's purchased. Been on a spending spree it would seem. So be it. Can't never have too much booze.

He opens the freezer for a chilled bottle of Vodka, uncaps it and downs a couple of good-sized gulps. Johnson welcomes the slow burn in his gut. He looks around the kitchen, spots a cane, he must have got somewhere, near the sink. Not a problem now that he has some vodka in him. He reaches it after several careful steps. While there, he decides to run his head under faucet knowing his hair must look like shit after several days now without washing. He uses his dish-washing liquid for shampoo. Satisfied, he combs his thinning hair back into place with his fingers. He need now only piss and visit his room and safe and he'll be ready to get the show on the road.

Relieved, Johnson makes it to his room and safe. He has to move a stack of cash to get to what he seeks. He finds it right where he expected too, a large vitamin bottle filled to the brim with crack rocks. He also digs out a throwaway, a chrome-plated, snub-nosed 38 Special that only holds five rounds. Not much of a gun, but it will do.

Slowly, but with renewed purpose, Johnson makes it to his truck and he's out of there.

Chapter Twenty-Two

Mikhail pulls to a stop in front of the Dumpster behind Sears. He scans for a security camera and finds one to his right. The camera for all practical purposes poses no threat. The Sears has been closed for a couple of years now and it's unlikely that even if the camera's functional that there's anyone monitoring it. Igor nods his approval as he opens the glove box and pops the trunk. Pavel gets out alone. He needs no help, Peter weighing a mere 75 kilos or so. With not so much as a grunt of effort, Pavel pulls the wrapped body from the trunk and tosses it over his shoulder. After another quick look around, Pavel lifts one of the lids on the Dumpster and tosses Peter in. He joins his crew back in the Caddy. They pull away.

Igor breaks the seal on a fresh bottle of vodka, takes a long pull. He wipes his mouth and lets out a satisfying ahhh. "To Peter, da," he says before passing the bottle.

Truth be known, Igor could give a shit about the death of Peter who most likely brought his death upon himself by getting careless and sloppy. Peter was probably even skimming from his organization. Fuck Peter, that's what Igor truly believes. Peter's death being a mere inconvenience. But now, he has two men he'll have to replace and finding two loyal men in his profession is not always the easiest thing to do.

Mikhail glances over at Igor. "Where to boss?"

"Back to warehouse. Igor need think."

~~~

"We've got some responses to my e-mails," Amy says prompting Eddie to move his chair in closer. She clicks on the first e-mail. "Hmm, this one doesn't know who she is, but he's attached a photo. Let's see what we've got." Amy opens the attachment. It's another group photo with the mystery woman in the background, but this time the photo catches the woman facing forward. "I'll just crop her out once more and do another Google Image Search and you can always print us out some hard copies, too."

"Ten-four, Detective," Eddie says.

It only takes moments to ascertain that the remaining e-mails, likewise, don't provide the answer to the woman's identity. Amy blows out her breath in frustration.

"Well, the consensus is she may be a maid, maybe with the catering service, or maybe a mother or mother-in-law or something, and Goggle Image Search is also a bust." Eddie reaches across the table to retrieve the printout from his wireless printer. "But we do have a hardcopy now. Should I print some extras?"

"Might as well. Print a dozen of her. Hey, here's something. They actually have a viewing of both the Smiths starting at noon today. The announcement just popped up on my news aggregate."

"I take it that neither of them was shot in the head then."

"It would appear not. "

"Same theory for viewings?"

"I don't see why not. Plus, now we have a second and better photo of the mystery woman. I don't see why we shouldn't go."

Eddie shrugs. "Let's do it then. Nothing ventured, nothing gained."

Amy sighs. "Such wisdom." Her expression causes them both to laugh. "Hope you have something decent to wear," she adds.

"And I hope you know how to iron."

"Touché."

Eddie and Amy prepare for the viewing. The viewing, a move that might just pay off.

~~~

It doesn't take long for Johnson to locate Karen, the young, white, crack-addicted prostitute. He knows her east-side haunts well. She's not pleased to see him.

"Get in Karen and don't make me say it twice."

Karen steps foot-to-foot. The last thing she wants to do is get into Johnson's truck and a truck she's never seen before. "I don't think so. I hear tell you ain't even a cop no more."

"Suit yourself," he says lifting the pill bottle where she can see it. He rattles it. "But I got something here for you." He twists the cap off the bottle, shakes out a fat 20-dollar rock and holds it up for Karen to see. He breaks off a good nickel and tosses it out the window at her feet. She's hesitant to pick it up, but her need wins out. Her hand's a little shaky picking it off the ground. She knows Johnson and he ain't no good. It could be a trap, Karen thinks. And maybe it ain't dope at all. Maybe's only some bunk, maybe even wax. Though it sure looks real. She looks all around her to make sure no other cops are around. Johnson's grin broadens.

"Try it. It will ring your ears. And I got plenty more, girl."

Karen feels like running, knowing Johnson ain't no cop no more but the bottle sounded like it's full. With one more look around, she digs into the bottom of her purse and extracts what's left of her Kleenex-wrapped glass stem. Karen wills her hands to quit shaking long enough to pack the rock into the end of the stem. She digs out her best lighter, cups her hand and turns her back to the slight breeze.

Karen hits the pipe hard. Holds the toke in her lungs as long as possible. She blows out the hit and her knees near buckle. And yes, it rings her ears. Wouldn't it be nice to get that whole bottle, she thinks? Fuck that's some damn-good shit. She reaches for the passenger door handle. Hesitates for only a few seconds before opening the door and climbing in. If she has to, to get her hands on the pill bottle, she'll even give the old bastard some pussy, but she sure ain't going to like it none.

"Shut the door, Karen," Johnson says breaking off another piece. "Load me up a hit."

Karen looks askance at him. She ain't never heard of Johnson smoking crack and she don't want him hitting her stem. "I ain't got but this one stem, Johnson."

"You about a dumb bitch. I'll buy you a handful of the goddamned things. Fucking load me a piece!" He smacks the steering with the palm of his hand. "Is the whole fucking world going to hell in a handbasket?" He shakes his head. "Jeez."

"Okay, okay. Look, we can't just smoke dope here in the middle of the street. The cops might roll up on us."

"Yeah, yeah. You would know," he says taking the stem. He's only tried crack a couple of times, but what the fuck. "Give me your lighter, too." Reluctantly, she does. She watches Johnson hit the piece and his eyes go round. Maybe the asshole will have a stroke. Wouldn't that be nice? He doesn't and silently passes the stem back. It's smoking hot to the touch. She rolls it on her jean leg to cool it.

"We can't just sit here, Johnson. But give me a piece okay. You ain't even left a good push, you know."

Johnson's heart is still pounding in his ears as he passes over an entire 20. Karen's suddenly beginning to look appealing to him. He swallows as he puts the truck in gear. Maybe a little pussy ain't out of the question. The thought passes. He chuckles. He's got bigger fish to fry. He's got better plans for Karen. He reaches under his seat for a bottle of Jim Beam. He uncaps it and takes a healthy pull from it. He offers the bottle to Karen.

She reaches for the bottle. Fuck it. Maybe now that he ain't a cop no more, maybe he's a little nicer now. She shakes her head in her own mind. No fucking way. He ain't never going to change. Never forget that girl. Concentrate on what's important: the bottle. Suspicion reasserts itself.

"What's up, Johnson? Why you give me dope?"

Johnson's grin returns. He pats her on the leg. "All in good time, Karen. I've got plans for you to earn this whole bottle. First, let's take a ride."

Porno crosses her mind. She ain't ever made a porno. Hell, she can do that. "Okay," is all she says as Johnson pulls onto the on-ramp to I-35 and they head north.

~~~

"Nothing to report, Igor. Dorbandt neither come nor go," Pavel says.

"Pussy not answer phone," Igor says in response. "What the fuck? Maybe we should whack, da?"

Pavel shrugs. "Da, could be." Maybe takes Igor's mind off Eddie the American and the ex-cop woman he secretly hopes. Though he too, for a moment, wanted to kill the American. He's starting to believe no good would come of it."

"And the American," Igor adds.

Of course.

Igor spits the end of his fresh Cuban to the floor. "Send man to get racks of ribs. Igor feel like eating barbecue ribs. Then we decide who to kill first."

Pavel nods. Of course, he thinks again.

~~~

Amy doesn't wait for Eddie to round the truck and help her down. As nice as the gesture is, it's unnecessary. She reaches back into the truck for the copies of the photo of the mystery woman. "Stay, Bobo," she says before closing the door. "And behave," she adds through the window. She joins Eddie in front of the truck.

"Looks like there's going to be a busy viewing," Eddie says taking Amy's empty hand. Together they walk up the sidewalk leading to the entrance of the funeral home where the viewing is taking place. They're greeted at the door by an elderly somber-looking gentleman who hands them the funeral service pamphlet for the Smiths assuming correctly that they were there on account of the Smiths. The pamphlet directs them to the front parlor, the larger of the home's parlors.

Much like their greeter, the parlor's ambiance is a somber one and a hushed one at that. Holly crosses Eddie's mind. She'll be identified through her DNA at any time meaning yet another funeral and funeral service, albeit one lacking a viewing, Holly being among the decomposed bodies discovered upon Lori's rescue. He swallows as his eyes begin to blur at her memory.

A squeeze of his hand brings him back to the present. Amy draws them to a stop, nods in the direction of the open caskets and an elderly woman paying her respects before the first casket.

They turn to each other. Could it be? They both think in unison. Amy urges them forward. Wouldn't that be something? "Ahem," Amy says softly as they come to stand behind the woman. The woman turns, dabs at her eyes with a tissue.

"Pardon me," the woman says.

It's instantly obvious to both Eddie and Amy. They both deflate with the realization that the woman before them is not the woman in their photo. Amy for a moment is at a loss of something to say, the disappointment having unbalanced her, uncharacteristically so. She regains her balance.

"Sorry to disturb you, but we're unofficially investigating the deaths of Mr. and Mrs. Smith."

"I know who you are. Both of you. Seen you often enough here lately on the news. What's your interest other than having discovered the murders?"

"Would you give us just a moment of your time, please?" Eddie interjects. "Perhaps we could step to the back to talk a sec and let the others come up and pay their respects."

Reluctantly, the woman nods and allows Amy to direct her toward the back. They still haven't answered her question, though she's pretty sure she knows what the pair's interest is. Out of earshot of the others, she once again poses her question.

"Well, again, what's your interest?"

Eddie notices the woman's no longer dabbing at her eyes. Her posture now seems overly formal, almost hostile. Perhaps he's reading her wrong. "Ma'am, we have reason to believe that

Russians were involved in the murders. It's possibly a complicated situation. May I ask your name and your relationship to the deceased?"

"I'm Ellen's mother. My daughter and son-in-law were outstanding members of the community. Obviously, it was a robbery gone wrong. Russians, phew! If you so much as think about slandering their good names, you both will be sued ten ways to Sunday."

The animosity takes Eddie and Amy both aback. "We're sorry for your loss," Amy says. "The last thing we want to do is to bring dishonor to your daughter or your son-in-law. Surely though, you want to catch the killers?"

"That's what we have the police for," she scoffs.

"And routinely they ask the community for help in solving cases like this, ma'am," Eddie softly points out.

Ellen's mother remains deadpan, unmoved.

"Okay," Amy says. She offers a copy of the photo. "If nothing else, perhaps you can tell us who this woman is?"

"Never seen her before," Ellen's mother says a bit too quickly.

Amy sucks in her bottom lip, counts to ten. Unbelievable. They're clearly going nowhere with this woman. She looks at Eddie and shrugs. Eddie returns the shrug. Nods in the direction of the exit. Together they make their way out, photos still in hand. They step back into the day, a beautiful day that's going mostly unnoticed by the people coming and going.

"Thank you for coming," the greeter says.

"If you have a second sir," Eddie says, "I'd like you to take a look at this photo."

The three hover around the photo. Going unobserved, a late-model Audi RS3 slowly passes by on the street out front. The driver, an elderly woman with graying hair clutches at the lapels on her blouse.

"Oh, my goodness," she utters. She recognizes the pair standing before the funeral home. Her heart flutters at the recognition. She attempts to make herself even smaller in her seat and silently prays they won't turn and spot her.

"Sorry," the greeter says. "Haven't seen her as of yet."

Amy frowns, "Hmmm. Okay. Thank you for your time. I'm going to leave this photo with you. Would you please call any of the numbers on the back of the photo if this woman should arrive?"

The Audi takes a right at the end of the block. Disappears from view. And along with the Audi, if not a major clue, some serious answers.

"Sure," the greeter says. "I can surely do that."

With nothing left to do, short of staking the place out, Eddie and Amy head back to the truck. Eddie opens the door for Amy.

"What's the plan now, Detective?" he asks.

"Well, we're dressed nice enough. Buy a woman something to eat?"

Eddie's smile produces the dimple in his cheek. "Is that all you ever think of?"

Amy hikes her skirt to reveal lots of firm thigh. Her mouth forms an O, causing them both to laugh. Shaking his head, Eddie shuts the door and rounds his truck. He's got a live one on his hands and damn if he isn't pleased about that. He knows of a small, high-end Italian joint on South Congress and decides to take Amy there.

"In the back," he tells Bobo, before climbing into the truck. He cranks the truck and they're off again.

~~~

"Whose house is it?" Karen asks. "And why are you pointing it out?"

This stupid bitch never shuts up, Johnson thinks. "That's not important, Karen. Just pay the fuck attention." He turns down a small dirt alley, just beyond the apartments, a block west of Eddie's.

The alley backs up to a number of small businesses and ends in an overgrown lot that's host to a dozen-plus, broken-down vehicles. Johnson does a three-point turnaround and puts the truck in park, nose facing back out the way they entered. He uncaps the pill bottle and shakes out another fat 20, breaks off a corner and passes it over to Karen whose jaw is working overtime when she not talking. She takes the offered dope with a shaky hand.

Karen packs the end of her stem. Damn, the dope is good to her. She can't remember the last time she smoked shit this good. Johnson's up to something no good, she can feel it. Feels the bad vibes that engulf him. And what's up with the house that he pointed out?

Karen hits her stem hard. The dope still rings her ears, but not like the first hit earlier. They've yet to buy the new stems that Johnson promised and she's loath to let him hit hers again. But what can she do? It's his dope after all. She rolls what's left of the stem on her jean leg to cool it. Johnson breaks off another piece for himself. To Karen, it seems, his piece is always bigger. The old fucker. If she can get her hands on the bottle, maybe she can bail on him and run. She fanaticizes about bolting all-the-while intently focusing on her stem. The stupid fuck really doesn't know what he's doing. A waste of perfectly good dope in her opinion. She absently scratches at her arms and old scabs. At 22, Karen appears years beyond her age. Her downward spiral seldom registers these days, so consumed by the crack. She exhales audibly.

"You going to get it too hot. There ain't much stem left, you know. When you going to buy me some more stems like you promised?"

Johnson backhands her causing her to draw up against the passenger door. Fleeing never crosses her mind. Johnson waits for a second for the pounding in his ears to reside. "You about the most talkative bitch. Don't you ever shut the fuck up?" He tosses what's left of the stem out his window and eyes Karen, challenging her to say something. He likes the way she's cowering—making herself small. His cock stirs ever so slightly. He can't remember the last time he was more than remotely interested in pussy. He reaches over and squeezes Karen's right breast hard. She yelps in response causing him to stir a little bit more.

"Lift your shirt. I want to see them tits, girl." Slowly Karen complies. She's not wearing a bra. Her breasts are pert but bruised in spots from one of her previous tricks. Her stomach flat from all the walking and the little nourishment that passes her lips. Johnson grins. Maybe later, he thinks. First things first. He fires up the truck and puts it into gear. First, they'll do another drive by and have a look-see and see if lover boy and his slut have made it back home. And, of course, buy some new glass stems so the stupid bitch will get some act right. His tires spin before gaining purchase.

Foster Cares

268

Chapter Twenty-Three

Igor pats his full belly and belches. He commences picking at his teeth with a wooden toothpick from the dispenser Mikhail pinched from the barbecue joint. He belches once more before kicking back in his recliner. He takes in his men who watch him warily. Inwardly, he smiles. His men should fear him to a degree. A healthy degree, that is. That's only a rightful show of respect, he thinks.

"No movement still at pedophile's?" he asks the room at large.

"No movement, boss," Pavel says. "He just seems to be holed up in his house." Though Pavel hates to say it, he does. "I think Lawyer now a liability." He twirls a big index finger at the side of his head. "I think, lose marbles. Da, maybe time."

Igor nods. Another asset gone bad. He's had a string of bad luck the past few days and it all seemed to start with an altercation with American. "Fuckin' American," he mumbles.

"Huh?" Pavel asks.

"Fuckin' American. Ever since day, things go to shit."

"I don't know, Igor."

"Then what fuck do you know? You tell Igor what fuck you know?"

Pavel raises his hands in surrender. Sometimes Igor is more than just frustrating. Maybe as the Mexicans say, "muy loco." Things are coming to a head and Pavel feels it with all his being. "Fine, Igor. We do whatever you want, da."

"Fucking A," Igor says though he doesn't know exactly what it means. He likes the way it sounds. He slaps the armrest of his recliner. "Fucking A," he repeats. He shoos them. "Give Igor time to think. Then we go kick ass and take names!" He chuckles as his men take their leave. God, he loves America. He interlocks his fingers and covers his heart. Within seconds Igor begins to snore.

~~~

"Well, I have to admit, that was definitely some fine Italian food," Amy says opening the fridge and getting them both a beer. "Expensive, but good. You do realize you have at least one message on your home phone," she adds, nodding in the direction on the blinking answering machine.

Eddie takes the offered beer and joins Amy before the answering machine. "Yeah, I guess I should check it," he says punching the play button.

They sip their beer as Eddie plays the first of his five, new messages. The first three are apparently robocalls. They both wince at the fourth message, each for their own reasons. It's from Lori saying hello and asking that Eddie give her a call. The fifth message gives them both pause. Eddie replays it.

"Please leave us alone," the shaky voice says. "It's the lawyer, Dorbandt, that's part of the real evil. Accept this information in exchange for leaving the innocent be. I beg of you, please."

Amy runs her hands through her hair. Sucks on her bottom lip for a long second. "Huh, now that's strange. Clearly an older woman. You think?"

"I think someone discovered we're looking for her."

"The greeter give us up?"

Eddie takes a sip of his beer. Turns and leans back against the counter. "Possibly..."

"And the lawyer? What's that about? He's clearly not a Russian. Dorbandt. It seems like I've heard that name before."

"I'm actually pretty sure I know who she's referring to. He's a bottom feeder. If you ever met him, you'd know what I'm talking about. He looks like a snake in the grass."

"So, what's the connection here?"

"Russians, a non-English speaking little girl and a bottom-feeding lawyer. It all points to human trafficking. Probably illegal adoptions. And, that's likely the tip of the iceberg. "

"I got the impression the little girl didn't speak Russian either. I wonder where she came from."

"She had blue eyes."

"Which doesn't really tell us anything other than she's valuable." Amy blows out her breath in frustration.

"So, where do we go from here? Share this new information with my former colleagues?"

Eddie sets his beer on the counter. Balances it on its edge. "I can't really tell you what to do, but I say we take a crack at Dorbandt first. As citizens, we don't have to read him his fucking Miranda rights first. "

Amy smiles. "Devious fellow, aren't you."

"Well, when I've got people trying to kill me, I mean us..."

"And beating you up. Don't forget the beating you up part."

Eddie smirks much like Amy does, causing her to laugh. "And there's that. How can I forget that? But it does tend to make me take things personally."

Amy steps in close. Sets her beer on the counter. Unbuttons a button on Eddie's shirt. "I suggest we get out of this formal wear, then follow up on our latest lead." Amy rises up on tiptoes, kisses Eddie on the lips. It sounds like a plan that will work for Eddie.

~~~

Johnson grins at the sight of Eddie's truck in the drive. They're home. Lover-boy and his slut are home. He takes a right at the next crossroad. Circles back around toward Burnet. Karen fidgets in her seat. She, too, noticed the truck in the drive. Something's about to come to a head. By the look of Johnson, he's clearly coming uncorked. If only the dope would stop his heart. Wouldn't that be the shit? Then she could just dump him somewhere and all the dope would be hers.

Johnson turns to eye Karen for a moment. He don't trust the whore much. What's the saying? "Can't make a housewife out of a crack whore." The street whores are devious to say the least. Never trust one, the key. He turns into the 7-11. Digs out a five to hand Karen.

"We need some new Brillo, too. That and maybe a ten-pack of lighters," she says.

"Why don't we advertise we have a truck-load of crack, too, while we're at it."

"I'm just saying. "

Johnson digs out an additional $20. "Get us a 12-pack of Bud, too, while you're at it. You are old enough to buy beer, ain't ya?"

Karen tentatively takes the cash. "Yeah, they don't hardly card me no more." She should take the $25 and bolt, but she knows she won't. Not until she has the dope. She exits the truck.

"Stupid whore," Johnson mumbles as Karen disappears into the store. She does look better from behind, he thinks. The thought of pussy crosses his mind once more. Maybe if he didn't have to look at her, he could actually fuck her. Well, if the old piece would get hard, that is. He snickers. If she makes it back from lover boy's, mission accomplished, he might just get him a good-ol' hardon. Hell, he might even be inclined to kiss the whore. Well, after smoking a little more dope that is. Karen returns with the beer and a small paper bag full of paraphernalia. She pulls the door shut behind her, looks over at the again grinning Johnson. To her, it looks like he's losing it. His hair sticking out in odd places. Whatever he's scheming, it can't be good, she thinks for the umpteenth time.

"What?" he finally asks.

"Let's go... And quit looking at me like that."

Johnson's grin fades. He debates on backhanding the bitch. Who the fuck does she think she is anyway? He reins in his ire. But for his plans for the bitch. Reluctantly, he puts the truck into gear and backs out of his spot. Hell, he may even kill the bitch when things are done. Keep the fucking dope for himself. He grins again, but in a grin that Karen can't see. He'll circle back around to take another look-see to make sure his prey is still at home.

And they are. Johnson has a hard time containing his mirth. He parks once more in the overgrown lot. Kills the engine. Karen's still playing with the Brillo. Burning the copper coating off the shit. Her hands shake so hard the lighter keeps going out. Finally, she appears to be satisfied with Johnson's perspective. He watches her wad a small piece and packs it into the end of a fresh glass stem.

"Well, are you going to give me a piece or what?" Karen says.

She's skating on thin ice, Johnson thinks. He turns and stares a hole in her.

"Don't never forget the nature of our relationship," he says. "You fucking understand me?"

Karen licks her lips. Swallows. "Sorry."

Johnson breaks her off a good half from what would sell on the street as a fat 20. After all, he does need her a little longer.

Karen hits the stem hard. Her head disappears in a cloud of smoke. The hit rings her ears as if a first hit. Her heart pounds in her chest. She cowers in her corner for a good 30 seconds before she can mentally regroup. Johnson snatches the stem from her fingers. Packs him a hit of his own.

"Hey, I was going to rig you up one for yourself."

"Well, you fucking took too long. Let me take this hit and I'll break down our plan," Johnson says.

~~~

"Well, now that you're completely sated, I guess we can roll," Amy says adding a smile.

Eddie returns her smile. "You going to roll with that just-fucked look or are you going to hit that mop with a brush?"

"You know, women pay their hairdressers top dollar for this look."

"But not that added flush. That they have to sleep with me to get."

Amy makes a face. "Right. Nevertheless, that ain't happening."

Eddie turns, hides his expression. "Ooookay, well then," he says stretching it out before turning to face Amy again. "If Dorbandt's address hasn't changed, we might just find the fucker."

Amy frowns. "Not to change the subject, but shouldn't you call Lori?"

Eddie snatches his truck keys off the kitchen counter causing Bobo to prance at his feet. "I'll call her when we get back."

"Awkward," Amy says.

"You're telling me. Calm down, Bobo, you're going."

"Hold his collar for a second. Let me pour Smoky some milk really quickly. Then I guess we'll be set to go." Eddie does while Amy fills the bowl. The meowing, ever-hungry Smoky climbs Amy's pant leg in an effort to get to the milk.

"Jesus," Amy says peeling Smoky from her leg as if he was stuck to her with Velcro. "You'd think we were starving the poor little fellow the way he acts." She sets them both on the floor.

All set, Eddie opens the door for Amy. Bobo barrels past her almost tripping her up.

"Dammit, Bobo! Men, ugh!" They both laugh as they step from the garage and into the day. A dark, ominous cloud picks that exact moment to block the sun. It reminds Eddie of a similar cloud he encountered the day he hooked up with Lori. Eddie starts to say something but thinks better of it. He shakes it off and opens the passenger door for Amy. Bobo beats her in. Jumps over the seat and into the back. Eddie shakes his head. What a dog. He shuts the door after Amy and rounds the truck to his side.

~~~

Johnson waits for the ringing in his ears to subside. Turns in his seat the best he can to face Karen. They're both sweating despite the truck's AC.

"Now listen up, Karen. This is real fucking important. You're going to do exactly as told. And in exchange, you're going to get this whole bottle of dope... You know, I'm going to even sweeten the deal, the pot, because I like you..."

"... You were always harassing me—shaking me down..."

"Would you please shut the fuck up and listen! Jeez! If you do as you're told, you get the dope and all the money in my pocket. Maybe a thousand or better."

Karen swallows and licks her lips. Whatever it is, she already doesn't like it. She waits for Johnson to continue. She watches as he extracts a chrome revolver from under his seat. She vigorously shakes her head no. Johnson could strangle the bitch at the way she's shaking her head and she ain't even heard him out. He takes a long moment to get his thoughts in order. She'll do as he asks. It'll just take a little psychology to get her to act right.

Johnson smiles to himself as he sets the revolver on the seat between them. He uncaps the bottle, shakes himself out a good piece and packs the stem with all of it. It takes a couple of good hits to smoke it up. His plan is to outwait Karen and her needs.

It's a short time coming. Karen begins to fidget in her seat.

"Johnson," she finally manages.

"What? "

"You going to hook me up a piece?" she asks.

Johnson notes the desperation in Karen's voice—notes with satisfaction. That's more fucking like it.

"Here's the deal, Karen. Your free ride is up. You can either sit there and watch me smoke up all your dope or you can listen. Or your final choice, don't let the door hit you in the ass on your way out. Not to mention, you'd have to suck and fuck a hundred motherfuckers just for the money in my pocket."

With a shaky and clammy hand, Karen reaches for her door handle. There's an audible click as the locking mechanism releases. But, try as she may, Karen can't will herself to push the door open.

"Can... Can I have just one more hit? Pleeeaasse!"

That's better. "No!" Karen swallows again, releases the door handle. She ain't got no choice.

"I'm... I'm listening. I'll do it."

Johnson grins. Of course, she will. He pats Karen on a bare leg. "That's better," he says. "It's really simple. You're going to take this revolver here, knock on the folk's house with the truck in the drive, ask if you can use their phone..."

"What if they ain't got no home phone?"

Johnson holds his breath. Blows out his cheeks. "They got a fucking home phone. Again, ask to use their phone and once inside, you're going to pull this revolver from under your shirt and shoot both of them. And then you'll calmly walk out and back to the truck."

"I ain't never killed no one before."

"It's simple, Karen, just point and pull the trigger. People kill each other every day," he says.

Tears cloud Karen's vision. She blinks them back. "Who are they?" Johnson's blood pressure spikes.

"It really doesn't matter, Karen, but for the record, they're white trash. Now take the gun, Karen."

Karen's heart races. Her fear close to debilitating. She ain't never even hurt anyone, much less killed anyone or anything other than a roach or a spider or such.

Change of plan, she thinks. She takes a deep breath. Here goes nothing. She reaches for the revolver. She don't know much about guns, but she's almost certain revolvers don't have safeties.

The revolver's heavy in Karen's hand. She sighs. Here goes nothing, she thinks again, doubling up on the pistol's grip. She cocks the hammer. The audible double-click fills the cab. Karen spins in her seat and levels the gun bringing it to bear on Johnson. The gun shakes in her hands.

"I'll kill you, Johnson! I swear I will! Just... Just give me the dope... Just give me the dope. Keep your money. Please. I mean it, Johnson!"

Johnson slowly turns to face Karen, his expression unreadable. He slowly raises both hands. "Don't shoot, Karen," he says as his expression changes to one of bemusement.

"I mean it! I swear!"

With speed and strength that defies Johnson's age, he swipes grabbing the barrel in a firm grip and twists lifting Karen off her seat. She screams out in pain, her finger caught in the trigger guard.

"Ow! Ow! Ow! You're breaking my finger!"

Johnson twists harder driving the revolver into the seat between them and lifting Karen even farther off her seat by the sheer pain alone.

"Please! Please! Johnson! I give!"

The rewarding snap of the finger doesn't materialize. Reluctantly, Johnson eases off allowing Karen to free her finger and yank her hand free of the revolver. Karen makes to escape. Johnson catches her by the hair with his free hand and pulls her back into the truck.

"Ow! My hair! Let me go!"

"Quit your fucking struggling." Johnson taps Karen on the top her head with the revolver's short-barrel. Not hard enough to inflict real damage, but hard enough to get her attention. Karen grows still. "Karen, Karen, Karen," Johnson says and adds a chuckle. He moves the revolver and presses it against Karen's temple.

Karen squeezes her eyes shut. Johnson pulls the trigger.

The hammer snaps on an empty cylinder.

Karen wets herself and begins to cry in earnest.

Johnson cocks the hammer once more. The double-click of the hammer's tiered action eerily amplified in the truck's cab.

Johnson pulls the trigger.

The hammer snaps on an empty cylinder.

Johnson erupts in laughter. Drops the revolver in Karen's lap. Digs into his front pocket and extracts the revolver's loose rounds. He lets them trickle through his fingers and into her lap.

"You about a dumb cunt, you know that? You think I'd give a crack whore a loaded gun?"

The pungent smell of urine hits Johnson. He grimaces. "Goddammit! Why'd you have to go and piss on yourself? Karen remains mute, silently continues to cry. Johnson pounds the steering wheel in frustration. "Shit," he says. "Had to go and stink up the truck."

Chapter Twenty-Four

Igor yawns wide and shakes himself awake. He reaches for his cigarettes only to find the pack empty. "Motherfucker," he mumbles as he wads the empty pack and tosses it to the floor. He flips the lever collapsing the footrest and rocks himself forward.

"Well?" he says to those present that expectantly watch on.

Mikhail finally bites.

"Well, what?"

"Give Igor fucking cigarette, Moron." Igor snaps his fingers. "And light, Igor need think."

Pavel shakes out one of his own and tosses it to Igor. He leans in and offers a light. Igor inhales deeply, lets out a plume of blue smoke followed by a series of smoke rings. Igor decides.

"Okay, fuck it. Let's pay pedophile visit, da. Erik, you stay."

~~~

"According to the GPS, it should be the house coming up on the right," Eddie says.

"The one with the Mercedes in the drive?"

"Yeah, check out the mailbox. That's it." He pulls to the curb.

"So much for my I-phone. It shows were still a block short," Amy says. Eddie grins—throws the truck into park and raises both hands.

"Well, what can I tell you, you should have bought an android," he says. "He doesn't believe in keeping his yard up, does he?"

"Nor his car. Why do I feel like we've been through this before?"

"Yeah, I feel you. Well, let's see if he's home."

~~~

The phone in Pavel's shirt pocket vibrates. He pulls it out and checks the caller I.D. "Yeah," he answers, then listens for a good 30 seconds. "Hmm. Okay, hold a sec." He covers the mouthpiece and steers with a knee. The news takes some processing. He turns to face Igor.

"You're not going to believe this boss, but the American and the ex-cop just pulled into Dorbandt's drive."

Igor does a double-take. Punches the dash with his good fist. "Fuckin' American! What fuckin' going on, Igor ask? You tell me, Pavel."

"What should I tell Grigori?"

"Stay put. Keep watch. And you, Pavel, get there, hurry!"

~~~

Eddie knocks on the front door. Amy rings the bell and Bobo barks. The TV can be heard from within and nothing else. They wait and try again. Nothing, no answer. Yes, it seems like they've been here before.

"Let's look in the backyard," Eddie says leading the way. They step through a cedar, picket-fence entry. The backyard's in even worse condition than the front. It clearly hasn't been mowed in some time. There's a sliding glass door facing the back patio and it's open 12 inches or so. Off to the right and beyond the clutter, the

282

AC unit is humming. Eddie and Amy stop and look at each other. Bobo shoots through the opening and into the house.

"Bobo!" they both yell. Bobo barks but does not reappear.

"Shit," Eddie says." I don't like this." He pulls his 1911.

Amy extracts her own 9mm.

"I'm with you. I don't like this a bit... Bobo! Damnit boy, get out here!" Amy adds a whistle. Despite this, Bobo fails to materialize.

"That dog. He's probably in there eating something," Eddie says.

Amy almost bites a nail. She quickly drops her hand to her side, hoping Eddie didn't notice. Eddie cautiously sticks his head through the opening.

"Dorbandt... Anyone at home? Hello. Bobo come here now!"

Bobo trots back, an open potato chip bag in his mouth. He drops it before Eddie and paws it spilling out some of the chips. They're instantly wolfed down.

The rear sliding-glass door leads to what's obviously the den. Eddie uses his elbow to open the door wider as Amy crowds in behind him.

"Jesus, what a mess," Amy says. "And it smells like shit, too."

"Or possibly death," Eddie adds. "What do you think?"

"Well, I'm no longer a cop so the fourth amendment no longer applies..."

"There is that."

"I think we better find out the source of the smell."

"I was afraid you'd say that," Eddie says crossing the threshold, his 1911 extended before him.

"I got your back, literally," Amy says. Eddie stops, causing Amy to run into him. He turns to face her for a second.

Amy shrugs and smiles—prods Eddie forward. He shakes his head and continues with his cautious pace. To their right is a short hall leading to what Eddie expects are three bedrooms and a spare bath. The first door is ajar and Eddie eases it open with his boot. It's a cluttered bedroom that looks like it's mostly used for storage. He lets out a breath and continues forward. The smell getting more pronounced with every step.

"I'm not feeling really good about this," Amy says as they come upon the next door. This one, however, is closed.

Eddie uses the tail of his shirt ensuring he leaves no prints. He wonders why he's suddenly worried about prints, but he is.

He slowly turns the knob—hears and feels the bolt disengage.

Again, he eases the door open with his boot, his apprehension mounting.

A home office. An empty home office. Another cluttered room.

Two remaining. Eddie sighs, but continues forward.

Bobo cruises past, disappears into the room at the end of the hall. No doubt the source of his potato chips.

"Damn, it, Bobo," Eddie mumbles. He tries one last hello is anyone home. Nothing.

The next room turns out to be the guest bath. It too is empty. Eddie and Amy eye each other and then eye the door at the end of the hall which they notice is now obviously the source of the smell.

They cautiously continue on. Stop at the quarter-open door.

~~~

"What are they doing now?" Pavel asks Grigori trying to ignore Igor's rants. Igor hasn't shut up since they got the news of the American and ex-cop. Pavel puts his cell on speakerphone hoping to silence Igor temporarily.

"They went through the fence into the backyard two or three minutes ago and haven't come back out," Grigori says.

"YOB tvo-YU mat! Fuck your mother!" Igor yells.

"Huh?" Grigori asks.

"Igor kill both!"

"Stay put," Pavel says. "We're minutes away." He ends the call, steps on the gas a little harder.

~~~

"Are you about done there, Karen?" Johnson asks in a bored tone.

Shit, things aren't going quite as anticipated, Johnson thinks. Not only does the truck now smell like piss but his bandaged knee is beginning to bleed through his trousers. Not to mention, his knee throbs a mite. Karen stops with her struggles. She can't believe the old bastard has such a strong grip. She can't believe she pissed on herself either, but there for a moment, she was sure she was dead. She can still hear the snap of the hammer, a sound she may never forget.

"Okay, Johnson, you win. You can let go of my hair now. I give. I promise."

"Okay, but let's not forget that my gun actually has rounds in it," Johnson says. That's one thing she ain't likely to forget.

"Can we do another hit. You know, so I can get my shit together. I kinda freaked there for a minute."

"You think? But no. You burned up your free dope long ago."

Karen frowns. She really needs a hit to get her mind straight. She extends her shaky hand for Johnson to see.

"I don't think I can even hold the gun straight. I'm just shaking too hard, you know." Johnson' s kind of in the mood for another hit himself. Shit, the crack's kind of good to him, too. Maybe he ain't going to be able to give her the whole bottle. Hell, he ain't got any more. He'll just have to take some out while she's doing the hit on pretty boy and his whore.

"Change of plans. One more hit. Then I'm going to drop you off in front of the house and circle back. Fuck the cameras if there are any. Sometimes, Karen you just have to take one for the team."

Karen eyes Johnson and his inane grin. "I ain't sure what you mean, Johnson. What team? And, how come you want to kill these folks?"

"You've never wanted to kill an asshole or two, Karen?"

Yeah, you. "I mean, sure, but not really, you know."

"Take my word for it and hand me your stem. But this is it, by God. No more fucking around. And, I fucking mean it, Karen."

"Okay, but make it a good one. Killing folks is some really scary shit."

Johnson pats her on her bare leg careful not to get too close to her wet crotch. "You got a deal there, girl."

~~~

"You ready, Amy?" Eddie asks. Amy nods her assent. Eddie draws back a boot and kicks the door open.

Centered in the room is Dorbandt – hanging from the ceiling fan – his face puffy and bloated—his tongue sticking out between blue lips.

The bile rises, nearly gagging Eddie. It's not necessarily the sight of a dead Dorbandt, that gets to Eddie, but the sight of flies that fester the slits of Dorbandt's eyes.

"Jesus," Eddie manages.

"Oh, shit," Amy adds. "Not good. Definitely not good."

"Bobo, get off that bed now!" Bobo looks up from whatever he's chewing and reluctantly hops to the floor. "Amy, I'm not sure, but I think we better get the fuck out of here."

"I think I concur..."

The buzz of a cell phone cuts Amy off. They're both drawn to an end table where a phone does lazy circles and continues to buzz.

The buzzing finally comes to an end. The display reads four missed calls.

"I don't think he's in position to make any returns calls," Eddie says. "I wonder who's calling?" he adds as he uses a knuckle to tap on the screen. Eddie notes that all four missed calls are from the same number and a relatively easy number to associate and remember.

"Forget the phone, let's get the hell out of here while we can." Eddie nods, grabs Bobo by the collar and gives him a good tug in the right direction to get him moving. Bobo drops the brush that he's been chewing on. Eddie picks it off the carpet, deciding it might not be a good idea to leave it behind considering it doesn't appear that Dorbandt has any pets. It's bad enough that Bobo likely left dog hairs on Dorbandt's bed. But it is what it is. Not much he can do about it now.

They exit through the sliding-glass door leaving it slightly open like the way that they found it. They exit the yard and hurry towards the truck.

Nobody appears to have noticed them, a quick look around assures Eddie. There's nothing he can do about any cameras in the area, but Dorbandt's clearly been dead for some time now— his first missed call from earlier that morning.

Eddie forgoes the gentlemanly gesture of opening the door for Amy. Bobo rounds the truck with him and loads up.

The squeal of tires and the roar of an engine causes both Eddie and Amy to turn and look down the street. At first, Eddie thinks it's the cops somehow responding, but then the car speeding toward them registers as a Cadillac. Not only a Cadillac, but a Cadillac with more than one occupant.

Eddie withdraws his 1911 once more. "Get in!" he yells across the truck at Amy.

Amy wastes no time getting in, clearly recognizing the threat. Their doors slam simultaneously.

The diesel rumbles to life.

Amy spins in her seat. "Oh, shit! Go, Eddie!"

Eddie shifts the truck into drive—slams down on the accelerator.

The squeal of the Cadillac's protesting rubber drowns out the diesel's roar.

The Cadillac fills Eddie's rearview.

Eddie raises a protective arm between Amy and the dash. He braces for the impact.

The truck's tires gain traction—the impact fails to materialize. The Cadillac's doors fly open.

Four men exit.

"Duck!" Eddie screams as the Cadillac diminishes in size in his rearview.

The pops are barely discernible.

The truck's rear window implodes—the windshield spiders.

Eddie winces at the sound of every pop and the new hole in his windshield.

Got to get out of the line of fire, Eddie thinks as his adrenaline spikes and his body's flight mode kicks into high gear.

Eddie lays hard on the brakes as the next intersection nears.

The truck shudders as the big tires fight for grip. Bobo yelps as he's flung to the other side of the truck. Eddie steers into the turn, bounces off the curb and straightens the truck out.

Amy scrambles to pull herself from the floorboard. She comes up with automatic in hand. "Shit!" She turns in her seat once more. Looks for the Cadillac through the missing rear glass. "What the fuck have we gotten ourselves into?"

"Get ready because I'm not going to be able to shake them," Eddie yells over the roar of the diesel. He steals glances at his rearview. Cocks the hammer on his 1911. "Oh, shit! They've rounded the corner."

"Fuck 'em, Eddie! Stop the truck!" Amy braces herself against the dash as Eddie slams on the brakes.

The truck shudders again as the big tires bark and squeal but rein the truck in. She's right, they have to make a stand.

Eddie spins in his seat. Levels his 1911.

The Cadillac's coming strong, but only one occupant hangs out the window with a pistol drawn.

Booms fill the cab. Spent cartridges ping off the truck 's interior. Holes punch through the Cadillac's windshield.

Igor takes a round through his right shoulder, drops his automatic and sings out. "y e-BA-tsa-SRA-tsa! Fuckin' Shit!"

Mikhail slumps over in his back seat.

A front tire blows—the steering wheel spins in Pavel's hands.

The Cadillac follows suit, spins and clips a parked car—crosses the street and slams into another parked car.

The deployed airbag knocks the wind out of Pavel. He struggles to push it out of his way so that he can see what's happening. The shooting's stopped. He realizes that Igor's moaning and clutching his shoulder. Pavel's surprised that he hasn't been hit, all the rounds the Cadillac's taken. He pulls on the door handle and leans his considerable weight into the door. The door protests with a screech but opens. Pavel tumbles out and onto the hot pavement. He rolls partially under the vehicle to shield himself. He draws his automatic.

"Holy shit!" Amy says slapping a new mag into her 9mm.

She glances over at Eddie. "You alright?"

"Yeah. Uh-oh. It may be reinforcements. You see the Explorer?"

"No doubt. Matches the description of the SUV casing your house."

"And, at least the driver made it out. I'm pretty sure he exited the car. Suggestions?"

"Let's get the fuck out of here, Eddie." Not having his spare mag, that sounds like a rational plan to Eddie. He romps back down on the accelerator pinning them both back into their seats. Bobo yelps once more as he's flung around once again.

Foster Cares

Chapter Twenty-Five

Grigori's Ford Explorer slides to a stop behind the wrecked Cadillac.

Already, the house curtains are being drawn. He can't believe what he just witnessed. He exits the car in a crouch but can already see that the American and his whore are leaving the scene.

"They're gone, Pavel," he says. Pavel stands, looks back inside their car. Igor's clutching his shoulder and moaning. Mikhail, in the back, is slumped over but still breathing. But their fourth man, Hugo, took a round right between the eyes and he's clearly dead as all get-out. Pavel's not exactly sure what that means, other than he knows it means extremely dead.

Pavel reaches into the car and grabs ahold of a big chunk on Igor's shirt. He's tempted to leave him behind, but just barely. He really does owe Igor in more than one way. He sighs, such is life.

"Get Mikhail. We need to go, now!"

Grigori yanks the door open and reaches in for Mikhail. Mikhail's bleeding profusely from the head, but he is in fact breathing. Mikhail's right ear flaps as if barely held on. Grigori pulls him from the car and drags him to the Ford.

Pavel helps Igor into the Explorer and slams the door shut behind him. He helps Grigori with Mikhail. Works him into the back of the SUV. "Get in," he orders Grigori. "Tend to Mikhail. Make sure he lives, da."

Pavel backs the Explorer up a good 30 yards, puts it back into park and casually exits the vehicle. He levels his Barretta just below the Cadillac's rear bumper and fires off a round. He's rewarded with a stream of gasoline. He sparks the next round off the asphalt. The ensuing wave of heat rocks Pavel. The ensuing flame engulfs the rear of the Cadillac.

Pavel hops back into the Ford and gives the flaming Caddy a wide berth. This is not good, he thinks. This escalates things with the American and the ex-cop to a whole other level. He removes his belt and hands it over to Igor.

"Cut off the bleeding, Igor, while I make this call."

~~~

Amy pats her chest. "I think that was scarier than the shootout with Johnson."

Eddie shakes his shirt out. Several spent cartridges fall out. "I think every one of your ejected shells hit me somewhere. And I'm here to tell you, they're quite hot against bare skin." He leans across the seat to check on Bobo. Eddie lets out his breath in relief. Bobo appears to be just fine. "I think it's safe to get out of the floorboard now, Bobo." Bobo decides to remain where he is for now.

Amy blows out her cheeks trying to get her ears to pop. "He probably can't hear you. My ears are still ringing. Probably be deaf for a week."

"I hear you, no pun intended." Eddie smiles. "You made the right call. We sure couldn't have outrun them."

"Head back to the scene. I think I hear approaching sirens." She turns to stare out the missing rear window. "I see smoke, too.

Maybe the bastards burned up." She turns back. Digs her phone out of her purse." I guess I'll call it in. Not 911, but to Howard."

"You going to tell him about Dorbandt?"

"I think I'm going to just suggest a welfare check."

"Devious woman."

"Thanks." They share a laugh in relief. It's amazing what survival will do for one's outlook in life, Eddie thinks, having experienced yet another brush with death. He counts the holes in his windshield, six. Combined, he and Amy shot 22 rounds and in the confines of a truck, it was not a pleasant experience. Eddie pulls to the curb a good half-mile from the scene. He taps Amy on the shoulder.

"Be sure and get Howard to notify dispatch that we're returning to the scene. We don't want to be shot by over-zealous friendlies."

Amy covers the mouthpiece for a second. "Already done. They'll be expecting us." She goes back to talking with Howard, Eddie only privy to her side of the conversation. He pulls away from the curb. Additional sirens can be heard in the distance. Amy ends the call.

"They put out an APB on the Explorer, again. I'm assuming it's the same Explorer that was keeping tabs on your house, Eddie."

"It fits the description."

They come to the intersection two blocks up from Dorbandt's and take a right. A half-dozen cop cars and one fire truck have already arrived. Soon the media, too. Here we go again, Eddie thinks. Amy's expression mirrors his for she's thinking the same thing.

~~~

The big hit renews Karen's jitters. She's once more antsy in her seat. Worse even, she smells of piss. She can't believe she went and pissed on herself. But damn if she didn't think she was dead there for a moment. She looks over at Johnson expectantly. Time's running out and she does really need that dope. And a thousand dollars, too. With that, she can rent herself a nice room and layup and smoke for a week.

"You about ready?" Johnson asks. She nods her head meekly. Not an encouraging sign. In retrospect, it ain't much of a plan. But nothing ventured—nothing gained. He puts the truck into drive.

"Let's do this... Oh, and you can put the shells in the pistol when I let you out."

"What if they look outside and see me with the gun?"

"They're probably in the house screwing their eyes out. Hell, I don't know, Karen. Jeez."

Johnson makes a right, turns on Eddie's street. His blood pressure spikes. Eddie's fucking driveway is empty. The motherfuckers ain't even home. He blows the horn in frustration.

Karen. It's all Karen's fault. All her bullshitting around. His jaws clench. He pulls his 9mm and cocks the hammer and points it at the cowering whore.

Johnson begins to hyperventilate. Dust motes appear in his peripheral vision. A sharp pain in his chest seizes him. His gun begins to waver. His foot slips from the gas pedal. The truck slows to a crawl. Johnson's non-gun hand clutches the swatch of shirt covering his heart. Karen stares at him slack-jawed.

"Johnson... Johnson, you okay?" Karen eyes the pill bottle. It's on the far side of Johnson between him and his door. Could it possibly be? Could the old bastard be having a heart attack?

"Johnson?" she tries again. Karen draws in a deep breath. This is what she prayed for after all. Well, not really prayed for, but kinda. She dares to reach over and shift the truck into park. The truck rocks back and forth for a few seconds. Johnson rocks with the truck.

Karen's afraid she may have her own heart attack the way her heart's beating. The pill bottle's so close but so far away. She swallows. She'll have to reach across Johnson's lap putting her awfully close to Johnson.

"Shit, do something, Karen," she tells herself. "You're parked right in the middle of the road."

Fuck it, Karen thinks. Can't just sit here. She bends over, reaches across Johnson.

Johnson's pain is blinding but not debilitating. He'll be damned if he lets the whore get his dope.

Karen's fingers touch the bottle, pushing it farther out of reach.

Johnson reacts, elbows Karen in the forehead driving her back to her side of the truck. She cries out.

"Ow!" Karen's eyes instantly water. She feels blindly for the door handle in yet another attempt to escape.

Once more Johnson's too quick for her and snatches her by the hair yet again and forces her head into the seat next to him. He puts the truck into drive and romps on the gas pedal.

"Don't make me break your neck, Karen! I ain't playing around!"

Karen's struggles slowly while Johnson drives. "That's better," he says as the pain in his chest slowly lessens. He's not sure what happened to him, but damn if it didn't hurt. He releases Karen's hair. She moves to sit up.

"I guess it's a change of plans… Temporary change of plans," Johnson says.

~~~

The garage door rattles shut behind them. Igor still moans from the passenger seat. Pavel looks over at him. Igor's ashen and his beady eyes are glazed. He might not make it, Pavel thinks, as he exits the Explorer and rounds the truck to Igor's side. He yanks the door open and has to catch Igor as he tumbles out. He lifts him as if he weighed nothing. The men waiting on them move out of Pavel's way and fall in behind him.

"Is the doc here, yet?" Pavel asks as he lowers Igor onto the cleanest bed in the warehouse, his own. Their main warehouse man, Kirill, appears almost as ashen as Igor.

"Not yet."

"Why the fuck not?"

"Umm, they say he's in surgery. I paged him." He shrugs, "That's the best I can do, but the midwife should be here any minute."

"Midwife," Pavel murmurs. "So be it. We'll have to make do. Get Pavel several units of plasma and the two AB positive and make sure you get the right ones."

"Here she is…"

"And the IV setup. Hurry, da."

The midwife looks frightened, even more so when she sees who the wounded man is. She makes the sign of the cross before hurrying to Igor's side. She digs out a pair of scissors and begins cutting away Igor's shirt.

"Hold him down, Senor, please," she says. "Maybe have something for pain. Si?"

Kirill returns with all the requested items. Being in the business they're in, they've prepared for most contingencies including the occasional gunshot wound. Kirill hands over the medkit and begins setting up the IV. Pavel rummages through the kit and comes up with a vial of morphine and a package of U-100 syringes. He passes both to the midwife and resumes holding Igor down.

"This is good, Senor, the bullet passed straight through." She probes some more. "No, hit bone, Si." She draws some morphine and expertly hits a vein. Igor's sigh fills the room. His eyes roll up in his head and the next moan dies on his lips. But his chest continues to rise and fall. Kirill tears the packaging on a catheter and gives it to the midwife. She inserts the needle in Igor's right hand and attaches the first unit of blood.

"Now we clean and stitch wounds, si, Senor. Then I can do no more. He be in Jesus' hands then, si."

Pavel watches over Igor while the midwife cleans, stitches and dresses the wounds. Mikhail has regained consciousness and joins the fray. He's holding a towel to his ear.

"Is he going to make it?" Mikhail asks.

"He should, considering. You?"

"Yeah, the ear's nearly shot off." He turns toward the midwife. "Mexican, go wash your hands and then stitch this ear back on. Then pray I don't lose this ear." He turns back toward Pavel. "You know, things have really turned to shit here lately." He nods at the inert Igor. "Igor's obsessions will get us all killed someday, do you not realize that, Pavel?"

"This American and ex-cop bring us much bad luck. Da, things go to shit, but what can we do now but kill the pair? What choice do we have?"

"Yes, we have no choice now. Unfortunately, it's now a matter of honor. We must make plans, da."

~~~

Nothing but the charred hulk of the Cadillac remains. Eddie and Amy are still on the scene two hours after the fact. Still answering the same old questions.

Amy throws her hands to her hips. Puffs out her cheeks in frustration. "I can assure you, Detective, we're not holding anything back and again, no, I don't know who the dead guy in the car is."

"But, again, you suspect whoever it is likely was hit by a round fired by you or Mr. Winston?"

"That is what I said, isn't it?" Amy glances at her watch. "Look, I'm not trying to be rude or uncooperative here, but we're going in circles. How about giving me your card and we'll call you if we can think of anything else."

"That was a lot of rounds you two shot considering this is a residential neighborhood."

"Is that a question or a statement?"

"It just seems reckless."

"So were the guys shooting at us. And, I am thankful that there wasn't any collateral damage." She checks her watch again. "Look, that's all the questions for today." Amy turns her back to the detective and motions Eddie over. She brings up her Uber app to summons them a ride. She's never actually used Uber before but seeing how Eddie's truck, or what's left of it, is being impounded, it seems like a viable option. "We're out of here," she tells Eddie.

"Well, that seems to have gone over well," Eddie says.

Amy bends to scratch Bobo behind the ears. "That's Williamson County for you. Cross over from Travis County and you're in a whole other world." The marked weight loss of her purse reminds her. "We need to stop by my house for my backup. I feel naked without my weapon."

"I hope you have a second backup."

Amy frowns. "Sorry. But I do have an old Mossberg pump my ex left behind out of..." She makes the finger quotes... "'concern' for my safety."

"Considerate."

"Yeah, a, real considerate bastard." They both laugh. "Here comes our ride," Amy adds.

"I still don't see why they took our weapons."

"I guess they figure we'll sleep better knowing who killed the shmuck in the Caddy. Actually, Eddie, it's not that uncommon. I've even done it on occasion, but usually only if the righteousness of the shooting is in question."

Eddie opens a rear door to the Chevy Bolt that is their ride. Bobo beats her in. They both shake their heads. Bobo.

The Uber driver is a talkative fellow, but Amy's quick to shut him down explaining that they've been instructed not to discuss the case. They have the driver drop them off at Covert Cadillac/GMC on the Motor Mile. Might as well, Eddie thinks, considering there's not much left of his current truck. It doesn't take Amy long to figure out Eddie is a no-nonsense shopper. He simply points out the truck he wants, calculates 20% off the MSRP and makes the salesman the cash offer. And, the truck is a beauty, another four-wheel drive GMC crew cab loaded to the gills. Even the unique teal color is beautiful, Amy thinks. And she sure wouldn't mind shopping in the same manner, however unlikely that might be for her. She shrugs. One never knows though, does one? Amy loops her arm through Eddie's. Yep, one never knows. Little does she know, but Eddie plans to buy her the Cadillac of her choice, but based upon the time of day, just not today. He smiles at the thought of Amy carefully viewing half the cars on the lot.

"What are you smiling at?" Amy asks.

"The most beautiful gal in Austin. "

Amy feigns looking all around before smacking herself in the forehead. "How silly of me—that would be I." They both laugh. Life can be good, especially during the breaks between everyone trying to kill you.

Chapter Twenty-Six

Karen eyes the house nervously as Johnson pulls into the drive. She fidgets in her seat. "What we doing here? Who lives here?"

Johnson stares across at her with contempt. "I do, you idiot."

"What we doing here?"

"You pissed all over yourself. You'd think you'd want to clean up," he says throwing the truck into park. "Not to mention, you stink."

"I ain't got no extra clothes."

"Duh. You don't think I have a washer and dryer?" He opens his door. The pill bottle drops to the drive. Johnson eases out. Shit, he doesn't know if he can bend enough to reach the bottle, but hell, he can't chance Karen with it because there's not a doubt in his mind that with the pill bottle in needy hand, she'll run on him. "Fucking knee. Fucking Foster." Johnson bends at the waist the best he can and in the moment of searing pain, he's just able to grasp the bottle. He buries the bottle deep in his front pocket as Karen slowly rounds the front of the truck.

Johnson can't temporarily speak. He nods in the direction of the open garage. Karen once again resigns herself to the fact that she can't live without another hit. Her shoulders slump as she shuffles toward the entrance. Johnson limps in after her, each step resulting in a wince. He'll have to be extra careful once inside the house. He doesn't trust Karen as far as he can throw her. He chuckles and at the moment he couldn't toss her across his own bed. Not that he'd really want to, well, absent a little ol' hit that is.

~~~

"Pavel, come. He's waking up," Mikhail calls out, thinking all the while, why couldn't the fucking GOP-nik, thug, just went and died.

Pavel moves to join Mikhail next to Igor's bed. "Da, his color's beginning to look good, too." Igor's eyes are somewhat cloudy, but he's clearly coming to. "How you feeling to-VA-risch, comrade," he says.

"LU-chshe vsyeky! Couldn't be better," Igor says struggling to get up. "Now we go kill American and whore." He snaps his finger. "TV, turn up, hurry!"

Mikhail does so as the camera pans to Dorbandt's house and the news reporter on the scene who continues with her story. They listen slack-jawed as the few details of the death of the currently unnamed deceased are given.

Igor rubs both hands down the stubble of his chin. Shit, fuckin' pedophile is dead. He shrugs—so be it. He never like sniffling slime ball no how. "Pavel, destroy phone now. Hmm, okay, Igor think. What news on shootout while Igor under?"

"They report only an investigation is underway," Pavel says.

"Okey-dokey," Igor says chuckles and winces in pain. "Maybe a little more medicine and Igor good, da?" Despite the situation, he's feeling euphoric but doesn't recognize it for what it is, the morphine. He eyes his Russian-made watch. "Prepare to kill American and whore!"

~~~

Eddie sets the Mossberg and box of birdshot on the kitchen counter and snatches Smoky off the floor. "So, your plan was to defend la casa, if need arose, with birdshot?" he says with mock incredulity.

Amy smirks. "I told you my ex was a considerate bastard. He bought the shotgun and the ammo. He was probably already saving up for his mid-life crisis—red convertible Corvette and blond bombshell. "

"She is a looker—I give her that."

Amy makes another face. "I think you're missing the point here."

"Oh?" Eddie innocently says.

"Right. Good one. Anyway, now that you're standing next to the phone, why don't you give Lori a call."

"I've been procrastinating. Can't you tell?"

"I figured as much. It feels equally awkward for me, too."

Eddie takes a deep breath and exhales. He lifts the phone from its base and dials, secretly hoping that Lori doesn't answer—she does.

"Hey, Eddie. Thanks for calling back."

Eddie hits the speakerphone button and sets the phone back on its base.

"Hey, Lori. How are..."

"You have me on speakerphone?"

Amy clears her throat, "Hey, Lori, it's Amy. How are you doing?"

"Recovering, but lonely."

"Ouch."

"Yeah, I guess I didn't think things through."

Amy looks over at Eddie and mouths a little help here. Eddie grows hot at the temples. The last thing he wants to do is hurt either woman. He's crazy about both and perhaps he shouldn't have rushed into a new relationship with Amy. But he was in desperate need of someone in his life and vulnerable. The silence drags on for a long moment. Amy steps over and gives him a nudge.

"Lori, I'm kind of at a loss for words here. You're young, beautiful, thoughtful. You have your whole life ahead of you and I'm old and a borderline alcoholic..."

"I don't care about all of that. You're a great guy. Never cut yourself short..."

"Okay..."

"...But I've put you in an impossible bind." Lori sighs heavily. "I'm coming back to Austin and I still want to be part of your life and if that includes Amy, so be it. She's a great person. By the way, you're a great person, Amy."

"Thanks."

"So, I guess I'll be seeing both of you soon. Please try to be careful. I'm not sure what's going on, but you two refuse to stay out of the news. Yes, I've been following the Austin news. It's easy enough to do these days. I stream it right to my phone. Anyway, I guess I better let you two go. I'll be seeing y'all soon. Later."

"Bye, Lori."

Eddie punches the end button. "Phew!"

"You handled it better than I could have."

"Yeah, real smooth," Eddie says causing them both to laugh.

Amy sits down at the kitchen table and flips open her computer. "I think I'll check my e-mail and then maybe call Howard, see if he's learned anything new."

"Sounds like a plan."

~~~

"You have anything for me to wear while my clothes dry. I don't like being naked."

"Jeez, you're a whore for Christ's sake. That's what you do. You get naked for a living."

Karen hugs herself, "Well, it's cold in here."

"Help me out of these trousers and then I need you to tend to this wounded knee. Clean it and patch me back up."

Trousers equal dope, Karen thinks to herself.

"And, I took the opportunity to stash the dope while you were showering, so you can get that out of your head. I know what you're thinking, Karen. I know before you do. Now help me out of these damn things and let's get this show on the road."

"What about a pick-me-up?"

"Duh, you about a dumb bitch. I kept us out a couple of rocks. But in order for you to get the whole bottle, you better make damn sure nothing happens to me. Now hurry up and help me with these."

Karen gives the cuffs of the trousers a couple of good tugs and off they come. The smell almost knocks her down. Johnson's tighty whities are no longer so white. In fact, the front of the briefs is entirely pissed-stained yellow.

"Help me with my underwear, too. Then, go in the bedroom and get me a clean pair of underwear."

Karen does her best to hold her breath. She's afraid she will be sick. Reluctantly she grabs as little of the underwear as she possibly can and still be able to get them off. She gives them a pull and they actually stick for a second, front and back.

Karen flees the room as her gorge rises. She drops the briefs en route to the bathroom and just barely makes it through the door before she begins to dry heave, there being essentially nothing in her stomach to expel. She opts for hanging her head over the tub having previously witnessed what the toilet bowl looked like.

Slowly, she catches her breath. Karen wipes the tears from her eyes. She not sure if she's ever smelled anything so bad. Rotten fish comes to mind. She shudders at the memory. Damn, if she doesn't need that hit now.

Karen's surprised that she's able to find a clean pair of underwear. She finds a bucket. Fills it with hot soapy water and grabs the largest, cleanest, looking towel that she can find and rejoins Johnson in the living room. Here she finds Johnson with his eyes round but dick so limp it reminds her of a frightened turtle. At least that's something to be thankful about. After a master blast from her well-packed stem, Karen sets to work cleaning the stinking bastard. It makes her wonder how anyone could work in the hospice field. Shit, she'd rather suck a dick as sad as that sounds. It takes Karen a good ten minutes to get Johnson cleaned, patched and redressed.

"Shit, you did good, Karen. When our little business is concluded I have a half a mind to let you hang around a bit."

Not a chance in hell, Karen keeps to herself. "Sure, whatever."

"Now don't go and get all uppity on me girl. I ain't got much tolerance for that. Get dressed. It's time we check up on lover boy and his whore."

"Who'd you say they were?"

"I didn't. I said go get dressed. It's time to go. And fetch a bottle of vodka out of the freezer. I need a little something to take the edge off."

~~~

Another hour passes and Igor's color continues to improve along with his mood. "It will be dark very soon now. It is time to go," he announces. "Bring Igor flak jacket and extra pistol and shoulder holster."

Pavel shakes his head. "Igor, we take care of American. You stay and rest up. Get your strength back."

Igor fists himself in the chest. "You think Igor pussy?"

Pavel sighs. His big shoulders sag. "Of course not. It's only that you've just been shot. You need to regain your strength."

"And who shot Igor? Da, that's what Igor thought." He pounds his chest once more. "Igor go, you stay."

Pavel throws up his hands. "Okay, fuck it, go. Erik, bring Igor what he requested."

"And your flak jacket?" Erik asks.

"Nyet. This time American not get away. I plan to kill him with my bare hands. I won't get shot."

"Okay, be right back." But personally, Erik plans to hedge his bet against getting shot and wear his vest. He smiles as he walks off.

This whole situation may prove an opportunity for him. Out of earshot, Erik chuckles. His stupid brother-in-law may die yet.

~~~

"Bingo!" Amy says tapping her finger at the photo on the screen of her I-Mac.

Eddie finishes rinsing Bobo's bowl, sets it back on the floor. "What?" he asks moving to Amy's side.

"Just received an e-mail in response to one of my own. We have a potential name for our mystery woman."

"Oh, yeah? We have a name, huh?"

"Well, almost. According to this e-mail, the mystery woman is the half-sister of the deceased's mother, but we still don't have a name. Mr. Smith's mother, that is."

Eddie pulls up the chair next to Amy and sits. "Now, why would Ellen's mother lie to us?"

"That's the $64,000 question. Is that the right number for the saying: $64,000?"

"I believe so, but I don't know its origin. So, at least we have another clue, if the e-mailer is correct."

Amy stifles a yawn. "It would seem. Hmm, don't know why I'm yawning. You want me to fix something for dinner?"

"No hurry as long as it includes a big juicy steak and a dessert."

"Moi?"

"Well, you're juicy enough, but I wouldn't say chewy as steak."

Amy elbows Eddie in the side. "I'm the dessert, you idiot."

Eddie leans in a kisses Amy on the cheek. "And that's why I love your pumpkin," he says causing both of them to laugh.

~~~

"Now, you know what to do, right?"

"But most people don't even have home phones anymore these days."

"Karen, goddammit. Tell them you need to use the fucking shitter for all I care. Just get your ass inside and take care of them. But anyhow, they do have a fucking phone, too. If the number in my old phone book is any good, that is."

Johnson turns left off of Burnet Road and onto Eddie's street. He's overcome with joy when he spots the big truck in Eddie's drive. Not a truck he's seen before, but no doubt Eddie's.

"They're home!" Johnson announces.

Karen nearly wets herself. Her bowels turn watery. She hopes she don't shit on herself. But what choice does she have? Johnson left the dope back at his house.

Johnson pulls to the curb 50 yards shy of Eddie's drive. "Hold the revolver by your leg as you load it. We don't want anyone to see you or call the cops. I'll circle around in a few to get you."

With trepidation like she's never experienced before in her life, Karen steps from the truck as Johnson drives away leaving Karen feeling naked and exposed. Fortunately, no one would likely recognize her in this part of town.

Karen fumbles with the shells, drops one, before managing to get five rounds inserted. She snaps the cylinder shut against her leg and tucks the revolver under her shirt and in her waistband.

Karen takes a deep breath and takes off walking the short distance to the house with the truck in the drive.

Karen's heart pounds in her ears. She cuts across the lawn to get to the front door that fronts the intersecting street.

Karen raises her fist to knock.

Bobo barks—skitters from the kitchen. His paws vie for traction on the slick, tile floor. Eddie and Amy laugh.

"Must be a friendly," Eddie muses out loud. "We know he doesn't bark when there's danger."

"You trained him well," Amy says shaking her head in amusement.

Eddie sets the shotgun on the table and together they go to see who it is.

"You don't think Lori is already in town, do you?" Amy asks.

Eddie shrugs.

Karen knocks.

Bobo barks.

~~~

Two miles north of Eddie's, a Ford Explorer with five Russians within take a left on Burnet and head south, it's occupants busy double-checking their gear.

~~~

Amy holds Bobo back by the collar as Eddie opens the front door to reveal the young blond outside. He pushes the screen door open. "Can I help you?"

Beyond Eddie, Amy's brow bunches. She of course recognizes the young prostitute Karen and the recognition is mutual. Amy steps nearer the door, her puzzlement evident.

"Karen, what in the world are you doing here?"

The last person Karen expected to see is Detective Foster and her surprise is also evident. "Detective, I... I... Was put out on the corner..."

"Yes?"

Oh my God! Johnson wants me to kill his partner. I can't kill her. She's always been nice to me. And the man, he looks really nice, too. I can't kill him. But... But I have to. I need the dope. Karen hugs herself. Boy, does she need the dope.

"Karen, are you alright? Are you high or something?"

I'm sorry, Detective, but I have to. God forgive me. "Um... I really need to use the bathroom."

"How'd you get here?"

Karen looks over her shoulder. "The man dropped me off. I didn't want to do what he wanted me to. Can I come in, please!"

Eddie pushes the door open wider, steps aside to allow her to enter. The coolness of the room raises goosebumps on Karen's bare arms. She hugs herself tighter. The revolver digs into her gut reminding her of the enormity of what she's about to undertake. Suddenly, she does need to go to the bathroom and needs to do so something fierce. She steps from foot-to-foot, her eyes scanning the room.

"Please, I really have to go."

Amy points. "Through the door to your left. First door on your right. Then we need to talk, Karen."

Karen nods meekly and hurries off.

Eddie and Amy look at each other and shrug.

~~~

A mile out, a Ford Explorer with five Russians within weave in and out of the evening traffic.

~~~

Johnson eyes the clock on the truck's dash. It's been five minutes now since he dropped Karen off and he'll be circling around for the second time. Shit, fucking whore. He smacks the steering wheel and runs his hands through his thinning hair. Of course, she'd fuck up a wet dream. What the fuck was he thinking, sending a whore to do a man's job. Who's the idiot here? You Johnson. He smacks the steering wheel again. One more pass and by God, he'll take care of the situation himself. He takes a long pull from his vodka. There'll be no turning back then. He'll have to gather what cash he has and hit the road. So be it, he decides. At least justice will prevail.

~~~

Karen's bowels turn to water. She just makes the toilet in time. Why does it have to be Detective Foster? Why couldn't it have been someone who she didn't know? And the man? What could he have possibly done to Johnson to want him dead? The revolver looks ominous at her feet. How could her life have gone so wrong? Karen sighs heavily and flushes the toilet. What choice does she really have? Life's been so unfair.

Karen plucks the revolver off the floor and tucks it back under her shirt. She'll try and make it as painless as possible for the pair. Maybe after the bottle of dope is all gone, she'll check herself into rehab and quit the crack for good. Right, who you kidding, Karen? You'll always be a junkie and a street prostitute.

Karen takes a deep breath and steps from the bathroom. She can hear Detective Foster and the man talking in the living room but can't make out what they're saying. She'll just pull the pistol and shoot them both dead and then get the hell out of here.

Karen rejoins the pair in the living room.

"Karen..." Amy begins.

Bobo shakes Amy's grip, bounds over to Karen and jumps up on her dislodging the revolver in the process.

The revolver thuds to the carpet. All eyes are drawn to the weapon.

The brakes squeal as the Ford Explorer pulls to the curb just beyond Eddie's drive.

Bobo barks and jumps atop the couch and parts the new curtains with a paw.

Eddie turns in reflex. Spots the Explorer through the gap in the curtains.

"Shit! We've got company!" Eddie yells out. He scrambles for the dropped revolver.

"Shit!" Amy echoes as the threat registers. Karen's frozen in place. Johnson?

Four men exit the Explorer with weapons drawn. Igor's hyped and clearly in his element once more.

"Erik, breach the rear. Pavel, front door and Kirill, you come with me. We'll enter through the garage." Igor eyes his watch. "T-minus 20 seconds, let's go!"

Igor spots the curtain's movement and brings his silenced automatic to bear. He systematically empties his magazine into the four living room windows as he casually crosses the lawn en route to the yawning garage doors that are seemingly always open.

"Duck!" Amy screams, at the sound of broken glass and the sight of the puffing curtains. She tackles the frozen Karen and takes her to the ground as holes materialize and pucker the wall opposite the windows.

"Go! Go! Go to our bedroom now!" Eddie frantically urges. "Stay down! Crawl dammit! Now!"

"My pistol's in my purse in the kitchen!"

Eddie scampers from the living room and into the kitchen. He snatches Amy's purse off the table and tosses it to her. "Go! Dammit!"

Staying low, Eddie snatches up the shotgun, as well. Pumps a round into its breach. Blindly, he feels for the box of shells knocking the box to the floor. The box bursts scattering shells across the kitchen floor. "Shit!" He gathers a few of the closest and stuffs them into his front pocket.

Johnson takes his foot off the accelerator as he watches the scene down the road unfold before his very eyes. He chuckles, "Holy crap!" He smacks the steering wheel again, but this time in total amazement. Eddie's house is under assault. He looks through his windshield to the sky. Talk about divine intervention. There truly is a God. And what a beautiful thing it is indeed, he thinks. He'll just ride in and mop things up. What a fucking break! He might even come out of this like he rode in to save the day!

Pavel literally tears the screen door off its hinges. He raises a massive boot and gives the inner door a kick near the knob that would make a mule proud, splintering the door and banging it off the inner wall. He rolls through the opening and comes up automatic at ready.

The living room's empty.

The sound of the shattering living room door has Eddie on nerve but at ready. Inanely, he recalls that the door wasn't even locked.

Slowly, Eddie begins backing down the hallway toward the bedroom.

The kitchen door bangs open.

Like the sacrificial lamb, Igor pushes Kirill through the opening. Sensing where the kitchen door is from his current position, Eddie puts two rounds from the revolver in that direction.

The boom in the confined hallway is deafening.

Through the walls, three guns open up in his perceived direction. The walls on both sides of Eddie pucker with holes. Chunks of sheetrock and dust rain down. His walls offer him no real protection. Eddie continues his scamper backward toward the bedroom.

Amy peers around the doorjamb. "Hurry Eddie! I have you covered!"

The last 15 feet seem an eternity away. Eddie turns and raises to a crouch.

He bolts for the door.

Eddie draws up short as a figure fills one of his bedroom windows.

With a one-handed grip, Eddie raises the Mossberg and pulls the trigger.

The shotgun bucks in his hand. The recoil nearly tearing it from his hand.

The boom shakes the bedroom.

The figure's blasted from the window.

Erik hits the ground with a thud. A moan escapes his lips. His chest feels like it's been caved in. He's surprised his heart's still ticking. "Fuck the window," he mumbles.

Erik rolls to his stomach, gets his knees under him, then his feet. In a crouch, he gets the hell away from the window. He cuts across the backyard. He'll breach the house in a safer manner.

"Cover the windows," Eddies murmurs. He moves to his dresser, topples it and pushes it toward the bedroom door.

Smoky comes flying down the hall, his tail pointed straight up in the air and clears the door. Eddie finishes pushing the dresser in place. Filled with clothes, it just might provide some protection.

All hell breaks loose.

Eddie grabs Karen and forces her prone to the floor. He drags his mattress across her.

Amy returns fire from her crouched position. She uses her limited rounds sparingly, mostly shooting blindly, however.

Eddie pumps the shotgun—chambers another round. Clumsy fingers dig a shell out of his pocket. He manages to inject it.

There's a lull in the gunfire. Miraculously, no one seems to have been hit. Smoky zips around the room. Bobo's taken refuge in the closet. Dust and cordite chock the bullet-riddled room.

Eddie and Amy make eye contact. The unspoken question—what now?

Amy locates her purse, digs out her I-phone. She dials 911 and hits speakerphone. The sound of the ringing line fills the room.

Igor chuckles. He ejects his magazine and snaps another into place. "Having fun, big American?" he calls out.

Pavel taps his wristwatch indicating time is running out. Their plan is a two-minute assault, tops.

Igor waves him off. "Come out and maybe Igor let woman live. Maybe keep for self." Assuming anyone's still alive, that is. "Okie-dokie. No want to speak. Okay, here we come," Igor nudges Kirill with the barrel of his automatic. Nods, go.

Kirill's head shake indicates a staunch no. Igor cocks the hammer on his automatic and places it against Kirill's temple effectively changing Kirill's mind.

With a banshee cry and guns blazing, Kirill streaks down the short hall with the intention of hurdling the toppled dresser. The boom of Eddie's shotgun sends Kirill sprawling back into the hall. He's dead before he hits the ground.

Igor shakes his head. Still alive, it would seem. And where is that no-good brother-in-law?

Amy's phone comes alive.

"911. What's the nature of your emergency?"

"Eddie Winston's house on Woodrow is under attack by multiple assailants. Gun battle in progress. Need assistance now!" Amy screams.

"Foolish Americans. Cops will not be in time to save you," Igor calls out. He follows up with a hearty laugh that brings on a moment of a fit of coughing. Igor nods, in Pavel's direction. It's time to employ their one and only tiebreaker, the flash grenade clipped to Pavel's belt.

Pavel unclips the grenade and pulls the pin.

~~~

Johnson draws his 9mm and chambers a round. A grin stretches the skin on his face taut. He can't believe his good fortune. What a turn of events. He continues slowly down the block. There's a lone man in the Explorer and his attention seems to be solely on the house. Through his open window, Johnson can hear muffled gunfire. The assault is clearly underway.

Johnson pulls to the curb 30 feet behind the Explorer. His arrival goes unnoticed by the man within. Johnson eases open his door and carefully exits, ever mindful of his knee, which at the moment isn't hurting him in the slightest.   He chalks it up to more divine intervention.

Johnson closes the gap. Raises his Beretta. Levels it at the rear window. Pulls the trigger. The safety glass cubes.

The Beretta bucks in his hand. The boom echoes off the houses. The man slumps at the wheel.

His head settles on the horn.

The shrill of the horn parts more curtains.

Pavel tosses the grenade.

It bounces off the dresser but clears the threshold.

Eddie and Amy respond in similar fashion, curl into fetal positions, doing their best to protect their heads and vitals.

The blast and flash blow the bedroom windows out, curtains and all. The percussion stunning all.

Amy can't see or hear the grenade having landed closer to her. She struggles to catch her breath and blindly searches for her dropped weapon.

Eddie's sight is cloudy. He can make out shapes but too can't hear. I thank God it was only a flash grenade. For a second, he knew they were all dead. He senses more than sees Amy's movement. Thank God she's alive. He'd call out but knows it wouldn't do any good. His head's splitting, his ears ringing. Get ready, Winston, he tells himself. He levels his shotgun at the door's opening.

Igor chuckles. Nods at Pavel. What a fucking blast, Pavel thinks as he moves down the hall. He's amazed at the magnitude. How can anyone survive that kind of explosion? He shrugs, perhaps they didn't.

Pavel reaches the doorway.

He puts a heavy boot against the dresser and gives it a good shove.

Pavel steps across the threshold temporarily dimming the light cast from the hall.

Eddie pulls the trigger. He feels but barely hears the blast.

Pavel's rocked back on his heels but doesn't go down. He looks down at his chest in confusion as the blood blossoms through his shirt.

Eddie blinks, the image in the doorway's still there. He chambers another round and pulls the trigger.

The figure in the doorway disappears.

"Nyet!" Igor screams at the sight of Pavel crumbling to the floor. He's blinded with rage. Takes off down the hall wildly shooting through the open door.

Igor leaps over the nearly decapitated Pavel who took the brunt of the blast under the chin. He lands just inside the doorway panning the room for someone to shoot.

Amy continues to grope for her missing weapon. Eddie pumps the shotgun, chambers another shell. Igor swings to train his automatic on Amy.

Eddie pulls the trigger. The blast takes Igor dead in the chest, sweeps him off his feet. He screams out in pain. Rubs his chest as if to put out the fire within.

"i-DI k CHOR-tu! Go to hell!" Damn if that didn't hurt, Igor thinks, as he scrambles to get off his back and swing his gun in Eddie's direction."

Eddie pumps the shotgun. Pulls the trigger.

The shotgun merely clicks, the hammer having fallen on the empty chamber. The wind's figuratively knocked out of Eddie's sails. It doesn't take a rocket scientist to figure out what happened, the shotgun's been plugged to limit it to hold three rounds.

Igor can't believe the shot didn't materialize. He laughs with gusto, though it hurts like a motherfucker to do so. A grin splits his face as he gets his feet under him, stands. Thank God that he had the foresight to wear the vest or he'd be dead as a doornail right about now. He laughs once more and shakes his head. "Dead as a doornail," he mumbles to himself. God, he loves America. But not the stupid American that's now killed most of his crew. For that, he'll die a slow death along with his cop whore. Hell, he'll kill his dog, too, he decides.

Igor steps near Amy and kicks her pistol beyond her reach. What a shame, she is a good-looking woman after all.

Eddie blinks, Igor comes more into focus. He recognizes the Russian from the first day at the Arboretum. So, this is how it ends. But damn if he'll grovel, beg, give the Russian the satisfaction.

Eddie looks over at Amy, makes out her shape. Such a good woman.

There's so much he'd like to say to her, but in all likelihood, she wouldn't be able to hear his words. He mouths the words, nevertheless, "I love you, Detective Amy Foster."

Amy resigns herself to her fate. She, too, knows it's over. But damn if we didn't kill a bunch of the fuckers. She sighs, just when life was beginning to look so promising. She smiles. At least she got to experience a few days of sheer happiness.

Igor looks from one to the other. For some reason, they both look content. He shakes his head. But, why?

Igor ejects the magazine, lets it fall to the floor. He slaps in a fresh one and releases the slide. In the distance, he thinks he hears the first of the sirens. Unfortunately, he won't get to spend the quality time with the pair that he would have like to, but so be it.

He draws a bead on Eddie's right knee.

Eddie braces himself. Damn this is going to hurt.

Chapter Twenty-Seven

A shadow precedes Erik into the room. Igor fails to sense his arrival. But what he does hear and sense is the double click of the action as Erik cocks the hammer on his automatic.

Igor turns and once again stares down the barrel of Erik's weapon. "Huh? What is this, brother-in-law?"

Erik smiles. "Ex," he says pulling the trigger and shooting Igor right between the eyes.

A cloud of blood precedes the exodus of gray matter. Igor collapses as if a length of dangling rope was released. Erik spits on the fallen body. There's a new sheriff in town. "Fuck you, Igor. And, oh, that's a message from your sister."

Erik looks down at Amy, then at Eddie. He grins. "It's been fun," he says spinning on his heels and leaving a stunned Eddie and Amy to wonder what the hell just happened. Erik's walking on air. All he has to do is get away and then put himself together with a new crew, most of a new crew, that is. He begins to whistle a Russian childhood tune.

Just outside the garage, Johnson lurks, his arm extended, his weapon at ready. Man, he's heard a shit-load of gunfire concluding with a single shot. He's overjoyed, the wicked witch is surely dead along with pretty boy and the law can't blame it on him. What a stroke of luck. Yes, divine intervention. Hell, he can even claim that if he'd arrived a few seconds earlier, he may have saved his former partner and Mr. Winston. He hears some whistling.

Johnson's grin broadens.

Erik with his determined pace steps from the garage, his automatic in a relaxed grip at his thigh. He has to make an abrupt stop. What the fuck?

Johnson pulls the trigger. His pistol booms, spits fire, lights up the early evening. The chest shot rocks Erik but doesn't take him down.

"Oh fuck! That hurt," Erik says taking another round to the chest as if the shotgun blast wasn't enough. The old fucker in front of him looks familiar.

Johnson looks on dumbfounded. It doesn't register that the man he just shot is wearing a bullet-proof vest. He blinks and finds he's looking down the barrel of Erik's automatic. His last earthly thought, huh?

The boom's still reverberating in Erik's head as he steps over the inert body of Johnson. His ears are ringing but he's pretty sure he hears sirens in the distance. Time to pick up his pace. He has a choice to make between the two running vehicles—an older Chevy truck he knows nothing about or an Explorer with a missing back glass.

Erik opts for the Explorer, steps around to the driver's side and gives his dead comrade a good tug toppling him from the vehicle and to the asphalt. Erik slides in. Pulls the door shut behind him. If he's lucky enough to avoid the eyes in the sky, he might just make it. Erik feels good about his odds as he pulls away from the curb.

Eddie injects the last two shells into the shotgun and pumps the shotgun as Amy digs at an ear with her finger as if that might help her hearing. The room's suddenly eerily quiet. Eddie shrugs as he looks over at Amy, his sight getting better with every blink.

"Did you hear that?" he yells, not realizing just how loud he is.

"I think so. Sounded like two distinct shots," she yells back then coughs as the dust gets to her. She locates her pistol and snatches it up. The breach is not locked open so she knows she has at least one round remaining, the chambered one. "I'm not sure what it means, though."

Eddie nods. Shit, the whole thing's odd, but he thinks he just witnessed a change of command. But why weren't they shot? Well, that's beyond him.

Movement causes both Eddie and Amy to jerk, their attention is drawn to the mattress as Karen kicks it off of her and sits up, her eyes as round and frightened as does, her cheeks streaked with tears. Eddie motions her to stay put as Amy moves to her side to comfort her.

Karen hasn't a clue as to what just went down, but she knows one thing for sure, the people she was sent to kill both made efforts to save her life and by god, she's still alive. The thought that she was going to go ahead and kill the two brings fresh tears to her eyes. To think someone would actually try to save her life.

Karen leans into Amy and cries in earnest.

The 911 operator chimes in to fill the silence.

"Officers en route. ETA, approximately three minutes. Fire Department and EMS en route, as well. Are there any injuries? Are the assailants still on the scene?"

Amy speaks up. "This is ex-Detective Amy Foster. There are multiple casualties. The remaining assailant or assailants have likely fled in a 2000 to 2005 tan Ford Explorer. Please advise responders that us survivors are holed up in the home's rear master bedroom. Please advise them not to shoot us."

"Yes, ma'am. Please remain where you are and keep this line open in case your circumstances should change."

"Ten-four," Amy says. She turns her attention to Karen. She still doesn't know why Karen showed up at the house, but she doubts it was a coincidence. She's not one that too much believes in coincidence, but whatever the situation is, Amy believes Karen's not beyond redemption. That she's a soul that might still be saved.

Amy covers her phone with her hand. "Listen, Karen, I'm not sure what you're doing here, but will figure that out later. For now, stick to your story. You asked to use the bathroom. That's all you know." Karen nods into Amy's shoulder and cries even harder.

"Fuck 'em," Amy mouths to Eddie. Eddie's a really fast study. He's pretty sure Amy wants to protect Karen and hey, he's alright with that. They obviously know each other and Amy must have her reasons. He winks at Amy, takes Karen's empty revolver, wipes it off and tosses it into the hall. In for a penny, in for a pound, he thinks as the sirens draw ever nearer.

Smoky darts from his concealment from under the box spring, his tail once more pointing skyward. He loves against Pavel's big boot before disappearing down the hall. Eddie shakes his head. Amazing. He whistles for Bobo, drawing him from the closet. Bobo shakes himself as if to dry and damn if he doesn't appear to be smiling, Eddie thinks. Probably thankful to be alive. Eddie grabs Bobo by the collar as Bobo's bark announces the police arrival. The last thing Eddie wants is his dog to be shot by some overzealous cop.

"We're in the back bedroom," Eddie yells out.

And Eddie and Amy's ordeal with the investigators begins anew. It's a trip downtown this time, but at least they were allowed to drive themselves. Unfortunately, Karen wasn't allowed to ride along. She is transported downtown by a detective with whom Amy didn't always see eye-to-eye. Ouch. Amy thinks, still not knowing Karen's story.

Four hours later, at midnight and after answering the same old questions Eddie and Amy are free to go.

"So, what now Detective Amy Foster?" Eddie asks cranking the truck and looking over at the yawning Amy who's unconsciously stroking the sleeping, yet purring Smoky.

Amy stifles her yawn. Smiles wanly. "To the Motel 6, I suppose seeing how the home 20 is once more in disarray and a crime scene." Her phone vibrates in her lap before she can think of something witty to add. She checks the caller ID. It's from Detective Howard's personal cell. "It's Ron, Eddie. Let me see what's up."

Amy taps the screen on her I-phone. "What's keeping you up so late, Ron?" she says tapping the phone again to put it on speakerphone.

"Heard they just cut you two loose. Thought you'd be interested in the latest..."

"They know more than they're letting on..."

"Probably, but that's not what I'm talking about."

"Oh."

"It's about your ex-partner. Believe it or not, he's still alive."

"But he got shot in the head."

"You have me on speakerphone? Your phone sure is echoing."

"Yeah, we're in the truck. And Ron, how could the fucker possibly be still alive? Does the asshole have nine lives or what?"

"They've got him in a medically induced coma. He's critical but apparently stable."

"Jesus Christ, he's like Freddy Kruger, a fucking nightmare."

"The question Amy, is, what in the hell was he doing there at the scene?"

Amy shrugs though Ron can't see her. "I have my suspicions, Ron, but I'd rather not say."

"Well, if it concerns the prostitute that was there, I hear she claimed to know nothing. That she just asked to use the restroom."

"Do you know if they turned her loose, Ron?"

"Apparently, she was nodding out. Probably been smoking crack for days. Anyway, I think they took her to one of the local hospitals to keep her overnight for observations."

Amy sighs. "Yeah, maybe she'll decide to get some help."

Eddie parks before the motel's office. Throws the truck into park. "I'll go pay," he says.

"Hey, Mr. Winston. I haven't had the pleasure of meeting you. Look after my girl, there."

"It's 'Eddie,' but that's a given."

"He will. He's a good guy. Ron, listen, got to run. Thanks for the update. Keep me in the loop."

"Anonymously. Later Amy."

Room paid for, Eddie hops back into the truck and pulls around back to park before their room. Kitten in hand, Amy alights from the truck before Eddie has a chance to round the truck and open her door for her. As nice as the gesture is, it really is unnecessary, Amy thinks. Bobo hikes his leg and waters the tire on the truck parked next to theirs. Amy laughs, shakes her head.

"At least he doesn't piss on your tires," she says.

Eddie smiles. "He wouldn't."

"Why? Because he knows it's your truck?"

"No, because mine is an American-built truck and you notice the truck he picked is a Toyota."

Amy looks at Eddie askance. "He couldn't possibly know the difference." Eddie shrugs and smiles. "Right," Amy continues. "Anyway, it might be prudent if I find a patch of ground for the little one here, just in case he needs to take care of business. Leave the door ajar, Eddie, and I'll be right back."

"Sure thing," Eddie says admiring Amy's backside as she wanders off in search of a suitable place for Smoky. Amy finds an ideal spot beneath a pecan sampling, but Smoky's only interest is batting around a fallen leaf.

"That is enough," she says snatching him off the ground. Amy finds Eddie kicked back on the bed with his boots off and snoring softly with Bobo curled and sleeping at his feet. Good naturedly, Amy frowns and gently tosses Smoky to the bed. "Hmm," she says then giggles. "Talk about a short honeymoon."

Amy showers and crawls naked in bed next to Eddie. Within moments, she too is asleep.

~~~

The aroma of fried food and coffee wakes Amy. She realizes she must have been sleeping pretty hard for Eddie to rise and leave the room and return without waking her.

"Morning, Sunshine," Eddie says smiling down at her.

Amy returns the smile, "I guess the honeymoon truly is over."

Eddie's smile broadens bringing out his lone dimple. "How so?"

"Duh, Eddie, I happen to be naked here."

"But the only thing showing was your feet." His statement inadvertently draws Amy's gaze to her feet which are in fact sticking out from under the covers. Eddie fakes an involuntary shudder.

"Hey! I happen to have small, sexy feet, I'll have you know!"

"It's the green polish. It just doesn't do it for me."

Amy throws her pillow at him. "Right. So, what else is in the bags besides coffee?"

"Well, let's see. I got you some local yogurt..."

"Asshole," Amy says causing them both to laugh.

After a hearty breakfast and a shower in which Amy happily discovers the honeymoon's far from over, Eddie and Amy dress in yesterday's apparel.

"So, what's on today's agenda, Detective Amy Foster?" Eddie asks.

"I guess we go by the Santa Fe and see if they'll let us retrieve any of our things. Then we can set up temporary shop at my place." She smiles. "I mean our second home."

"So, though most of the players now appear to be dead now, I take it the investigation continues."

"Of course. The ultimate mystery still needs to be solved, to wit: where's the little girl that started all of this?" Amy plucks Smoky from underfoot. "Let's roll, tiger."

~~~

Eddie parks the truck at the curb in front of the house careful to avoid the literally chalked outline in the street where a dead Russian had been removed. Eddie attaches Bobo's leash before alighting from the truck. "I'm surprised with today's technology they still use chalk to outline the deceased," he says.

"Old habits die hard. No pun intended."

Only two unmarked police cars remain on the scene. The investigation is clearly winding down. A toot of the horn announces the arrival of Lori in her battered Honda Civic. She wheels it to the curb behind Eddie's truck. Lori's arrival sparks a mixed bag of emotions in both Eddie and Amy, each for their own personal reasons. They return Lori's wave and wait for Lori to exit her vehicle. Other than the large shades obviously concealing her still black eyes, Lori looks remarkably well considering the harrowing ordeal through which she recently lived.

"Hi, you two," Lori says for a sudden lack of anything else to say.

It's a slightly awkward moment prior to Amy closing the gap and giving Lori a hearty hug.

"You look great," Amy whispers in Lori's ear prior to giving her one last squeeze before letting go and allowing Eddie and Lori their hug.

Amy clears her throat. "Um, I'm going to go in and see if they'll let me retrieve my Mac. Be right back."

Lori holds Eddie tight and watches Amy over his shoulder as she retreats into the house. "You're a lucky man, Eddie," Lori says finally freeing Eddie from the embrace. "That's some woman."

Eddie smiles. What can he possibly say? "You're looking well. It's really nice to see you."

"Thanks. I still have my ups and downs." She pushes her glasses up revealing her eyes for Eddie. "I'll be needing the glasses a bit longer and I'll never be a hand model, but other than that, I think I'm doing okay." She frowns a second. "And I miss you something fiercely. You know, I'm also still conflicted about giving you two my seal of approval. I think I'd have been really good for you, Eddie."

Again, uncharacteristically, Eddie's at a loss for words. He can only smile in a sad sort of way.

Lori steps back a bit, looks over at Eddie's house. "So, what really happened here, Eddie? You two just can't stay out of the news."

"It would appear that we stumbled onto a case of human trafficking."

"That's what I gathered. The big question is, is it over?"

Eddie shrugs. "I believe so. At least most of the players seem to be deceased at this time."

Lori steps in close again, rises up on tiptoes and kisses Eddie on the lips. Her eyes settle on Eddie's. "I guess I better run along. You're still my hero, you know." She bends to pet Bobo. "And you, too."

"And you're mine. But for you, I'd still be wallowing in self-pity."

Lori lets her glasses fall back into place. "Gotta run." She steps around the back of her Honda. Glances back at Eddie. "See you around lover boy. Say goodbye to Amy for me."

And with that Lori hops in her car and is gone. Eddie is startled to find Amy at his side, clutching her Mac to her breast. "Think she'll be alright?" she asks.

Eddie nods. "You know, I actually think so."

"Good. And I have good news and bad news for you. The good news is that they allowed me to retrieve my Mac. The bad news is, they're not finished with their investigation here so we're not allowed to take anything else at this time. But, perhaps tomorrow."

"Figures. But it is what it is. So, what's the plan, Detective?"

"Wrap up the investigation and find the girl, of course."

Eddie smiles and lays his arm across Amy's shoulder. Draws her near. "Women,"' he says.

Chapter Twenty-Eight

"Got her," Amy says with evident pleasure. "The whole shebang. Name, address and all."

"And?"

"And, if the address is any indication, I believe it's a nice, upscale area."

"Do a Google street view and let's take a look and pan the area."

Amy does so on her Mac which is already logged onto the net through her I-phone. She turns the screen so that Eddie can see.

"Nice, very nice," he says. "And, though it's not in real-time, there's an Audi parked in the drive which I suspect to be hers." Eddie answers the unasked question. "And, I suppose we're dutybound to check it out."

Amy leans in and kisses Eddie on the cheek. "And, that's why we make such a great team."

Eddie can't argue with that. "Plug the address into my GPS and I'll get us there."

Smoky stirs on the seat between them, yawns wide and digs his claws into Amy's leg to help him stretch. Amy responds with an "ow" and works Smoky's claws free. "The little sucker's got some sharp claws," she says. Smoky replies with a hearty meow. Amy sets him in her lap, adds, "And I think he's telling us he's hungry."

Bobo sticks his head between the seats. He, too, yawns wide then looks to Eddie, then Amy, and then back to Eddie.

"And, I guess he's hungry, too," Eddie says causing Bobo to lick his snout. They both laugh and both think the same thing, what a family.

They make good time in the semi-light mid-morning traffic. The GPS indicates to take a right at the next stop sign. Eddie slows the truck to a crawl as he makes the turn, surprised to see coming from the opposite direction is the Audi associated with the address.

"Yeah, I see it," Amy says. "Pull to the curb. Let's see what happens."

Eddie does so as the Audi turns into the drive. Simultaneously, the front door to the residence opens and out steps what they both perceive to be the woman's black maid holding the hand of the little girl.

"Bingo," Amy says. "I'll be damned."

They both watch in silence as the woman exits the Audi and steps to her lush lawn. She bends and opens her arms as the little girl streaks across the lawn and into the waiting arms. Up in the air, the little girl goes unleashing obvious giggles before the woman lowers her and hugs her tight.

The girl stares at the truck and tentatively waves as she's carried to the front door and the three disappear within.

"It looks like she spotted us, Eddie."

Eddie indicates to the rear of the truck causing Amy to turn and look where she finds Bobo half sticking out of the rear passenger window. "Of course," she says. "She clearly has a fixation with that dog of yours."

"Well, we found her. Now what, Detective?"

"I think I've seen enough. I think she's in good hands for now."

"And the cops? Do you think they'll figure it out too? I mean we've mentioned the little girl more than once."

Amy sighs. "Probably, but who knows." She looks over at Eddie in earnest. "It shan't be because of me though."

"Nor me," Eddie says trusting Amy's judgment. He watches as she digs through her purse and extracts a short piece of ribbon and fashions it into a small bow which she then attaches to Smoky's flea collar. "There," she says with obvious satisfaction. Amy digs through the center console next and withdraws an open pack of beef jerky. She removes a sizable chunk. "Pull up in front of the house but keep the motor running."

Eddie does as instructed and pulls to the curb. "Stay, Bobo," Amy says opening her door and hopping to the ground. She jogs across the lawn, places Smoky and the piece of jerky before the front door and rings the bell.

Amy sprints across the yard, hops back into the truck and slams the door. "Go! Go! Go!" she yells as if she'd just committed a youthful prank.

With a slight squall of the all-terrain tires, they're out of there, Amy watching the house over her shoulder as it slowly grows smaller. Eddie in his rearview does the same the best that he can.

The front door to the residence opens just as they make their turn a block and half down the street and the woman steps out.

Unsettled by the sight of no one at her door, she takes a step farther out allowing her to look up and down the street. She just spots the turning truck and smiles. God's answered her prayers, at least for now. She bends to pick up Smoky who refuses to relinquish his piece of beef jerky just as the little girl appears at her side.

The sight of the kitten brings a huge smile that lights up her face. "Kitty," she manages to say in her Syrian accent as her feet begin to dance as if she needed to pee, her hands outstretched and her fingers begging.

The woman smiles down at the child as she hands her the kitten. "I believe it's for you, Katrina," she says. She strokes the overjoyed child's hair a couple of times before corralling her back into the house and pulling the door shut and whispering softly, "Thank you, Lord."

~~~

"We used to call that..."

"Don't say it," Amy says reigning in her giggles. "Shit, that was fun!"

"Reminded me of a porch pirate captured on a security cam."

Amy giggles again. "And, I even felt somewhat guilty. Imagine that."

"Well, I guess this means the case is closed, right Detective?"

Amy leans in to kiss Eddie on the cheek. "As far as I'm concerned."

"Good," Eddie says. "I'm tired of Russians and tired of trying to be killed. Something I'm wondering about, though. Our first clue, the expensive teddy bear. I just don't see where it fits in? One would naturally associate the expensive bear with Germany and the girl then likely one of the hundreds of thousands flooding their country, but in that scenario, the Russians don't fit in. Personally, I'm thinking Syria where the Russians are so heavily involved in propping up the government."

"Good read. I agree wholeheartedly. It's called a 'red herring.' No telling where she got the toy."

"I know what a 'red herring' is," Eddie says. "I used to read once upon a time."

Amy smiles and squeezes Eddie's hand. "And that is why we make such a good team. 'Foster & Winston' even has a good ring to it."

Eddie returns the smile. "I think I'll have another go at the name change," he says.

With a backhand, Amy smacks him in the chest. "Bastard!" She says. They both laugh as Eddie steers the truck toward their second home and the beginning of their new lives and careers.

The End.

Note from the author

If you've enjoyed this novel but have yet to read its predecessor, "The Girl in the Attic," I suspect you will enjoy it as well, so please check it out. It's the hard-core thriller that ultimately brings Eddie and Amy together. And should your tastes also include a bout of humor, please check out the "Steven Paul" Series and the youthful antics and indiscretions that lead Steven Paul and his fellow teenage crew into seeming no-way-out peril. Happy reading.

Sincerely,

Steven Paul Wilson

About the Author

Steven Paul Wilson is the author of six novels in the Steven Paul Series and two in The Eddie Winston Series. He was raised in Austin, Texas and considers it and Lexington, Texas home. He currently writes from his prison cell in the Texas Department of Criminal Justice where he's currently working on his ninth novel. He's an avid reader and animal rights advocate who hopes to someday be freed and to convert the family ranch into an animal sanctuary. He also hopes his colorful life translates into good reading. To learn more about the author, visit him at stevenpaulwilson.com.

Steven Paul Wilson

Donations: Please scan this QR Code to donate to this Indie author. Thank you for your generosity!

9 780998 165127